RESEARCH IN MARKETING

Volume 15 • 1999

THEORETICAL FOUNDATIONS IN MARKETING ETHICS

RESEARCH IN MARKETING

THEORETICAL FOUNDATIONS IN MARKETING ETHICS

Editor: JAGDISH N. SHETH
Goizueta Business School
Emory University

Co-Editor: ATUL PARVATIYAR
Goizueta Business School
Emory University

Volume Editors: SCOTT J. VITELL
School of Business Administration
University of Mississippi

DONALD P. ROBIN
Calloway *School of Business and Accountancy*
Wake Forest University

VOLUME 15 • 1999

United Kingdom – North America – Japan
India – Malaysia – China

Emerald Group Publishing Limited
Howard House, Wagon Lane, Bingley BD16 1WA, UK

Copyright © 1999 Emerald Group Publishing Limited

Reprints and permission service
Contact: booksandseries@emeraldinsight.com

British Library Cataloguing in Publication Data
A catalogue record for this book is available from the British Library

ISBN: 978-0-7623-0566-7
ISSN: 0191-3026 (Series)

Awarded in recognition of
Emerald's production
department's adherence to
quality systems and processes
when preparing scholarly
journals for print

INVESTOR IN PEOPLE

CONTENTS

LIST OF CONTRIBUTORS

Sherry Baker

Department of Communications
Brigham Young University

Lucette Comer

Department of Consumer Sciences
and Retailing
Purdue University

Linda K. Ferrell

Department of Marketing
University of Northern Colorado

O. C. Ferrell

Department of Marketing
Colorado State University

Neil C. Herndon, Jr.

Chair, Department of Management,
Marketing, and International
Business
Stephen F. Austin State University

Ronald E. Hopson

Department of Psychology
University of Tennessee

Roxanne Hovland

Department of Advertising
University of Tennessee

Gene R. Laczniak

College of Business Administration
Marquette University

Debbie Thorne LeClair

Department of Marketing,
Quantitative Analysis, and
Business Law
Mississippi State University

James H. Leigh

Graduate School of Business
Texas A&M University

Patrick Murphy — College of Business Administration, Notre Dame University

Russ Robertson — Quality Assessment Manager, Baxter Health Care Corporation

Donald P. Robin — Calloway School of Business and Accountancy, Wake Forest University

Katharina Jolanta Srnka — Department of Marketing, University of Vienna

Arturo Z. Vásquez-Párraga — Institute for International Business Research, University of Texas - Pan American

Scott J. Vittell — School of Business Administration, University of Mississippi

Joyce M. Wolburg — Department of Advertising, Marquette University

THEORETICAL FOUNDATIONS
IN MARKETING ETHICS:
A LOOK BACK

Scott J. Vitell

In their classic review piece on marketing ethics Murphy and Laczniak (1981) stated that, "As marketing moves into the 1980s, the theoretical foundation for marketing ethics remains very much at sea" (p. 253). Fortunately, however, over the last two decades this has changed, and a considerable amount of scholarly work has been devoted to the establishment of marketing and business ethics theories designed to help explain and predict the behavior of decision makers faced with marketing and business dilemmas that involve ethical issues. These theoretical models have been crucial to the development of our understanding of what influences behavior, either ethically or unethically, in business, and they have helped to guide and focus the research in this area.

The primary purpose of the present review is to examine the contribution of some of the more prominent theoretical frameworks in marketing and business ethics. The emphasis here is on business ethics, in general, rather than just marketing ethics because it is impossible to effectively separate the two given the

Research in Marketing, Volume 15, pages ix-xiii.
Copyright © 1999 by JAI Press Inc.
All rights of reproduction in any form reserved.
ISBN: 0-7623-566-5

degree of overlap that exists between them. Nevertheless, the majority of major theoretical models posited have appeared in the marketing literature.

Specifically, the objective of this review is to take a brief look back at the major theoretical models and the principal contribution of each. While some empirical findings are cited, it is beyond the scope of this synopsis to provide a complete review of all of the empirical findings relative to each theory. Rather, the purpose of this review is to highlight the major theoretical contribution, or the "addition" to existing theory, of each of the works cited.

A LOOK BACK

The first major theoretical model of decision making within the business ethics context was that of Ferrell and Gresham (1985). Besides the obvious contribution of being the first comprehensive theory of individual decision making in business ethics, its principal contribution was that it explicated many of the constructs that influence the individual in decision making. Most particularly, it included "significant others" and "opportunity" as influences on the individual decision maker. Citing the theory of differential association, the authors theorized that top management as well as peers and immediate supervisors influence the "ethics" decision-making process either positively or negatively. They further theorized that the system of rewards and punishments within the organization, including codes of ethics and their enforcement, could influence decision making in ethical situations by either providing an opportunity for unethical behavior or by preventing such an opportunity. The social and cultural environment as well as the individual's own personal characteristics were also theorized as influencing decision making. Many of these relationships have been supported in empirical findings including the influence of top management and peers on ethical behavior (e.g., Ferrell, Zey-Ferrell, & Krugman, 1983; Hunt, Wood, & Chonko, 1989).

Hunt and Vitell (1986) similarly included the cultural, organizational, industry, and personal environments in their "general theory of marketing ethics," but the major contribution of their theory was in terms of explicating the individual decision-making process by breaking it down into deontological (rules-based) versus teleological (consequences-based) evaluations. These ethical perspectives (deontological and teleological) were borrowed from moral philosophy. The authors further examined the individual components of each of these ethical perspectives or evaluations by stating that one has norms or rules (i.e., the deontological evaluation) that one lives by and that can often be applied to various situations. These rules may be general, that is, it is "wrong to steal," or they may be more specific to a business setting, that is, it is "wrong to pad one's expense account." They also posited that a decision maker determines the consequences of an action by looking at factors such as the likelihood and desirability of outcomes for important stakeholders. The decision maker then judges the ethics of various perceived alternatives based on a combination of these deontological and teleological evaluations. This dependence on both deontological and teleological evaluations by decision makers has subsequently been borne out by various studies (e.g., Hunt & Vásquez-Párraga, 1993).

Another early theoretical model is that of Trevino (1986). The major contribution of this work was the inclusion of the concept of cognitive moral development (CMD). This is the hierarchical concept developed by Kohlberg (1968, 1976) that includes six stages, two within each of three distinct levels of moral development: preconventional, conventional, and principled. While not specifically designed to explain behavior, one's stage of moral development may have an impact on decision making in situations having ethical content. Thus, a business decision maker who is at a higher stage of moral development, as compared to peers, might not only behave more ethically, but might also engage in very different ethical decision making processes from those at a lower stage of moral development. Various empirical studies have, in fact, supported the role of CMD in ethical decision making within a business context (e.g., Goolsby & Hunt, 1992).

In 1989, Ferrell, Gresham, and Fraedrich developed a synthesis model that combined each of the three previous models: Ferrell and Gresham (1985), Hunt and Vitell (1986), and Trevino (1986). While not adding any new concepts to the theoretical models that already existed, this model did successfully integrate the contributions of the previous three models.

Wotruba (1990) developed a framework based on Rest's (1986) four-component model of moral behavior, specifically focusing on ethics within sales organizations. Within this framework, he cited superiors, peers, and corporate culture, as well as customers and competitors as significant moderating factors to the decision-making process in ethical situations. While this represents the first framework specifically modeling decision making in the sales area, it too is primarily a merger of the three major comprehensive models already mentioned (e.g., Ferrell & Gresham, 1985; Hunt & Vitell, 1986; Trevino, 1986).

Jones (1991) posited a comprehensive model that clearly explicated the role that each unique situation would have on a decision maker. He termed this construct "moral intensity," and suggested that it has six unique dimensions: magnitude of consequences, social consensus, probability of effect, temporal immediacy, proximity, and concentration of effect. Thus, he theorized that not all situations involving ethics are alike. He further theorized that decision makers may behave differently depending on the intensity of the moral issue involved. That is, the same individual might behave more ethically if the situation involves a higher degree of moral intensity than when it involves a lower degree of intensity due, in part, to the fact that the ethical nature of the act would be more likely to be perceived when the moral intensity is higher. For example, while an employee might make a single copy of a short personal document on a company copy machine (low magnitude of consequences), that same person would never pad an expense account (high magnitude of consequences). The relationships between the moral

intensity construct and both recognition of an ethical problem as well as intentions, in situations involving ethical issues, have been supported by empirical
findings (e.g., Singhapakdi, Vitell, & Kraft, 1996).

In 1993, Hunt and Vitell revised their earlier theory primarily by adding a professional environment. This was not a new concept because Ferrell and Gresham
(1985) had mentioned this element in their original model. However, more significantly, Hunt and Vitell also stated that their theory could apply to ethics decision
making in a general sense, not just to individual decision making within organizations. This could be accomplished by simply eliminating the following three environments: professional, organizational, and industry. Thus, for example, by
eliminating these three environments from the model, it could be used to examine
the ethics of consumers as well as that of other types of decision makers.

Finally, two recent models have included the "business relationship" dimension
and the impact that the types and structures of relationships have on behavior in
situations involving ethical issues. Based on a social network perspective, Brass,
Butterfield, and Skaggs (1998) developed a model that incorporates the types and
structures of relationships as factors that interact with the organizational, individual, and issue-related factors common in other models. Thus, unethical behavior is
influenced by the types and structures of relationships. For example, one might be
inclined to act more ethically where the strength of a relationship is greater (i.e., a
good friend) then where it is weaker because the consequences of the unethical
behavior would be greater in the former instance. This is consistent with Jones'
moral intensity construct, especially the proximity and magnitude of consequences dimensions.

Similarly, Pelton, Chowdhury, and Vitell (1999) propose a model where decision behavior in situations involving ethical issues depends on the relationships
between the decision maker and other stakeholders, such as channel members, that
might be impacted by the decision. Thus, a decision maker would be likely to vary
behavior depending upon the nature of the relationships with relevant channel
members (i.e., one might act more ethically where there is a stronger and more
permanent relationship). This too is consistent with the moral intensity construct.

These latter two models are too recent to have been empirically tested. However, they represent an area that marketing ethics theorists need to examine
more closely—namely, issues of ethics and trust within existing business relationships. A related area in need of additional examination is that of group decision-making processes in situations involving ethical issues. Very little research
has been conducted to date that facilitates our understand of the dynamics of
group decisions having an ethical component. Finally, as a scholar working in
the marketing ethics area, I look forward to the coming decades with eager
anticipation as existing theories are further tested and modified and new theories developed.

REFERENCES

Brass, D., Butterfield, K., & Skaggs, B. (1998). Relationships and unethical behavior: A social network perspective. *Academy of Management Review, 23*(January), 14-31.

Ferrell, O.C., & Gresham, L. (1985). A contingency framework for understanding ethical decision making in marketing. *Journal of Marketing* (Summer), 87-96.

Ferrell, O.C., Gresham, L., & Fraedrich, J. (1989). A synthesis of ethical decision models for marketing. *Journal of Macromarketing, 11*(Fall), 55-64.

Ferrell, O.C., Zey-Ferrell, M., & Krugman, D. (1983). A comparison of predictors of ethical and unethical behavior among corporate and agency advertising managers. *Journal of Macromarketing* (Spring), 19-27.

Goolsby, J.R., & Hunt, S.D. (1992). Cognitive moral development and marketing. *Journal of Marketing, 56*(January), 55-68.

Hunt, S.D., & Vásquez-Párraga, A. (1993). Organizational consequences, marketing ethics, and salesforce supervision. *Journal of Marketing Research, 30*(February), 78-90.

Hunt, S.D., & Vitell, S.J. (1986). A general theory of marketing ethics. *Journal of Macromarketing, 6*(1), 5-16.

Hunt, S.D., & Vitell, S.J. (1993). The general theory of marketing ethics: A retrospective and revision. In Quelch & Smith (Eds.), *Ethics in marketing.* Chicago, IL: Richard D. Irwin.

Hunt, S.D., Wood, V.R., & Chonko, L.B. (1989). Corporate ethical values and organizational commitment in marketing. *Journal of Marketing, 53*(July), 79-90.

Jones, T.M. (1991). Ethical decision making by individuals in organizations: An issue-contingent model. *Academy of Management Review, 16*(April), 366-395.

Kohlberg, L. (1968). The child as a moral philosopher. *Psychology Today, 2*(4), 25-30.

Kohlberg, L. (1976). Moralization: The cognitive-developmental approach. In T. Likona (Ed.), *Morality: Theory, research and social issues.* New York: Holt, Rinehart & Winston.

Murphy, P.E., & Laczniak, G.R. (1981). Marketing ethics: A review with implications for managers, educators and researchers. In B.M. Enis & K.J. Roering (Eds.), *Review of Marketing 1981.*

Pelton, L., Chowdhury, J., & Vitell, S.J. (1999). A framework for the examination of relational ethics: An interactionist perspective. *Journal of Business Ethics.*

Rest, J.R. (1986). *Moral development: Advances in research and theory.* New York: Praeger Press.

Singhapakdi, A., Vitell, S.J., & Kraft, K.L. (1996). Moral intensity and ethical decision-making of marketing professionals. *Journal of Business Research, 36,* 245-255.

Trevino, L. (1986). Ethical decision making in organizations: A person-situation interactionist model. *Academy of Management Review, 11*(July), 601-617.

Wotruba, T.R. (1990). A comprehensive framework for the analysis of ethical behavior, with a focus on sales organizations. *Journal of Personal Selling and Sales Management, 10*(Spring), 29-42.

THEORETICAL FOUNDATIONS
IN MARKETING ETHICS:
A LOOK AHEAD

Donald P. Robin

This discussion takes the broader perspective of business ethics, which of course includes marketing ethics. After considering the history of business ethics theory development, two areas seem particularly important as we look to the next millennium. One issue simply asks, "Who are we?" and "Who should we be?" The other area of interest is that of model building and testing, outlined in the discussion offered by Scott Vitell. How we handle each of these topics can change the face of business ethics throughout the next millennium.

WHO ARE WE?

The field of business ethics has yet to define itself clearly. There is a clear dichotomy in much of the work on the topic. Many of the prestigious professorships in business ethics are filled by professors who are trained in moral philosophy, and most of the textbooks are written by them. While there seems to be a movement toward using professors trained in business for these professorships, and more

Research in Marketing, Volume 15, pages xv-xvii.
Copyright © 1999 by JAI Press Inc.
All rights of reproduction in any form reserved.
ISBN: 0-7623-566-5

textbooks written by them, the current situation favors the moral philosopher. However, I expect (hope for?) more synergistic cooperation, rather than a contest, between these two groups for the next few decades, but improvement will not come easily.

The principle difficulty in bringing the views of these two groups together is their difference in perceptions about theory building. Those professors trained in moral philosophy naturally view theory as normative theory, and they are concerned with applying normative theory to business in new and innovative ways, as with stakeholder theory. However, it is just as natural for those of us trained in the business disciplines to take a positive theoretical approach to the discipline by modeling the empirical question of why people behave ethically or unethically. There is, at best, an ambivalent view by each group of the other's work. At worst, there is antagonism between the groups.

This discussion brings us back to the questions of "Who are we?" and "Who should we be?" The answer to the first question is that we are now a dichotomy of beliefs, and of course, the result is less productive than it should be. I believe (hope? guess?) that a concern by each group for the other's work will develop eventually.

The answer to the second question is that the two groups need each other and should work together to provide the most productive theories for business use. A comment about the work of each group illustrates the point. From the empirical, positive theory side, we must ask what it is that we are modeling. If the answer is ethical or unethical behavior, then we must define what we mean by "ethical." If we rely solely on what individuals believe about ethics in a work setting, we can easily be faced with the problem of accepting prejudice in the workplace. Accepting the judgment of top management can produce the same type dilemmas. Furthermore, the law, which represents another option, is not always a good guide. We must have standards of ethical behavior to be able to aid management and to give our models meaning.

From the other side, it has never been acceptable business ethics to simply label specific business behaviors "unethical." Every professional ethics group has two agendas. One is the ethics agenda, which involves judging what is and is not ethical in a professional setting. The second agenda is that of satisfying the fundamental mission of the profession. To me, the job of a business ethicist is to discover ways in which both goals can be achieved synergistically. That is, both goals must be satisfied as efficiently and effectively as possible. Thus, the business ethicist must be concerned with helping to accomplish the business mission, and that is something that has been missing in most of this group's work. To achieve this dual goal, the moral philosophers must recognize the importance of empirical work performed by those of us with business training.

MODEL BUILDING AND TESTING

In the area of model building, we have played the role of good social scientists, and our progress indicates it. We have used traditional social science paradigms to hypothesize how ethical decision making takes place. In addition, we have added what is specifically known about the ethical character of individuals to the models. While some empirical testing has occurred, the near future will undoubtedly produce more. We are also likely to see more, and perhaps better, constructs to use in our testing procedures. In addition to this linear progress with model building and testing, I believe that we will see three other directions for research. There will no doubt be others.

Ethical decision making seems to have a strong situational component, due in part to the existence of the sympathy and empathy emotions. Jones' construct of moral intensity, mentioned by Professor Vitell, represents an attempt to capture that situational influence. I suspect that we will see much more work done in this area as future research develops. Concepts like "moral involvement" with the ethical situation, following the marketing work on product involvement, offer exciting possibilities.

A second direction of interest is moral segmentation. Obviously, moral segments must relate to specific ethical situations and are time dependent. However, it seems clear that the causal factors hypothesized by existing models impact groups differently. Thus, within the same company different groups of employees may feel differently about the same ethical issue. Employees, customers, and other stakeholders are all suitable targets for segmentation on a broad set of ethical issues. The usefulness of the approach to company leaders could be substantial. For example, if management discovers several employee segments with widely disparate views toward bribery, one conclusion is that their culture lacks cohesiveness, and another is that their ethics training may not be achieving its objective.

A third area for possible development includes the concept of corporate moral development. Empirically based standards are needed for true ethical audits by corporations. I visualize these standards as hierarchical measures of corporate moral development. Once established, universally and by industry, individual businesses can audit their own performance and compare it to these standards.

CONCLUSION

I believe that the evolution of business ethics is in its very early stages. Compared to other business disciplines, we have much to discover—including a clear definition of the subject. During this early stage of evolution, the discipline is likely to experience many frustrations. However, there is also a world of opportunity for exploring new and exciting avenues. Creative thinking and persistent exploration of the area are welcome!

THE ENTITLEMENT MODEL:
A MORALLY BANKRUPT BASELINE FOR
JUSTIFICATION OF MARKETING PRACTICES

Sherry Baker

ABSTRACT

The term "entitlement model" is coined for the position that all clients, legal products, and causes are entitled to professional assistance and representation despite
their moral indefensibility; that professional persuaders have a right to advocate for
legal products and causes, even if they are harmful; that *caveat emptor* is a morally
acceptable position; that clients and advocates have no responsibility for the negative effects on others that result from their legal persuasive communications; that
professional communicators have a responsibility to serve their clients well despite
potential harm to society or personal moral aversion; and that if a product or cause
is legal, its promotion is ethically justifiable. The model is defined and described,
and its assumptions are delineated. The marketing of cigarettes, a legal but harmful
product, is discussed as a paradigm example of the application of the model in marketing practice. The ethical defensibility of the model is refuted in light of a variety
of ethical perspectives including classical ethical theories, communications ethics
theories, and marketing-specific ethical treatises. The paper concludes that the entitlement model is an assertion of communicator rights and entitlements without the

Research in Marketing, Volume 15, pages 1-23.
ISBN: 0-7623-566-5

balancing acceptance of ethical responsibility for one's behavior and for the welfare of others; that the model fails the basic ethical requirement that people take responsibility for the effects of their actions on others; and that the entitlement model is a morally bankrupt position that should be rejected as a baseline for justification of marketing practices.

INTRODUCTION

Among the key ethical issues in professional persuasive communications is the acceptance of morally questionable clients and/or the promotion of harmful products and causes. This paper suggests that there is a cluster of justifications for these practices that are closely related, and that naturally adhere into a distinct construct of reasoning and rationalization for these behaviors. The paper coins and introduces into the literature the term "the entitlement model" to represent this cluster of interrelated arguments, assumptions, and assertions. The purposes of the paper are to: (1) identify this justificatory position, (2) give it a name, (3) provide an archetypal case that represents the position in practice, and (4) refute the ethical defensibility of its assumptions.

The entitlement model integrates related arguments from which appeals are made in personal and public justification of behavior. The archetypal or paradigm case suggested, the marketing of cigarettes to vulnerable audiences, establishes and epitomizes application of the model in professional practice, and also provides an example against which other cases can be compared and differentiated for purposes of moral reasoning and ethical nuancing. Moral analysis of the model is the heart of the paper. The discussion aims to establish that appeals to the entitlement model are ethically indefensible in the case of promotion of clearly harmful products and causes.

THE ENTITLEMENT MODEL

Within the discourses of both academe and professional persuasive communications (marketing, public relations, advertising), certain arguments are advanced and/or refuted as justification for the promotion of morally questionable clients and of harmful products and services (for example, see Barney & Black, 1994; Black, 1992; Blair & Hyatt, 1995; Bovet, 1993; Crowley, 1993; Davidson, 1995, 1996a, 1996b; Gregson, 1994; Griffin, 1997; Grunig, 1989; Hyman, Tansey, & Clark, 1994; Martin, 1994; Martinson, 1994; Nantel & Weeks, 1996; Nelson, 1994; Newsom, Turk, & Kruckeberg, 1996; Pearson, 1989; Pratt, 1994; Roschwalb, 1994; Sautter & Oretskin, 1997; Seib & Fitzpatrick, 1995; Seitel, 1995; Takala & Uusitalo, 1996; Thomsen, 1998; Zinkhan, 1994). In this section the entitlement model is defined as a construct that consists of these related justifications, and the assumptions of this construct are delineated. Note that this discussion quotes from the writing of several authors who have identified and discussed, often in highly critical terms, various aspects of what this paper is calling the entitlement model. Reference to these authors in no way suggests that they are supportive of the entitlement position.

An overview of the entitlement model is that it draws its strength from the assertion of rights as opposed to responsibilities, specifically the rights of all clients to be represented and the speech rights of professional communicators to advocate for all legal products and causes, and for all clients.

The entitlement model assumes the basic egoistic or Machiavellian perspective that clients and businesses have the right to use society for their own benefit, even if it is damaging to the social order (Martinson, 1994, p. 105). This egoistic perspective is expressed in its *caveat emptor* (let the buyer beware) position; a self-interested "stonewall egoism" and "look out for number one" stance (Nelson, 1994, p. 228). It assumes that "everybody is entitled to present a point of view and is entitled to professional assistance" (Seitel, 1995, p. 11), that everyone has a right to promote a legal product, that professional persuasive communications (marketing, advertising, public relations) are forms of professional behavior that are protected by the First Amendment (Barney & Black, 1994, p. 238) and that "if it's legal, it's ethical" (Black, 1992, p. 242).

The entitlement model asserts that the primary duty of professional advocates is to "vigorously defend the client in public arenas," and that "an advocate must relegate society's immediate interest to a secondary position behind that of a client" (Barney & Black, 1994, pp. 239-240). A professional communicator must distribute the client's (or product's) message without concern for balancing messages (Barney & Black, 1994, p. 243), must wear "the mantle of single-minded advocate in the arena of public opinion" and not apologize for it (Barney & Black, 1994, p. 240), and must submerge his or her own ethical values on behalf of the client (Martinson, 1994, p. 104) "accepting any client regardless of character or conscience" (Seitel, 1995, p. 11).

The entitlement model adopts the position that persuasive communicators are equivalent to lawyers in advocating the cause of their clients in an adversarial society (Barney & Black, 1994). Lawyers must vigorously defend their clients, despite guilt or the heinousness of the crime, because in an adversarial system, truth and justice are ultimately best achieved through professional advocacy of all interests. Professional persuasive advocacy is likewise valuable to society despite any harm it might cause (Barney & Black, 1994, p. 238), and it is not the role of the advocate to censure the messages that will be or should be communicated.

> [Although] there is no guarantee in the court of public opinion that adversaries will square off...just as a lawyer has no obligation to be considerate of the weaknesses of his opponents in court, so the public relations person can clearly claim it is another's obligation to provide countering messages (Barney & Black, 1994, p. 241).

Table 1. Synopsis of Entitlement Model Assumptions and Justifications

1. All clients, legal products and causes, are entitled to professional assistance and representation despite their moral indefensibility, and should therefore be represented.

2. Professional persuaders have a right to advocate for legal products and causes, even if they are harmful. Their advocacy is therefore justified.

3. *Caveat emptor* (let the buyer beware) is a morally acceptable position.

4. Clients and advocates have no responsibility for the negative effects that result from their legal persuasive communications.

5. Professional communicators have a responsibility to serve their clients or employers well despite personal moral aversion or potential harm to individuals and society.

6. If a product or cause it legal, its promotion is ethically justifiable.

This legal advocacy metaphor suggests a framework for professional persuasive communications in which all organizations and individuals (clients as well as advocates) have a right to promote legal products; clients have a right to advocacy, no matter who they are or what they wish to promote; and professional communicators have not only a right to speak and advocate for all legal products and positions, but a duty to serve the client well despite moral indefensibility of the client's position. "Ethical practitioners will, like lawyers, serve any client with loyalty whether or not they personally subscribe to the client's position" (Newsom et al., 1996, p. 199). A synopsis of the entitlement model's assumptions and justifications are captured in Table 1.

An example of practitioner articulation and defense of these assumptions is documented in Thomsen's (1998) examination of an on-line debate among public relations practitioners about the ethics of representing tobacco interests. In his review of a 14-month thread of this discussion involving 91 different participants and 216 posted messages, Thomsen found that the focus of the debate, "marked by intense disagreement and an inability to achieve a consensus," centered on the right of an organization to promote a legal product versus a practitioner's obligation to protect the welfare and safety of society (Thomsen, 1998). Participants in the debate who defended the right of the tobacco industry to retain public relations counsel appealed to the legality of the product as a justification for representing that industry. They drew comparisons between and defended the roles of public relations counselors and defense attorneys in representing clients for "purely professional reasons" despite personal feelings about the client, and also presented public relations practitioners as mere technicians unconnected to organizational policy and, therefore, not morally accountable for its activities (Thomsen, 1998).

The heart of [this] argument was that an individual's ethical baseline could not be challenged or called into question for simply carrying out assigned responsibilities passed downward to the practitioner through the organizational chain of command. Performing assigned duties in a professional and competent manner was assumed to be the more accurate ethical litmus test (Thomsen, 1998).

Thomsen's study illustrates at least two points relevant to the present article: that the assumptions of the entitlement model adhere naturally for practitioners into a construct of justification for persuasion practices, and that practitioners appeal to this construct in their reasoning and in their explanatory and justificatory discourse.

AN ARCHETYPAL CASE:
THE MARKETING OF CIGARETTES
TO VULNERABLE AUDIENCES

Cigarettes are perhaps the most obvious example of a legal but clearly harmful product, the marketing of which has sparked much public, professional, and academic debate (Cosco, 1988; Crowley, 1993; Davidson, 1995, 1996a, 1996b; Gregson, 1994; Martin, 1994; Nantel & Weeks, 1996; Pitts, 1998; Sautter & Oretskin, 1997; Thomsen, 1998). Cigarette smoking has been shown by scientific study to cause or to be an important risk factor in cancer, heart disease, stroke, lung diseases, and birth defects (including mental retardation), to pose a serious risk to nonsmokers and children resulting from second-hand smoke, and to inflict heavy social costs on society at large. "More than 400,000 deaths in the U.S. each year [are] attributed to tobacco, and the social costs—health care, fire department services, etc.—[are estimated] at more than $68 billion every year" (Davidson, 1995, p. 3).

Nevertheless, cigarette companies continue to move aggressively to market their products in national as well as international markets (Gruner, 1996; Nantel & Weeks, 1996; Vateesatokit, 1990).

> For example, at the very moment when major tobacco companies were getting ready to launch an advertising campaign in the United States encouraging adolescents not to smoke (*Marketing News*, 1991), these same companies were investing heavily in the development of Asian and African markets, among others, by distributing free cigarettes in places often frequented by 13 and 14 year-old children ("Asia: The New Front," 1991; Levin, 1991) (Nantel & Weeks, 1996, p. 11).

The World Health Organization projects that "by the year 2000, tobacco consumption is expected to be the leading cause of death in the less-developed world" (Gruner, 1996, p. 2), with particular impact on the world's population of children and women (Gruner, 1996).

Clearly cigarette smoking increases human suffering and can be deadly. The marketing of cigarettes, especially to children and to women (potential child-bearers whose smoking will affect their fetuses and whose second-hand smoke will affect their children) in the less-developed world, or to other vulnerable audiences in all parts of the world, is an archetypal example of, and a paradigm case for, the application of the entitlement model.

Paradigm cases are "straightforward instances of acceptable or unacceptable behavior" (Jaksa & Pritchard, 1994, p. 23). They can be used for moral reasoning by differentiating between and among the facts, circumstances, and details of the clear-cut paradigm case and those of other morally problematic situations (Conrad, 1993, pp. 140-143). "A paradigm case is a *kind* of case. This is what makes it useful in discussing more complicated cases" (Jaksa & Pritchard, 1994, p. 24, emphasis added). Moral reasoning from this case perspective, called casuistry, requires the identification of the relevant features of the paradigm case that can be compared with the relevant features of similar cases (Boeyink, 1992, pp. 112-113; Jonsen & Toulmin, 1988). For example, consideration of the moral defensibility of marketing other potentially harmful products and causes, such as casino gambling or state lotteries, could be approached by identifying the ways in which these cases are similar to or different than the relevant features in the marketing of cigarettes.

This paper suggests that (1) the marketing of cigarettes is a paradigm case demonstrating professional behavior, the relevant feature of which is the promotion (especially to vulnerable audiences) of a legal but clearly harmful product; (2) the justification for this behavior is grounded in entitlement model assumptions; and (3) the entitlement model is not ethically defensible in cases that involve the marketing of clearly harmful, though legal, products and causes.

ETHICAL ANALYSIS OF
ENTITLEMENT MODEL ASSUMPTIONS

The following section discusses the assumptions of the entitlement model from various ethical perspectives. It addresses first the legal metaphor that equates ethical persuasive communications with the practice of law, and with the attorney-client relationship. It then moves on to ethical theory, communications-specific ethical theory, and practice-specific ethical thinking. This approach presents breadth rather than depth of ethical analysis as a way of demonstrating that the entitlement model is not supported by any of these relevant perspectives as a baseline for ethical justification of professional persuasive communications and advocacy. The entitlement model holds that professional communicators have a right to advocate for all clients and for all legal products and services. The question to be explored here is not whether this legal right exists, but whether the appeal to this right is a legitimate moral justification for advocacy of clearly harmful, though legal, products and causes.

The Legal Metaphor

The model assumes that if an action is legal, it is therefore morally permissible or ethical. This assumption misunderstands the relationship between ethics and law. Whereas law in some sense may be considered to be ethics codified, there is a vast area of appropriate human behavior that is not codified, and that is governed by ethics rather than by law (Kidder, 1995, pp. 66-76; Pojman, 1995, pp. 3-6). The legality of an action does not necessarily equate to its ethicality.

Furthermore, there are several major flaws in the model's analogy equating the attorney/client relationship in the courtroom with that of the professional communicator representing a client, product, or cause in the court of public opinion. The primary problem with this analogy is that in law, an advocate for the alternative or conflicting point of view (the other side of the dispute) is guaranteed. It is the guarantee of countering messages (guaranteed advocacy for both sides of a legal dispute) that defines and produces justice in the attorney advocacy model of the American system of law. In marketing, advertising, and public relations, by contrast, there is no guarantee that counterbalancing messages will surface to offset and mitigate false or exaggerated claims, or harmful persuasive messages. The contention that the "public relations person can clearly claim it is another's obligation to provide countering messages" (Barney & Black, 1994, p. 241) is flawed in the case of potentially harmful persuasion. For the attorney/client analogy to stand, countering messages must be guaranteed; the lack of this insured advocacy destroys the comparison with professional persuasive communications.

The issue of client partiality is also at the core of the attorney/client analogy for professional communications. Attorneys are expected in this view to be loyal solely to their clients. In professional persuasions, however, does a communicator similarly owe loyalty or partiality solely to the client or management? Is there not also a requisite loyalty to the public interest? The Public Relations Society of America, Code of Professional Standards for the Practice of Public Relations, answers this question summarily in its first article which states: "A member shall conduct his or her professional life in accord with the public interest" (Seib & Fitzpatrick, 1995, p. 121). This responsibility to the public is also emphasized widely in scholarly and professional literature. For example, in their book about public relations ethics, Seib and Fitzpatrick (1995) write in depth about the duties to society that must be recognized by public relations professionals. Client and management partiality must be carefully balanced against the public interest. As Martinson (1996) has stated:

> Clearly, by the very nature of their position, public relations practitioners have particular loyalties to clients or management. At the same time, however, this does not relieve them of any and all obligations to significant third parties and/or the general public interest...Public relations practitioners' differentiated role, therefore, allows them to be partial toward client or management interests but not in a way that violates the rights of others or acts negatively on the public interest (p. 41).

The entitlement model's assumption that professional communicators may or must be loyal solely to client or management at the expense of the public interest is not a justifiable professional position.

Ethical Theory

This section briefly considers entitlement model assumptions in light of the following ethical theories: Kant's categorical imperative, W.D. Ross's prima facie duties, Rawls's veil of ignorance, Mill's (1987) principle of utility, and Judeo-Christian ethics. These particular perspectives have been selected because they are among the core of the canon of ethical theories frequently used for moral analysis in communications and media ethics literature (Baker, 1998). It is asserted that each of these perspectives refutes the ethical validity of entitlement model assumptions and justifications.

Kant's Categorical Imperative

Immanuel Kant, "the greatest philosopher of the German Enlightenment and one of the most important philosophers of all time" (Pojman, 1995, p. 137), formulated the categorical imperative as the "fundamental principle" in ethics (Jaksa & Pritchard, 1994, p. 127). Kant provided several different and progressive formulations of the imperative, including the following:

> Act only on that maxim [rule] through which you can at the same time will that it should become a universal law.

> Act in such a way that you always treat humanity, whether in your own person or in the person of any other, never simply as a means, but always at the same time as an end. (Kant, 1956, pp. 29-35).

The basis of Kant's categorical imperative is the dignity of other human beings; others must be treated as ends in themselves, and never merely as a means to one's own ends.

> For Kant, being capable of acting on the categorical imperative is a mark not only of our rationality but of our dignity....To have dignity is to have intrinsic, or inherent, worth. Money, for example, has only instrumental worth. It is valued not in itself but as a means to something else. Human beings, however, should not be treated merely as a means to an end; they are to be respected as ends in themselves. Human beings are said to be "beyond price." (Jaksa & Pritchard, 1994, p. 128).

The requirement to recognize and value human dignity precludes engaging in actions that cause harm to others (such as the promotion of harmful products) merely as a means of achieving one's own ends (such as financial reward). The entitlement model fails this test.

Kant's imperative also requires that moral actors engage only in those actions that they would wish to be universalized or engaged in by others as a universal practice. "For Kant, a course of action is not ethical unless the person who adopts it would see nothing reprehensible in its adoption by all others and unless this practice does not threaten the survival of society" (Nantel & Weeks, 1996, p. 3).

Universalizability also suggests the test of reversibility. In reversibility, if one would not want to be the recipient or victim of an action, one should not engage in imposing that action upon others. "In ethics one is not allowed to make exceptions for oneself that one would deny to others" (Martinson, 1996, p. 42).

The entitlement model assumes that because their activities are legal, and because they have a responsibility to represent effectively the interests of their clients, communicators have no responsibility for the negative effects on others that result from their persuasive messages. The test of human dignity, with its related concepts of reversibility and universalizability, require that ethical communicators consider if one would want to be victim of similar negative effects by the persuasions of others, and if one would want the persuasion and its effects to be universalized. As a baseline for ethical action, the model fails these Kantian tests.

Ross's Prima Facie Duties

W.D. Ross (1930) proposed that there are several basic ethical values, responsibilities, or prima facie duties to which we must be true, such as: fidelity (including veracity or truth-telling); promise-keeping; reparation for wrongful acts we have committed against others; gratitude for favors or good done to us by others; beneficence (doing good or bettering the lot of others); justice (ensuring the equitable distribution of pleasure or happiness, of benefits and burdens); self-improvement (bettering our lot); and non-maleficence (the duty not to injure others) (Pojman, 1995, p. 136; Patterson & Wilkins, 1998, p. 12; Ross, 1930, pp. 18-36). We must be true to all of these duties simultaneously, and may only violate one of the prima facie duties when it is in conflict, in a particular case, with another more compelling prima facie duty, given the circumstances.

The promotion of harmful, although legal, products and causes cannot be justified within Ross's framework of prima facie duties. Regarding the duty of justice, for example, Nantel and Weeks (1996) have written:

> The duty to justice goes beyond what is prescribed by the law. A good example [of the abuse of justice] is the distribution in Third World countries of certain products which have been banned in the West (p. 6).

The promotion of legal but harmful products or causes allowed by the entitlement model also fails the duties of beneficence and non-maleficence. The marketing of cigarettes, for example, does not contribute positively (as required by the duty of beneficence) to those persuaded by the message, and it causes great harm (thus violating the duty of non-maleficence). "The duty not to place the health or safety of others in danger is probably the most important" of Ross's prima facie duties (Nantel & Weeks, 1996, p. 6).

Some might argue that cigarette marketing results in beneficial financial returns for tobacco producers and marketers, but these outcomes cannot be offset or justified by the maleficence (loss of life and health) inflicted on others worldwide. In choosing between the duty of good to producers and marketers versus the duty to cause no harm to countless others, the ethical marketer must choose non-maleficence.

> In general, the principle is that certain rules or duties are required, and the burden of proof lies with any exception to them. For example, manufacturers and marketers could ask whether it is morally acceptable to produce and market a product which is potentially harmful to some individuals. Following the Kantian approach, the manufacturer [or marketer] of a harmful product would ask himself the question: "Would I be willing to live in a world where all producers were making products known to be harmful to some people in their normal use?" [Ross's] prima-facie response would obviously be "no" (Takala & Uusitalo, 1996, p. 6).

Rawls'Veil of Ignorance

In his book *A Theory of Justice* (1971), the Harvard philosopher John Rawls addresses issues of social fairness. "He presents a theory of just *procedures*, so that whatever results from these processes is itself just" (Pojman, 1998, p. 673, emphasis added). The goal of this process is to "nullify the effects of specific contingencies which put men at odds and tempt them to exploit social and natural circumstances to their own advantage" (Rawls, 1971, p. 136).

Rawls proposes a method of moral analysis that strips away social differentiation in deliberating about a course of action. In this mental procedure, one takes a conceptual stance behind a "veil of ignorance" and imagines there all other persons involved with or affected by the issue in question (Rawls, 1971, pp. 136-142). Behind the veil, all are in an original or initial position of equal worth and equality of rights with all others, and no one is aware of one's station in life or of how a decision made behind the veil will ultimately affect one personally.

> all parties step back from real circumstances into an "original position" behind a barrier where roles and social differentiations are eliminated. Participants are abstracted from individual features such as race, class, gender, group interests, and other real conditions, and are considered equal members of society as a whole.... Behind the veil, no one knows how he or she will fare when stepping out into real life.... As we negotiate social agreements in the situation of imagined equality behind the veil of ignorance, Rawls argues, we inevitably seek to protect the weaker party and to minimize risks.... The most vulnerable party receives priority in these cases and the result, Rawls would contend, is a just resolution (Christians, Fackler, Rotzoll, & Brittain-McKee, 1998, p. 16).

In the example of the marketing of cigarettes, taking a position behind the veil of ignorance allows an examination of the justice and equity of the action without foreknowledge of who will be the purveyor and who will be the recipient of the marketing message. The task behind the veil is to find a course of action that will be fair and equitable to all those affected by the decision, and especially to the weaker parties; to ensure "that the interests of some are not sacrificed to the arbitrary advantages held by others" (Cahn & Markie, 1998, p. 621).

The veil of ignorance requires professional communicators to step out of their roles as powerful disseminators of persuasive promotional messages, and to assume the perspective of the weaker parties (such as the recipients of messages persuading them to personally destructive behaviors). In the example of marketing tobacco products for harmful uses to vulnerable audiences, if one would not want to emerge from behind the veil to find oneself in the position of one of the weaker parties (such as a newborn child seriously affected by a tobacco-related malady), one should not engage in the promotion. In their discussion of Rawls' veil of ignorance, Takala and Uusitalo (1996) say his approach

> might define an activity as ethical if it involved true freedom of choice and actions, was available to all, injured no one, and was of benefit to some. Obviously, price fixing, bribery, and *marketing products which harm people*, are practices which are morally questionable (p. 7, emphasis added).

The entitlement model fails the veil of ignorance test.

Mill's Principle of Utility

John Stuart Mill, "one of the most important British philosophers of the nineteenth century" (Pojman, 1998, p. 189), argued for the utilitarian perspective that to test the morality of a course of action, one must assess the consequences that will result from that action. The right choice is that which will result in the greatest utility, good, or happiness for the greatest number of people. Under this utilitarian view, "an action is only ethical if it maximizes the greatest number of positive repercussions for the greatest number of people while at the same time minimizing negative repercussions to the smallest number" (Nantel & Weeks, 1996, p. 4).

> we are to determine what is right or wrong by considering what will yield the best consequences for the welfare of human beings....All that matters ultimately in determining the right and wrong choice is the amount of good promoted and evil restrained (Christians et al., 1998, p. 14).

The entitlement model fails this test in that it assumes that all clients, causes, and legal products are entitled to professional communication advocacy, despite the harm that may result to large numbers of people.

Utilitarianism requires an assessment of "a social cost/benefit analysis.... If the net result is positive, the act is morally acceptable, if the net result is negative, the act is not acceptable" (Takala & Uusitalo, 1996, p. 7). If many are harmed by the promotion of cigarette consumption, for example, while a relatively few are benefitted, the promotion is not ethical under utilitarianism. The entitlement model fails the test of utility because it is geared to achieving benefits for the few at the expense of the welfare of the many.

Judeo-Christian Ethics

Judeo-Christian ethics and other religious traditions require that human beings recognize their interconnectedness with other human beings and that they love and care for each other.

> the classic contribution of this religious perspective, in its mainline form, contends that ultimately humans stand under only one moral command or virtue: to love God and humankind. All other obligations, though connected to this central one, are considered derivative (Christians et al., 1998, p. 8).

The religious perspective requires that people consider the value of others; that they love others; that they consider what God would want them to do—how God would want them to treat others; and that they ask themselves, what is the loving thing to do? (Christians et al., 1998, pp. 17-19; Outka, 1972; Pontifical Council, 1997; Rachels, 1986).

> Judaism and Christianity teach that the world was created by a loving, all-powerful God, to provide a home for us. We, in turn, were created in his image, with the intention that we would be his children. Thus the world is not devoid of meaning and purpose. It is, instead, the arena in which God's plans and purposes are realized (Rachels, 1986, p. 40).

The Vatican's Pontifical Council for Social Communications has issued a publication titled *Ethics in Advertising* (Pontifical Council, 1997) in which the religious ethics perspective is articulated as a standard for practice in product promotion. The following are some excerpts from this pamphlet that exemplify this perspective (Pontifical Council, 1997):

> the Church stresses the responsibility of media to contribute to the authentic, integral development of persons and to foster the well-being of society (p. 6).

> advertising can itself contribute to the betterment of society by uplifting and inspiring people and motivating them to act in ways that benefit themselves and others (p. 12).

> If harmful or utterly useless goods are touted to the public...if less than admirable human tendencies are exploited, those responsible for such advertising harm society (p. 15).

> the media of social communications have two options, and only two. Either they help human persons to grow in their understanding and practice of what is true and good, or they are

destructive forces in conflict with human well-being....Against this background, then, we point to this fundamental principle....*Advertisers...are morally responsible for what they seek to move people to do* (p. 22, emphasis added).

[Advertisers have a duty] not merely to serve the interests of those who commission and finance their work but also to respect and uphold the rights and interests of their audiences and to serve the common good (p. 27).

The entitlement model fails as an acceptable justification for behavior according to the standards of religious ethics. In asserting individual and corporate rights and a *caveat emptor* perspective, the model assumes no responsibility for caretaking or loving kindness of others, or for human well-being and the common good.

Communications Ethics Theories

The following section discusses approaches to communications ethics that are relevant to the assumptions of the entitlement model including: (1) two-way symmetrical public relations communications; (2) dialogue as a model for public relations ethics; and (3) communitarian ethics. The assumptions of all three of these approaches differ markedly from those of the entitlement model.

Two-Way Symmetrical Model of Public Relations

James Grunig (1989) draws distinctions among four models of public relations: (1) press agentry/publicity, (2) public information, (3) two-way asymmetrical, and (4) two-way symmetrical. The press agentry/publicity model "seeks media attention in almost any way possible" (Grunig, 1989, p. 29). In the public information model, practitioners "disseminate what is generally accurate information about the organization but do not volunteer negative information" (Grunig, 1989, p. 29). The two-way asymmetrical model uses "research to identify the messages most likely to produce the support of publics without having to change the behavior of the organization" (p. 29). The two-way symmetrical model, by contrast, "has effects that are symmetrical effects that a neutral observer would describe as benefitting both organization and publics;" it uses strategies "to bring about symbiotic changes in the ideas, attitudes, and behaviors of both the organization and its publics" (Grunig, 1989, p. 29).

Some of the assertions of the two-way symmetrical model of professional communications as they relate to the entitlement model are as follows:

1. The major purpose of communication is to facilitate understanding among people....Persuasion of one person or system by another is less desirable.
2. People should be treated as equals and respected as fellow human beings.
3. People and organizations must be concerned with the consequences of their behaviors on others and attempt to eliminate adverse consequences.

4. Public relations should "improv[e] the societies in which we live" (Grunig,
    1989, pp. 38-41).

The entitlement model, with its emphasis on the rights of the speaker despite the
effects on the receiver, is antithetical to the goals of the two-way symmetrical
model of professional communications that emphasizes concern for others as well
as for self.

Dialogue as a Public Relations Ethic

In explaining the idea of dialogue as it relates to communication ethics, Ron
Pearson says a key value in this approach is the speaker's attitude toward and relationship with the listener. "Successful dialogue takes place only when speakers
treat each other as ends rather than means" (Pearson, 1989, pp. 123-124).

> Brockriede (1972) contrasted the rhetorical rapist, seducer and lover. The rapist's attitudes toward
> listeners are superiority and contempt; listeners are objects and methods are manipulative. The
> seducer and this is where Brockriede would likely put much of current public relations practice
> is deceptive, insincere, charming, and indifferent to the identity, integrity, and rationality of the
> audience. On the other hand, attitudes of the rhetorical lover toward an audience include equality,
> respect, and the desire to promote free choice among audience members envisioned as persons
> not objects (Pearson, 1989, p. 124).

Pearson explains that the conditions for dialogue are "honesty, concern for the
other person, genuineness, open-mindedness, mutual respect, empathy, lack of
pretense, non-manipulative intent, and encouragement of free expression. In contrast, monologue is characterized by deception, superiority, exploitation, dogma-
tism, insincerity, pretense, personal display, coercion, distrust, and self-
defensiveness" (Pearson, 1989, p. 125).

Discourse ethics is based in large part on the work of Jurgen Habermas (1970,
1984) and his theory of communication. "[Habermas] offers a theory of equal
negotiating partners and an opportunity for domination-free communication....The basic idea is that every individual has the right to domination-free
action....Every buyer-seller relation should be evaluated and reconstructed on the
base of ethics of mutual communication" (Takala &Uusitalo, 1996, p. 11).

In seeking to identify the ideal conditions for noncoercive communications,
Habermas would have us ask: "What ethical norms would members of an ideal
communication community agree represent their mutual interests?" (Griffin,
1997, p. 399). The ideal speech situation from Habermas's discourse perspective
is one in which people have access and "equal opportunity to participate in the
dialogue....[people are] allowed to sincerely express their attitudes, needs and
desires....Everyone is committed to a standard of universalizability. What makes
ethical claims legitimate [is their acceptance] by anyone *affected* by them" (Griffin, 1997, p. 400).

Pearson sums up his discussion of dialogue and its ethical imperative for public relations by saying that

> ethical business conduct is conduct that is sanctioned within the parameters of a dialogic communication process between a business organization and those organizations, groups or individuals that are affected or potentially affected by its conduct. No other source of ethical standards exists. Conduct that is not sanctioned or legitimized by that process is open to attack on moral grounds (Pearson, 1989, p. 127).

While discourse ethics may appear to be a utopian ideal for professional persuasive communications, the attitudinal orientations that require one to adopt the perspective of the listener and to take responsibility for the effects on others of one's communications are legitimate and applicable in professional practice. The entitlement model, with its focus on one-sided self-benefitting persuasion, is on the opposite end of the spectrum from the dialogic approach.

Crowley (1993) makes a suggestion for the advertising industry that is in keeping with the dialogic perspective. He recommends that the "advertising industry should take the lead in reviving antismoking advertising and instituting some truly informative advertising about the dark side of alcohol use. What better way could there be to prove the importance of advertising in presenting people with all the information they should have to make free choices? What is more, it is likely to do a great deal of good" (Crowley, 1993, p. 14).

Communitarian Ethics

The communitarian ethics position assumes much of the same attitudinal stance toward others as does the discourse ethic. As Kathie Leeper explains (1996a, p. 166), communitarianism as an ethic for professional communications is based in the 1990s movement spearheaded by Amitai Etzioni and others that seeks to balance the relationship between rights and responsibilities in society, and to focus on the health, strength, and vitality of the communities we all share.

> The "primary code of conduct" by which our behaviors are judged will focus on our social responsibilities to strengthen community....Communitarianism would suggest that creation and support of community must be at the base of [our] choices, that one has responsibility for one's actions and for the betterment of community" (Leeper, 1996a, pp. 168-173).

Communitarianism moves away from the "individualistic rationalism of John Locke and other Enlightenment thinkers" and toward a notion of mutuality in which people "live simultaneously for others and for themselves" (Griffin, 1997, pp. 400-401). "[Communitarianism is] a frontal assault on rampant individualism and libertarianism [in which the] focus is on relations between the individual and the community, the one and the many....individuals must act morally in ways that strengthen and perpetuate community" (Hodges, 1996, pp. 136-137).

An act is morally right in communitarianism when stimulated by interest in maintaining one's responsibilities to others in community, and "wrong if driven by self-centeredness" (Christians, Ferre, & Fackler, 1993, p. 73). By communitarian standards, the entitlement model's emphasis on serving individual interests at the expense of the well-being of others in the community is unethical.

Contemporary Thinking in Applied Professional Ethics

The following section summarizes in pertinent part two short articles (Davidson, 1996c; Divita, 1996) and two in-depth articles about marketing ethics (Thompson, 1995; Smith, 1995). The purpose is to illustrate current professional thinking about marketing ethics issues as they relate to the assumptions of the entitlement model.

"New Commandment: Ethics in All Marketing" (Davidson, 1996c)

In his ethics column of *Marketing News*, Davidson points to the "vulnerability of the buyer relative to the seller in the marketplace today" (Davidson, 1996c, p. 2). He says, "[t]echnology, in all its many and wondrous forms, has outpaced the learning ability of even sophisticated buyers so that they no longer have the skill to judge advertising claims and marketing pitches effectively" (Davidson, 1996c, p. 2)

> Long gone are the days of Adam Smith's glove maker and glove purchaser when buyer and seller came together with approximately equal standing and power in the market. Today, *consumers are at the mercy of marketers* for the vast majority of their purchases, with only limited resources, knowledge, and skill with which to judge the claims being made (Davidson, 1996c, pp. 2-3, emphasis added).

Davidson contends that in these circumstances, "it becomes increasingly important for marketers to consider the ethical dimension of their decisions as they put together their strategies and decide on their tactics" (Davidson, 1996c, p. 3). This contention argues against the entitlement model's self-serving perspective.

"Do Business with Integrity" (Divita, 1996)

In the context of reviewing Stephen Carter's book titled *Integrity*, Sal Divita writes that the system in which we operate "encourages people to place their own interests before those of their fellowmen...even at the expense of others" (Divita, 1996, pp. 1, 2). He contends that we must do business with integrity, which is "the ability to differentiate between right and wrong, to act accordingly based on this distinction even at personal cost, and to declare openly one's moral convictions" (Divita, 1996, p. 1). Divita (1996) says, "It is high time for people to stop and take stock of their own integrity to see if they have managed to retain it or they have allowed it to be eroded by the prevailing culture of greed" (p. 1).

This call for integrity argues against the entitlement model's position that one may justifiably submerge personal ethical values when representing a client or product.

"A Contextualist Proposal for the Conceptualization and Study of Marketing Ethics" (Thompson, 1995)

In his contextualist or naturalistic approach to assessing the ethics of marketing practices, Thompson explores the insights shed on the subject by Carol Gilligan's ethics of care (Gilligan, 1982). The care approach emphasizes "the roles that interpersonal connectedness and empathy play in moral reasoning" (Thompson, 1995, p. 3). "Gilligan emphasizes the importance of recognizing the interdependencies and social bonds that exist among people" (Thompson, 1995, p. 8). Thompson (1995) suggests that a contextualist approach to ethics has at least one normative implication: "the need to foster a caring orientation in the conduct of marketing ethics" (p. 16).

> If marketers care about customers or suppliers in the way that they care about the interest of close friends or family members, personal gain would be defined in a way that entails benefits to the other.... Gilligan's proposals regarding the ethics of care may offer a means to revitalize Smith's conception of a free-market system tempered by a social conscience: That is, a person's sense of his or her own well-being is fundamentally connected to the interests of society as a whole" (Thompson, 1995, pp. 17-19).

"Marketing Strategies for the Ethics Era" (Smith, 1995)

Smith asserts that the public increasingly is scrutinizing marketing strategies, and that *"caveat emptor* is no longer acceptable as a basis for justifying marketing practices" (Smith, 1995, p. 85). Smith says post-World War II growth market strategies were subject to the simple rule of *caveat emptor*, within the rule of law. "If it was legal to sell a product that might be harmful or might not live up to the seller's promises, then marketing the product was acceptable because the decision to buy was the consumer's. The consumer was expected to employ the maxim "buyer beware" (Smith, 1995, p. 85).

Smith (1995, p. 85) says times have changed, that the current period is an ethics era, and that standards of acceptable marketing practices have now shifted. He uses as an example the removal of the R.J. Reynolds Uptown cigarettes from the test market, and the public criticism of its plans to market its Dakota brand. Uptown cigarettes were to have been targeted specifically at the black community, and Dakota to "young, poorly educated, blue-collar women...the virile female'" (Smith, 1995, p. 88). R.J. Reynolds viewed pressure against these campaigns from "antismoking zealots" as an erosion of the free enterprise system (Smith, 1995, p. 88). Smith sees it instead as evidence of the new ethics era.

> But the [recent] controversies that resulted over product safety, targeting disadvantaged groups, and misleading pricing reflect the shift in society's expectations of business. While it may be that caveat emptor was never an adequate criterion for evaluating marketing practices as ethical, it was, at least, a justification for marketing practices that society hitherto was willing to accept. With consumer rights becoming more important, this is no longer the case (Smith, 1995, pp. 88-89).

Smith suggests that in moving away from the assumptions of *caveat emptor*, marketers should adopt the assumptions of "consumer sovereignty" which is grounded in the capitalistic assumptions of "consumers exercising informed choice" (Smith, 1995, p. 91). It is an idea that is embodied in "President Kennedy's Consumer Bill of Rights [which] included the consumer's right to choose and be informed (as well as the right to safety and to be heard)." The consumer sovereignty paradigm creates "an obligation for marketers to ensure that the consumers whom their marketing programs target have capability, information, and choice." In applying his Consumer Sovereignty Test (CST) to the marketing of cigarettes, Smith says "targeting potential smokers is unacceptable" (Smith, 1995, pp. 92-93).

An article by Leonard Pitts Jr. (1998) in a Knight Ridder Newspapers column exemplifies Smith's assertions that consumers no longer accept the assumptions of *caveat emptor*. Pitts' article refers to internal papers released by R.J. Reynolds Tobacco Company in which "tobacco executives speak of the need to develop aggressive marketing campaigns tailored to children as young as 14 years old—variously referred to them as 'beginning' smokers, 'pre-smokers,' and 'replacement' smokers" (Pitts, 1998). The following are Pitts' reactions to these revelations:

> Reynolds is, you will remember, the same company that has so loudly denied ever encouraging young people to smoke. The one that reacted with wounded indignation to suggestions that its Joe Camel cartoon mascot was a way of reaching kids....These people sold death sticks behind a smiley face, and even if you think that's OK, even if you think smoking is a decision adults get to make, you cannot condone the fact that they went after our children. And lied about it (Pitts, 1998).

An article by Nantel and Weeks (1996) is also supportive of Smith's consumer sovereignty position. Nantel and Weeks (1996, p. 1) assert that "of all the management fields, the field of marketing is undoubtedly that which raises the most controversy when it comes to the question of ethics." Among the ethical problems is that studies about the decisional processes used by consumers have provided information that can lead to dubious marketing practices and that can be used to "frame" consumers. "The understanding of the information processing mechanisms used by consumers permits the creation of messages which are sometimes dangerously effective" (Nantel & Weeks, 1996, p. 2).

Table 2. Summary of Ethical Perspectives Discussed and
Conclusions Drawn to Refute Entitlement Model Assumptions

Ethical Theory	
Kant:	Model fails tests of human dignity and respect, reversibility and universalizability.
Ross:	Model fails tests of justice, beneficence, and non-maleficence.
Rawls:	Model exploits privileged circumstances of communicators to their own advantage, and fails to protect vulnerable parties.
Mill:	Model does not maximize the greatest good for the greatest number.
Religious Ethics:	Model does not recognize the interconnectedness of human beings, responsibilities for caretaking and loving kindness of others, and concern for human well-being and the common good.

Communications Theory	
Two-Way Symmetrical:	Model's effects do not benefit both parties.
Dialogue:	Model is monologic, self-benefitting, and nonrepresentative of mutual interests.
Communitarian Ethics:	Model is based in individualism and rights rather than mutuality and responsibilities to community.

Applied Professional Persuasion Ethics Perspectives	
Davidson:	Model takes unfair advantage of buyer vulnerability.
Divita:	Model fails to value integrity over the prevailing culture of greed.
Thompson:	Model emphasizes individual rights and interests rather than interpersonal connectedness and care.
Smith:	Model allows consumer manipulation to the sole interest of the communicator. Model's *caveat emptor* position is not an acceptable basis for justifying marketing practices.

> In fact, the consumer is very substantially in the service of the business firm. It is to this end that advertising and merchandising in all their cost and diversity are directed; consumer wants are shaped to the purposes and notably to the financial interests of the firm....it is in this field that the distinction between a lawful practice and an ethical practice appears the clearest (Nantel & Weeks, 1996, p. 2).

Nantel and Weeks also point out that while the goal of marketing is to meet the needs of consumers, consumers are no longer content with having their needs met; they are now concerned with the ethics of *how* those needs are met.

> The consumer is no longer merely concerned with the satisfaction obtained from a product or service, but also with the way in which this product or service is obtained....the consumer is not only concerned with the final product, but also with the marketing process (Nantel & Weeks, 1996, pp. 7-8).

This observation gives insight into the changing expectations of the marketplace and to the concern for ethics held by consumers. The entitlement model, with its emphasis on the legal rights of the speaker (marketer) and on *caveat emptor*, represents an assumption about marketing that increasingly is not shared by the buying public.

Summary of Ethical Analysis

The core assumptions and justifications that constitute the entitlement model have been discussed based on a discussion of the inappropriate appeal to the lawyer/client metaphor for professional persuasive communications and advocacy, and by a discussion of ethical theory, communications theory, and marketing-specific ethical viewpoints. Table 2 provides a summary of the specific ethical perspectives discussed and conclusions drawn in refutation of the entitlement model paradigm.

CONCLUSION

This paper coins the term "entitlement model" for an interrelated cluster of arguments, assumptions, and assertions that frequently are evoked in professional and academic discourse to justify the marketing of legal but harmful products and causes (summarized in Table 1). The paper refutes the ethical justifiability of the entitlement model by taking a wide-ranging look at the ways in which it can be assessed as a legitimate ethical baseline. The model is held to the light of classical ethical theory, contemporary theories of communication ethics, and marketing-specific philosophical evaluation (summarized in Table 2).

The marketing of cigarettes, especially to vulnerable audiences, is presented as an archetypal example of the application by practitioners of entitlement model assumptions. The goal in focusing on cigarette marketing has been to provide a paradigm case by which to exemplify both the application of the entitlement model in practice, and the ethical refutation of that model. The discussion is not intended, however, to be limited or restricted to the marketing of cigarettes. The assumptions of the entitlement model, although somewhat extreme, are evidenced in the marketing of a wide range of legal put potentially harmful products and causes, and the ethical analysis and conclusions reached here are applicable to each, depending on the product and the marketing circumstances.

The entitlement model is an assertion of communicator rights and entitlements without the balancing acceptance of ethical responsibility for one's behavior and for the welfare of others. Essentially, the model fails the basic ethical requirement that people take responsibility for the effects of their actions on others. The entitlement model is a morally bankrupt position that should be rejected as a baseline for justification of marketing practices.

REFERENCES

Note: Some of the entries in this section have been accessed from electronic rather than hard copy source, namely *Infotrac SearchBank*. Where this is the case, page number citations in the text of this paper are to downloaded and site-printed pages rather than to original source pagination.

Asia: The new front in the war on smoking. (1991, February 25). *Business Week*, p. 66.

Baker, S. (1998). Applying kidder's ethical decision-making checklist to media ethics. *Journal of mass media ethics, 12*(4), 197-210.

Barney, R., & Black, J. (1994). Ethics and professional persuasive communications. *Public Relations Review, 20*(3), 233-248.

Black, J. (1992). Media ethics. In M. Murray & A. Ferri (Eds.), *Teaching mass communication: A guide to better instruction* (pp. 235-253). New York: Praeger.

Blair, M.E., & Hyatt, E. (1995). The marketing of guns to women: Factors influencing gun-related attitudes and gun ownership by women. *Journal of public policy & marketing, 14*(1), *117*(11). Accessed on *Infotrac SearchBank.*

Boeyink, D. (1992). Casuistry: A case-based method for journalists. *Journal of Mass Media Ethics* (Summer), 107-120.

Bovet, S. (1993). The burning question of ethics. *Public Relations Journal* (November), 24-29.

Brockriede, W. (1972). Arguers as lovers. *Philosophy and Rhetoric, 5*, 1-11.

Cahn, S., & Markie, P. (1998). *Ethics: History, theory, and contemporary issues.* New York: Oxford University Press.

Christians, C., Ferre, J., & Fackler, M. (1993). *Good news: Social ethics & the press.* New York: Oxford University Press.

Christians, C., Fackler, M., Rotzoll, K., & Brittain-McKee, K. (1998). *Media ethics: Cases & moral reasoning* (5th ed.). New York: Longman.

Conrad, C. (1993). *Ethical nexus.* Norwood, NJ: Ablex Publishing.

Cosco, J. (1988). Tobacco wars: the battle between titans heats up. *Public Relations Journal* (December), 15-38.

Crowley, J. (1993). The advertising industry's defense of its First Amendment rights. *Journal of Mass Media Ethics, 8*(1), 5-16.

Davidson, K. (1995, August 14). Tobacco critic shares views on cigarette ads. *Marketing News,* 29(17), 9(1). Accessed on *Infotrac SearchBank.*

Davidson, K. (1996a, June 17). Sure it's legal, but is it legitimate? *Marketing News, 30*(13), *13*(1). Accessed on *Infotrac SearchBank.*

Davidson, K. (1996b, July 15). Marketing of this brand could go up in smoke. *Marketing News,* 30(15), 4(1). Accessed on *Infotrac SearchBank.*

Davidson, K. (1996c, August 26). New commandment: Ethics in all marketing. *Marketing News,* 30(18), 4(1). Accessed on *Infotrac SearchBank.*

Divita, S. (1996, July 29). Do business with integrity. *Marketing News, 30*(16), 4(1). Accessed on *Infotrac SearchBank.*

Gilligan, C. (1982). *In a different voice: Psychological theory and women's development.* Cambridge, MA: Harvard University Press.

Gregson, J. (1994, September). The good, the bad & the ugly. *Management Today*, pp. 38-42.

Griffin, E.M. (1997). *A first look at communication theory.* New York: McGraw-Hill.

Gruner, H. (1996). The export of U.S. tobacco products to developing countries and previously closed markets. *Law and Policy in International Business, 28*(1), 217-254. Accessed on *Infotrac SearchBank.*

Grunig, J. (1989). Symmetrical presuppositions as a framework for public relations theory. In C. Botan & V. Hazleton (Eds.), *Public Relations Theory* (pp. 17-44). Hillsdale, NJ: Lawrence Erlbaum Associates.

Habermas, J. (1970). Toward a theory of communication competence. *Inquiry, 13*, 360-375.

Habermas, J. (1984). *The theory of communicative action* (Vol. 1, T. McCarthy, Trans.). Boston: Beacon Press.

Hodges, L. (1996). Ruminations about the communitarian debate. *Journal of Mass Media Ethics, 11*(3), 133-139.

Hyman, R., Tansey, R., & Clark, J. (1994). Research on advertising ethics: Past, present, and future. *Journal of Advertising, 23*(3).

Jaksa, J.S., & Pritchard, M.S. (1994). *Communication ethics: Methods of analysis.* Belmont, CA: Wadsworth.

Johannesen, R. (1981). *Ethics in human communication.* Prospect Heights, IL: Waveland Press.

Jonsen, A.R., & Toulmin, S. (1988). *The abuse of casuistry: A history of moral reasoning.* Los Angeles: University of California Press.

Kant, I. (1956). *Groundwork of the metaphysic of morals* (H.J. Paton, Trans.). New York: Harper Torchbooks.

Kidder, R. (1995). *How good people make tough choices.* New York: William Morrow.

Leeper, K. (1996a). Public relations ethics and communitarianism: A preliminary investigation. *Public Relations Review, 22*(2), 163-179.

Leeper, R. (1996b). Moral objectivity, Jurgen Habermas's discourse ethics, and public relations. *Public Relations Review, 22*(2), 133-150.

Levin, M. (1991). US tobacco firms push eagerly into Asian market. *Marketing News, 25*(2), 2.

Martin, C. (1994). Ethical advertising research standards: three case studies. *Journal of Advertising, 23*(3), 17-29.

Martinson, D. (1994). Enlightened self-interest fails as an ethical baseline in public relations. *Journal of Mass Media Ethics, 9*(2), 100-108.

Martinson, D. (1995). Ethical public relations practitioners must not ignore public interest. *Journal of Mass Media Ethics, 10*(4), 210-222.

Martinson, D. (1996). Client partiality and third parties: An ethical dilemma for public relations practitioners? *Public Relations Quarterly, 40*(4), 41-44.

Mascarenhas, O. (1995). Exonerating unethical marketing executive behaviors: A diagnostic framework. *Journal of Marketing, 59*(2), *43*(15). Accessed on *Infotrac SearchBank.*

Mill, J. (1987). *Utilitarianism.* Reproduced in *John Stuart Mill and Jeremy Bentham: Utilitarianism and other essays.* New York: Penguin Books.

Nantel, J., & Weeks, W. (1996). Marketing ethics: Is there more to it than the utilitarian approach? *European Journal of Marketing, 30*(5), *9*(11). Accessed on *Infotrac SearchBank.*

Nelson, R. (1994). Issues communication and advocacy: Contemporary ethical challenges. *Public Relations Review, 20*(3), 225-231.

Newsom, D., Turk, J.V., & Kruckeberg, D. (1996). *This is PR: The realities of public relations.* Belmont, CA: Wadsworth.

Outka, G. (1972). *Agape: An ethical analysis.* New Haven, CT: Yale University Press.

Pearson, R. (1989). Business ethics as communication ethics: Public relations practice and the idea of dialogue. In C. Botan & V. Hazleton (Eds.), *Public relations theory* (pp. 111-131). Hillsdale, NJ: Lawrence Erlbaum.

Pitts, L. (1998, January 24). Tobacco companies from land of Oz. *Knight Ridder Newspapers.*

Pojman, L. (1995). *Ethics: Discovering right and wrong.* Belmont, CA: Wadsworth Publishing.

Pojman, L. (1998). *Ethical theory: Classical and contemporary readings.* Belmont, CA: Wadsworth Publishing.

Pontifical Council for Social Communications. (1997). *Ethics in advertising.* Boston: Pauline Books & Media. (http://www.pauline.org)

Pratt, C. (1994). Hill & Knowlton's two ethical dilemmas. *Public Relations Review, 20*(3), 277-294.

Rachels, J. (1986). *The elements of moral philosophy.* New York: Random House.

Rawls, J. (1971). *A theory of justice.* Cambridge, MA: Harvard University Press.

Roschwalb, S. (1994). The Hill & Knowlton cases: A brief on the controversy. *Public Relations Review, 20*(3), 267-276.

Ross, W. (1930). *The right and the good.* Oxford: Oxford University Press.

Sautter, E., & Oretskin, N. (1997). Tobacco targeting: The ethical complexity of marketing to minorities. *Journal of Business Ethics, 16*(10), 1011-1017.

Seib, P., & Fitzpatrick, K. (1995). *Public relations ethics.* Orlando, FL: Harcourt Brace.

Seitel, F. (1995). *The practice of public relations* (6th ed.). Englewood Cliffs, NJ: Prentice-Hall.

Smith, N. (1995). Marketing strategies for the ethics era. *Sloan Management Review, 36*(4), 85-97.

Takala, T., & Uusitalo, O. (1996). An alternative view of relationship marketing: A framework for ethical analysis. *European Journal of Marketing, 30*(2), *45*(16). Accessed on *Infotrac Search-Bank.*

Thompson, C. (1995) A contextualist proposal for the conceptualization and study of marketing ethics. *Journal of Public Policy & Marketing, 14*(2), *177*(15). Accessed on *Infotrac SearchBank.*

Thomsen, S. (1998). Public relations and the tobacco industry: Examining the debate on practitioner ethics. *Journal of Mass Media Ethics, 14*(3).

Vateesatokit, P. (1990). Increase in tobacco marketing and advertising to developing countries. *Journal of the American Medical Association, 264*(12), *1522*(2). Accessed on *Infotrac SearchBank.*

Zinkhan, G. (1994). Advertising ethics: Emerging methods and trends. *Journal of Advertising, 23*(3), 1-4.

RELATIONSHIP OF INDIVIDUAL MORAL VALUES AND PERCEIVED ETHICAL CLIMATE TO SATISFACTION, COMMITMENT, AND TURNOVER IN A SALES ORGANIZATION

Neil C. Herndon, Jr., O.C. Ferrell,
Debbie Thorne LeClair, and Linda K. Ferrell

ABSTRACT

This study considers how individual moral values and the perceived ethical climate in a retail firm affect organizational outcomes. The findings reveal that most salespeople desire consistency between their own moral values and the ethical climate of their organization. Furthermore, salespeople who perceive the organizational climate as ethical have greater job satisfaction and organizational commitment. Individual moral values and ethical climate significantly influence job attitudes but not turnover intentions. Managerial and theoretical implications are provided.

Research in Marketing, Volume 15, pages 25-48.
Copyright © 1999 by JAI Press Inc.
All rights of reproduction in any form reserved.
ISBN: 0-7623-566-5

The marketing discipline has provided leadership in developing positive models of ethical decision making that have the potential to be used to describe, predict, and control elements of the ethical decision-making process (Dubinsky & Loken, 1989; Ferrell & Gresham, 1985; Hunt & Vitell, 1986). Models of ethical decision making in marketing include consideration of individual moral values, organizational culture, and work group influences as major determinants of ethical decision making (Ferrell & Gresham, 1985; Hunt & Vitell, 1986; Jones, 1991; Trevino, 1986). The basis of organizational culture as a determinant of ethical climate in the organization is grounded in employee organizational learning about ethical decisions through informal and formal socialization, expectations, and rewards (Akaah & Riordan, 1989; Trevino & Youngblood, 1990). Organizational culture, therefore, communicates to members the acceptable standards for behavior in the organization. Through this culture, organizational members socialize new employees as to the acceptable and correct way to think and act within the firm. One component of the organizational culture is the climate. "The ethical climate of a corporation, the shared perceptions of what is ethically correct behavior and how ethical issues should be handled, both reflects and helps define (the) ethics of a corporation" (Victor & Cullen, 1987, p. 52).

Marketing is often cited as the functional area of business with the highest incidence of unethical behavior (Goolsby & Hunt, 1992; Murphy & Laczniak, 1981). Within marketing, the boundary-spanning role of a salesperson is a major area of ethical conflict between the organization and the customer. According to Wotruba (1990), "the central nature of selling—a negotiation between buyer and seller—is inherently a laboratory of ethical scenarios" (p. 30).

Despite the importance of ethical decision making to sales organizations, there has been limited research in sales management to advance understanding of how the ethical component of an organizational climate affects key outcome variables such as job satisfaction, organizational commitment, and turnover.

Elements of corporate culture and ethical climate, such as opportunity (Ferrell & Gresham, 1985; Ferrell, Gresham & Fraedrich, 1989), are thought to influence ethical behavior and may also influence other sales force management constructs and practices. In 1984, Dubinsky and Ingram called for a better understanding of how ethical conflict influences a salesperson's job satisfaction and turnover. In 1991, Kelley and Dorsch noted the need for empirical research that examined both the antecedents and consequences of the ethical climate in sales organizations. Several studies have examined some of these relationships. For example, Hunt and Vásquez-Párraga's (1993) study of sales force supervision activities suggests that a climate emphasizing ethical values can be developed by making salespeople aware of what is "done" and "not done" in the organization. Hunt, Wood, and Chonko (1989) reported a positive association between corporate ethical values and organizational commitment and Schwepker, Ferrell, and Ingram (1997) found that salespeople's perceptions of a positive ethical climate are negatively associated with their perceived ethical conflict with sales managers.

Finally, in a more generalized work setting, Victor and Cullen (1987) noted that conflict between personal moral values and the ethical climate at work may be a source of dissatisfaction, turnover, and performance problems. To date, however, there are very few studies examining the role of individual values and organizational ethics in salesperson job-related outcomes.

As boundary-spanning generators of most business revenue, salespeople facilitate consumer decision making by supplying relevant information about products and the organization. Consequently, they have greater opportunity for exaggeration, untruthfulness, and dishonesty during these salesperson-customer interactions than other organizational members (Bellizi & Hite, 1989). The responsibility for meeting organizational goals can also contribute to an environment of ethical conflict for the sales force. Finally, as Levy and Dubinsky (1983) have noted, ethical difficulties in retail stores often relate to problems in providing close supervision of salespeople. Thus, there is a need to examine the issue of ethics in sales organizations.

The purpose of this research is to determine how individual moral values and perceived corporate ethical climate affect work related sales force outcomes. Individual moral values are hypothesized to influence perceptions of corporate ethical climate while the ethical climate embedded in the corporate culture is hypothesized to influence sales force outcomes including job satisfaction, organizational commitment, and turnover. The sample consists of salespeople and their supervisors from a nationwide retail chain of 725 company-owned specialty stores. First, we provide the theoretical foundation for this study and then present hypotheses, research methods, and results. Finally, discussion is provided with attention to both theoretical and managerial implications as well as limitations and directions for future research.

INDIVIDUAL MORAL VALUES, ETHICAL CLIMATE, AND SALES FORCE OUTCOMES

Ethics in the sales area has been explored from a number of perspectives. Salespeople attempt to balance the interests of the seller and the buyer, as well as those of the salesperson; therefore, ethical conflicts and choices are inherent in the personal selling process. Empirical studies have examined certain selling practices that are perceived by salespeople to be unethical (Dubinsky, Berkowitz, & Rudelius, 1980; Dubinsky & Gwin, 1981; Levy & Dubinsky, 1983). These practices include overstating product benefits, overselling or convincing a customer to buy more than he or she needs, and providing inaccurate information on the product or organizational policies. Recent research extended this work to include consideration of which sales practices having ethical content are actually addressed by company policy (Dubinsky, Jolson, Michaels, Kotabe, & Lim, 1992). The ethical decision-making process of sales managers has also been studied (Hunt & Vásquez-Párraga, 1993; Vitell & Hunt, 1990).

Harris (1990) reports that both sales and service personnel feel more pressure to compromise their values than other employee types included in the study. The salesperson's highly visible boundary-spanning roles and the somewhat autonomous nature of the selling situation may provide a weaker organizational support structure for salespeople than that which is afforded other employees (Laczniak & Murphy, 1993). However, a strong corporate culture that emphasizes ethical behavior may alleviate a salesperson's opportunity to behave unethically (Hunt & Vásquez-Párraga, 1993).

Ethical Climate

Organizational climates, including ethical climates, are a component of organizational culture (Ashforth, 1985; Sathe, 1983). In this view, the organizational climate is characterized by shared values and beliefs that become known through patterns of observable behaviors. Organizational climate, therefore, addresses the behaviors that are supported, expected, and rewarded (Schneider & Rentsch, 1988). Research findings support the view that organizational climates influence ethical behavior (Ferrell & Skinner, 1988), job performance and satisfaction (Downey, Hellriegel, & Slocum, 1975), and research and development innovations (Abbey & Dickson, 1983). Previous studies of work climate have focused primarily on employees' perceptions of control, organizational structure, and the nature of reward systems (Victor & Cullen, 1987).

The present study extends our knowledge of organizational climates and focuses on those aspects that guide individuals about how ethical issues are handled and what types of behavior are considered ethical. Thus, the ethical climate of an organization is one dimension of the overall organizational climate. Factors such as top management ethical actions, the influence of coworkers, and the opportunity for unethical behavior are all captured by the ethical climate construct.

Employees' standards of ethical conduct result from both their own set of moral values and the prevailing values of the organization (Clinard, 1983). Based on the ethical decision-making model of Hunt and Vitell (1986), it is assumed that personal ethical standards are used by the individuals to evaluate perceived corporate ethical climate. It is also possible that the ethical reasoning in a nonwork situation uses one set of criteria, and that the corporate culture influences in the business organization produce a different set of criteria for evaluation of perceived ethical climate in a corporate environment (Carr, 1968; Dubinsky & Gwin, 1981; Fraedrich & Ferrell, 1992). In either case, an individual's set of moral values will guide perceptions of the ethical climate of his or her employing organization.

Individual Moral Values

The discipline of moral philosophy has developed a complex framework for analyzing how individuals make ethical decisions. In the Western world, there are five main theories that characterize the different ways in which individuals reason through ethical issues (Beauchamp & Bowie, 1983; Donaldson & Werhane, 1983). First, utilitarianism is the theory which suggests that individuals should strive for the greatest good for the greatest number of people in a society. Second, deontology focuses on those duties that individuals have to other people and society; a deontologist uses a combination of rules and logic to reach ethical decisions. Third, egoism is the moral philosophy that is grounded on individuals' making decisions that serve their own best interests. Fourth, justice theory is concerned with the equal treatment of equal individuals; with justice reasoning, unequal individuals are treated unequally. Fifth, relativism is the ethical theory which holds that all normative beliefs are based on a certain individual's or culture's values and that there are no universal ethical truths.

Each of these individual moral philosophies can lead to conflicting evaluations of what is right or wrong and ethical or unethical. Researchers in marketing and sales ethics often assume that individuals use either deontology, utilitarianism, or some combination of both moral philosophies in making ethical decisions (cf. Ferrell & Gresham, 1985; Hunt & Vitell, 1986). In addition, Fraedrich and Ferrell (1992) found that marketing managers will vary their moral philosophies across different situations (work, home, etc.). Other researchers have utilized all five moral philosophies to better understand the decisions that marketers make and suggest that these frameworks be employed in future ethics research (cf. Reidenbach & Robin, 1988; Reidenbach, Robin, & Dawson, 1991). The present study employs this broadened view of individual moral philosophies.

In an organizational setting, individuals may have two sets of ethical standards: one a personal set and the other a business set (Carr, 1968; Dubinsky & Gwin, 1981; Fraedrich & Ferrell, 1992). It is possible that the personal set of ethical standards would more directly influence the individual moral values construct and that the business set would more directly influence the perceived corporate ethical climate construct. Individual moral values are shown to positively influence perceived corporate ethical climate because employees desire consistency or congruency between their own ethical value system and the ethical climate of the organization (Dubinsky & Ingram, 1984; DeGeorge, 1995). In general, individuals will strive to maintain congruency or a positive relationship between their personal values and the perceived values of their employing organization.

Hypothesis 1. Individual moral values have a positive relationship with perceived organizational ethical climate.

Organizational Outcome Variables

Organizational climate has been shown to affect a wide range of organizational outcomes. While ethical behavior can be one of the outcomes of an ethical climate, other possible outcomes include job satisfaction, organizational commitment, and turnover. Pervin (1968) found that when individual and organizational characteristics are congruent, performance and satisfaction tend to be high. The congruence between individual moral values and the ethical climate of the firm forms the basis for the following hypotheses.

Job Satisfaction

A salesperson's job satisfaction has been conceptualized as the individual's "affective state relative to several job facets" (Brown & Peterson, 1993, p. 64) or as an overall measure of the job itself and the work environment in which the salesperson operates (Churchill, Ford, & Walker, 1974). Although satisfaction can refer to diverse categories, a macro-organizational view of satisfaction is taken for this research. Satisfaction is defined as "the degree to which employees have a positive affective orientation toward employment by the organization" (Price & Mueller, 1986, p. 215). It appears to encompass all job characteristics that salespeople find fulfilling, rewarding, and satisfying. Churchill, Ford, and Walker (1976) found that about 40 percent of job satisfaction was explained by organizational climate variables, including closeness or management supervision and authority structure. A study of management information systems professionals found greater job satisfaction when top management stressed ethical behavior and when employees were optimistic about the relationship between ethics and success within their firms (Vitell & Davis, 1990). These studies indicate that an individual whose values are compatible with the organizational culture will view the company as more ethical and thus, is more likely to be satisfied with his or her job.

Hypothesis 2.   An ethical organizational climate has a positive relationship with job satisfaction.

Organizational Commitment

Price and Mueller (1986) equate commitment with organizational loyalty, where loyalty is directed at the macro-organization as opposed to work groups. High levels of organizational commitment are characterized by three factors, including (1) a strong belief in the organization's values and goals, (2) a willingness to exert considerable effort on behalf of these goals and values, and (3) a strong desire to maintain membership in the organization. These factors signify aspects of both behavioral commitment and attitudinal commitment (DeCotiis &

Summers, 1987). Mobley (1982) sees "the individual's belief in and acceptance of the goals and values of the organization...[as]...a major part of organizational commitment" (p. 74). Hunt, Wood, and Chonko (1989) report a positive association between corporate ethical values and organizational commitment. Kelley and Dorsch (1991) found that certain types of ethical climates were strongly related to purchasing executives' organizational commitment. Haughey (1993) also concludes that there is a relationship between loyalty, commitment, and the ethical character of the organization; when employees perceive an ethical corporate culture they are acknowledging a certain level of trust and commitment that they have to the firm. These studies support DeCotiis and Summers' (1987) finding that when the organization meets its members' expectations, then the members become more committed to the organization's values and goals.

Hypothesis 3. An ethical organizational climate has a positive relationship with organizational commitment.

Turnover

Turnover is defined as "the cessation of membership in an organization by an individual who receives monetary compensation from the organization" (Mobley, 1982, p. 10). In this study, turnover is conceptualized as an intention to leave the organization. This approach was taken because of its ability to predict actual turnover (Johnston, Varadarajan, Futrell, & Sager, 1987; Mobley, 1982) and because this approach has received broad acceptance by sales management researchers over time (Futrell & Parasuraman, 1984; Ingram, Lee, & Lucas, 1991). Apasu (1986), linking an ethical value ("honesty") to turnover intentions, found that individual value congruence with organizational values is negatively associated with turnover. DeGeorge (1995) indicates that "those who do not agree with the tone [of the corporate culture] and do not fit in usually do not stay long" (p. 104). Thus, those individuals whose moral values are congruent with the organization's ethical climate are less likely to leave the organization.

Hypothesis 4. An ethical organizational climate has a negative relationship with turnover.

Ethical Climate Related to Organizational Outcome Variables

The research model (Figure 1) shows the hypothesized relationships among the sales force outcome variables based on previous studies. Job satisfaction is positively related to organizational commitment (Bluedorn, 1982; Dubinsky & Skinner, 1984; Johnston, Parasuraman, Futrell, & Black, 1990) and negatively related to turnover (Dubinsky & Skinner, 1984; Futrell & Parasuraman, 1984; Johnston et al., 1987; Sager, Varadarajan, & Futrell, 1988).

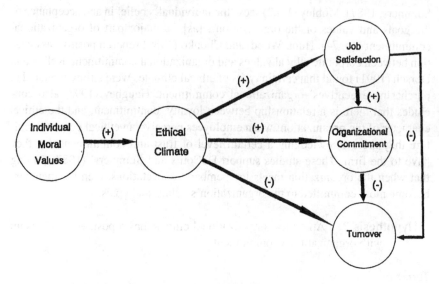

Figure 1. Hypothesized Model

Organizational commitment is shown to be positively related to job satisfaction (Dubinsky & Skinner, 1984) and negatively related to turnover (Cotton & Tuttle, 1986; DeCotiis & Summers, 1987; Sager & Johnston, 1989). Those individuals who have a high investment and attachment to the organization are less likely to leave the organization (Brown & Peterson, 1993). These hypothesized relationships among job satisfaction, organizational commitment, and turnover are frequently found in sales management studies (Sager, Futrell, & Varadarajan, 1989) and are included in this study primarily to evaluate their relationship to ethical climate.

Hypothesis 5. Job satisfaction is positively related to organizational commitment.

Hypothesis 6. Job satisfaction is negatively related to turnover.

Hypothesis 7. Organizational commitment is negatively related to turnover.

RESEARCH DESIGN

The present research attempts to improve our knowledge of the importance of individual moral values and corporate ethical climate on certain sales force outcome variables. As noted above, the hypotheses follow from conceptual models in both the sales management and marketing ethics literature. The relationships in

Table 1. Sample Characteristics

	Salespeople		Supervisors	
	Sample	Population*	Sample	Population*
Age (years)	33.53	21	34.48	34
Education (years)	14.23	n/a	14.45	n/a
Gender (% male)	90.0	83.9	88.7	93.5
Income ($)	22,316	18,500	31,541	37,500
Tenure (years)	1.94	<1	4.69	4.5
Sample Size	233		160	

Note: *The population statistics were provided by the company under study.

this study were tested using a structural equation modeling approach (LISREL VII; Joreskog & Sorbom, 1989) which requires explicit specification of variable operationalizations and hypothesized causal relationships among constructs (Hughes, Price, & Marrs, 1986).

Although LISREL VII can be used in exploratory research, this study takes a strictly confirmatory approach to determine whether the hypothesized model is consistent with the observed data. Because this study focuses on theory testing and employs previously validated measures, the primary focus is on the structural linkages in the model. However, attention is also given to the psychometric properties of the measures. The following sections detail the sample, operationalize study variables, measure assessment, model evaluation, and the show the results of the study.

Sample and Data Collection

The sample was drawn from a nationwide chain of 725 company-owned retail specialty stores. Anonymity was promised to both the organization and the respondents. Using a proportional random sample within divisions, full-time salespeople and their immediate supervisors were surveyed at 300 stores located in 43 states of the continental United States. Using a sample from one functional area (i.e., sales) within an organization reduces the influence of other corporate subcultures on the hypothesized relationships in this study.

Of the 1,500 questionnaires sent out, 468 were returned for a 31.2 percent response rate. Of the 468 returned, 393 or 84 percent of those returned were deemed usable. Seventy-five were eliminated due to significant missing data. Therefore, for the purposes of this study, the usable sample size is 393. A prenotification letter signed by a senior corporate executive and mailed two weeks in advance of the study was used to increase response rates (Martin, Duncan, Powers, & Sawyer, 1989), as was a cover letter in the questionnaire offering appreciation for participation. A detachable coupon to obtain a free summary of study results was also included. These activities were intended to implement Dillman's

(1978) method of maximizing survey response, as was the wording of both the prenotification letter and cover letter. The mail survey approach was utilized to reduce social desirability bias (Dillman, 1978). Of the questionnaires that were returned, 59.3 percent were from full-time salespeople and 40.7 percent were from their immediate supervisors. Characteristics of the sample are reported in Table 1.

To assess nonresponse bias, demographics of the first two-thirds of the sample were compared to the last one-third of the sample using t-tests with 388 degrees of freedom at alpha equals .05. There was no significant difference in age ($t = .4790$, $p = .6322$), education ($t = .4802$, $p = .6313$), gender ($t = -.1906$, $p = .8489$), or tenure ($t = 1.6859$, $p = .0926$). There was a significant difference in income ($t = 2.5592$, $p = .0109$) with early respondents reporting higher annual income than late respondents ($27,357 to $23,457, respectively). A lack of significant differences between early and late respondents indicates that nonresponse bias is not a severe problem, assuming that those who respond late are more like those who do not respond at all (Armstrong & Overton, 1977; Gatignon & Robertson, 1989). Therefore, considering there are only income differences among sample respondents, nonresponse bias is not deemed a serious problem.

Although respondents have the title of either salesperson or supervisor, the nature of retail sales and the small size of each individual store suggests that both are engaged in selling to customers and have few functional differences. A series of t-tests found no significant differences at alpha = .05 between salespeople and supervisors on age ($p = .3163$), education ($p = .2519$), or gender ($p = .6670$). There is a significant difference in income ($p = .0001$) and tenure ($p = .0001$), with supervisors having higher income and longer tenure with the firm. This would be expected because supervisors in this organization are typically salespeople who have remained employed with the retail chain for a longer time. Furthermore, there were no significant differences between salespeople and supervisors on the Individual Moral Values scales ($p = .3966$) or the Ethical Climate scale ($p = .5731$). Therefore, the sample was collapsed for further analysis.

Operationalization of Study Variables

A self-administered questionnaire containing five measures was used (see Appendix). All variables were measured with multiple-item scales validated in previous research. The Individual Moral Values scale (Reidenbach & Robin, 1988; Reidenbach, Robin, & Dawson, 1991) consists of three scenarios, each followed by eight seven-point semantic differential scales anchored by bipolar adjectives or phrases. The scale is intended to measure various individual moral frameworks including moral equity, relativism, and contractualism. Reidenbach and Robin (1988) report coefficient alpha for the measure to be .87. Both the scale and the scenarios have been used previously in studies of retail salespeople and sales managers (i.e., Henthorne, Robin, & Reidenbach, 1992; Reidenbach, Robin, & Dawson, 1991). The research made no assumptions about a desirable or appropriate moral framework. The summated measure was used to determine the existence of individual moral values.

The Ethical Climate Questionnaire (Victor & Cullen, 1987, 1988) consists of 26 statements followed by a six-point Likert-type scale. Victor and Cullen report coefficient alphas of .80, .79, .79, .71, and .60 for each dimension of ethical climate. The measure is designed to elicit five dimensions of ethical climate including caring, law and code, independence, instrumental, and rules-based. Victor and Cullen (1988) were able to identify different corporate climates using their scale. While it has been used successfully in a variety of organizational types (Victor & Cullen, 1987, 1988), this appears to be its first use in a retail sales setting. This research was based on a global measure of ethical climate and did not consider dimensions of ethical climate.

There is significant justification in defense of using a summated measure for the ethical climate and individual moral values scales for the purposes of this research. One of the fundamental postulates of factor analysis is the "postulate of parsimony." In this research, the key research focus is on the relationship between proven global measures, not the items within the construct. In other words, our purpose is not to break down ethical climate, for example, into its five dimensions, but we assume that ethical climate can be an overall construct that is a part of corporate culture. Our study is not about developing ethical climate, but relationships of ethical climate, individual moral values, and outcome variables. This study is consistent with Kim and Mueller (1978) who state that "we accept on faith the more parsimonious model…such an assumption is not provable but is widely accepted in other fields of research" (p. 44).

Bagozzi and Heatherton (1994) support the approach we have used in this study in that "scales are treated as the sum of many items, and the focus in their predictive properties" (p. 64). This study uses global hypotheses and global measures. Again, Bagozzi and Heatherton support such an approach in that "when global measures are under scrutiny, such as when the meaning of general self concept is desired, the total aggregation or partial aggregation models are appropriated" (p. 64).

The Job Satisfaction Index (Brayfield & Rothe, 1951) consists of 18 statements followed by a five-point Likert-type scale. Brayfield and Rothe report the reliability coefficient as .87, while Price and Mueller (1986) report that for four studies the range was .78 to .99, with a mean of .89.

The Organizational Commitment Questionnaire (Mowday, Steers, & Porter, 1979) consists of 15 statements followed by a seven-point Likert-type scale. They report coefficient alpha to range from .82 to .93 with a median of .90. Johnston et al. (1990) report LISREL-derived reliabilities of .883 and .926 in a longitudinal sales force study.

Table 2. Reliability and Variance Extracted

Scale	Number of Items	Reliability*	Variance Extracted**
Individual Moral Values (IMV)	23	.942	.320
Ethical Climate (EC)	26	.888	.598
Job Satisfaction (JS)	18	.919	.535
Organizational Commitment (OC)	15	.942	.596
Turnover (T)	4	.928	.859

Notes: Due to a printing error in the questionnaire, only 7 out of the 8 items for one scenario were used in the analysis for the Individual Moral Values scale.

* Nunnally (1978) recommends that reliability coefficients be at least .70.

** Guidelines indicate that variance extracted for a construct should exceed .50 (Hair et al., 1992).

The Turnover measure (Bluedorn, 1982), as modified by Johnston et al. (1990), consists of four statements followed by a seven-point Likert-type scale. Johnston et al. (1990) report LISREL-derived reliabilities of .924 and .963 in a longitudinal study of sales forces.

Scores on the multiple items were summed to obtain a global measure of the corresponding construct for all scales. This practice is common when using established scales and enables direct comparisons with past research results (Hair, Anderson, Tatham, & Black, 1992; Johnston et al., 1990). Because one of the main objectives of this study was to draw on past research and to facilitate comparisons in the future, we followed the traditional approach of deriving summed values from the multiple-item measures and using single indicators for each construct. We recognize that aggregation may not be appropriate when global hypotheses are not nested in multiple-item scales validated in previous research.

ANALYSIS AND RESULTS

Measure Assessment

The constructs used in the study primarily exhibit high reliability and variance extracted measures (Table 2). All constructs have reliability above the recommended level of .70 (Nunnally, 1978). The LISREL-derived reliabilities range from .888 for the Ethical Climate Questionnaire to .942 for both the Individual Moral Values scale and the Organizational Commitment Questionnaire measures. The Turnover measure exhibits a reliability of .928, and the Job Satisfaction Index has a reliability of .919.

Variance extracted refers to the overall variance in indicators that is accounted for by the latent construct and is a more stringent measure of reliability and convergent validity. Hair et al. (1992) suggest that the variance extracted value exceed .50. Ethical Climate, Job Satisfaction, Organizational Commitment, and Turnover exceed the threshold value of .50. The Individual Moral Values con-

Table 3. Correlations and Variances for Model Constructs*

	EC	JS	OC	T	IMV
EC	146.074				
JS	.357	160.495			
OC	.477	.785	359.532		
T	−.341	−.677	−.724	59.105	
IMV	.164	.043	.158	−.055	309.211

Notes: * Diagonal values represent variances and lower matrix contains correlations.

    Legend: EC = Ethical Climate

                JS = Job Satisfaction

                OC = Organizational Commitment

                T = Turnover

                IMV = Individual Moral Values

struct is somewhat below that threshold, although we deemed the measure sufficient for this research.

Table 3 shows the correlations and variances for the model constructs. Shared variance between two constructs is indicated by the squared correlation between the constructs. When the shared variance is lower than each construct's extracted variance value, then the constructs have discriminant validity (Fornell & Larcker, 1981). With one exception, all pairs of constructs' shared variance were lower than each construct's extracted variance. For example, the shared variance between Turnover and Ethical Climate is .116 ($-.341^2$). Turnover and Ethical Climate have extracted variance values of .859 and .598, respectively, and meet the requirements for discriminant validity. Job Satisfaction and Organizational Commitment have a shared variance of .616 ($.785^2$), extracted variances of .535 and .596, and do not have discriminant validity. However, theoretically these constructs are expected to be highly correlated (Brown & Peterson, 1993; Williams & Hazer, 1986).

Overall Model Analysis

Each construct in this study was measured by established scales with known reliabilities and was represented by a single indicator. Because only a single indicator was used, it was necessary to make certain assumptions about the values of the measurement parameters. These parameters were fixed prior to the analysis and are indicated in Table 4. Both Williams and Hazer (1986) and Kenny (1979) advocate fixing parameters in the following manner: the path from any construct to its measured variable is set at the square root of the reliability of the measured variable. Measurement error variance is equal to one (1) minus the reliability of the measure. Reliabilities of the five constructs in this study are found in Table 2.

The hypothesized relationships shown in Figure 1 were analyzed using the sample correlation matrix as input to LISREL VII (Joreskog & Sorbom, 1989). This

Table 4. Overall Structural Model Lisrel Estimates and t-values

Chi-Square (df = 3)			7.50 (p = .057)
GFI			.990
AGFI			.948
RMSR			.019
NFI-2*			.992
NFI*			.987
TLI*			.987

Linkage/Parameter		Estimate	t-value
λ_1		.971**	.000
λ_2		.942**	.000
λ_3		.958**	.000
λ_4		.971**	.000
λ_5		.963**	.000
δ_1		.058**	.000
ε_1		.112**	.000
ε_2		.081**	.000
ε_3		.058**	.000
ε_4		.072**	.000
γ_{11}	IMV → EC	.186	2.893***
β_{21}	EC → JS	.395	6.382***
β_{31}	EC → OC	.226	5.342***
β_{41}	EC → T	.023	.429 (not significant)
β_{32}	JS → OC	.753	18.048***
β_{42}	JS → T	−.275	−2.925***
β_{43}	OC → T	−.555	−5.456***

Notes: * Null Model: Chi-square = 584.55, df = 5, p = .000.
         ** Fixed parameter (preassigned based on scale reliabilities).
        *** Significant at $p < .01$.

type of analysis is useful for making causal inferences about both the pattern and magnitude of the hypothesized relationships (Bagozzi, 1980) and for theory testing (Hughes, Price, & Marrs, 1986). The variances and correlations among constructs are reported in Table 3.

The overall fit of the data to the hypothesized model was assessed using several types of tests, the results of which are reported in Table 4. The chi-square statistic is not significant, suggesting few discrepancies between the model and the data. However, because the chi-square test is susceptible to sample size effects, other fit indices were examined (Bagozzi, 1980). The goodness-of-fit index (GFI) and adjusted goodness-of-fit index (AGFI) both meet the .90 criteria suggested as a guideline for assessing the meaningfulness of the model (Anderson & Gerbing, 1984; Joreskog & Sorbom, 1984). The root mean square residual (RMSR) is very low (.017), indicating an adequate model fit (Marsh, Balla, & McDonald, 1988). Both normed fit indices (NFI and NFI-2) are much greater than .90, indicating an adequate model fit. Finally, the Tucker-Lewis Index (TLI) also exceeds the recommended level of .90. If the last three indices cited had been less than .90, then

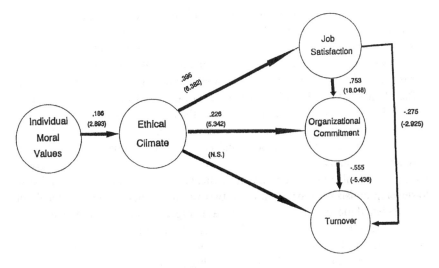

Figure 2. Structural Equation Model

this would suggest that the model could be improved (Marsh, Balla, & McDonald, 1988).

Structural Model

Examination of the structural coefficients reveals six significant relationships (see Table 4 and Figure 2). Individual moral values have a significant positive impact on perceptions of the organizational climate as ethical (Hypothesis 1 supported). Congruence between individual moral values and ethical climate has a significant positive impact on job satisfaction (Hypothesis 2 supported) and organizational commitment (Hypothesis 3 supported) but no significant effect on turnover (Hypothesis 4 not supported). Job satisfaction has a significant positive impact on organizational commitment (Hypothesis 5 supported) and a significant negative impact on turnover (Hypothesis 6 supported). Finally, organizational commitment has a significant negative impact on turnover (Hypothesis 7 supported).

DISCUSSION

The hypotheses reflected in the structural equation model were supported with one exception. Perceptions of organizational climate as ethical did not have a significant effect on turnover. However, the organization's ethical climate results in higher job satisfaction and higher organizational commitment. These findings and relationships between the organizational outcomes of satisfaction, commitment, and turnover are consistent with theoretical models and empirical research in the sales management literature. The significant relationship between individual moral values and their relationship to perceived ethical climate is consistent with our model and with theoretical models of ethical decision making in marketing.

Based on Hunt and Vitell's (1986) model of ethical decision making, it seems logical that an individual's set of personal ethical standards is used to guide the evaluation of perceived organizational ethical climate. This study supports the positive relationship between individual moral values and perceptions of ethical climate. Apparently, employees strive for consistency or congruency between their own ethical value systems and the ethical climate of the organization. Failure to develop consistency between these two variables could result in ethical conflict, lessened job satisfaction, and decreased organizational commitment.

This research has shown that individuals who find the ethical climate of the organization to be comfortable and congruent with their own values (i.e., perceived as ethical) are more likely to score higher on the measure of job satisfaction. It is logical that consistency between individual moral values and ethical climate should result in greater job satisfaction because individuals tend to feel more satisfied and fulfilled in an organization where they are comfortable.

Consistency between individual moral values and the ethical climate is also positively related to organizational commitment. Commitment has been associated with loyalty. To some extent, organizational commitment relates to "the individual's belief in and the acceptance of the goals and the values of the organization" (Mobley, 1982, p. 74). As an organization meets members' expectations, then the employee commits to serve the organization's missions and activities. Higher levels of commitment have been shown to reduce role ambiguity, role conflict, and work alienation for both salespeople and sales managers (Michaels, Cron, Dubinsky, & Joachimsthaler, 1988). A negative relationship was found between job satisfaction and turnover as well as between organizational commitment and turnover. These findings are consistent with numerous studies cited in the review of sales management research (Dubinsky & Ingram, 1984; Johnston et al., 1987). Those who find the ethical climate of the organization to be less consistent with their own beliefs have less job satisfaction and less organizational commitment. Also, these individuals may be more likely to leave the organization.

There was no significant relationship between ethical climate and turnover, but there may be a logical explanation. It appears that turnover is mediated through job satisfaction and organizational commitment. For many reasons, some employees' moral values may not be consistent with the firm's ethical climate, but they have not left the organization. Salespeople often do not leave the organization until they find another job. They may go through a complex process of evaluating many concerns in the organization, not just ethical climate. However, because this inconsistency between the employee's and the organization's values may lead to lower job satisfaction and organizational commitment, the individual may eventually be compelled to leave the organization.

The respondents in this study had one year of tenure beyond the average salesperson or supervisor in the organization. Current employees who find congruence with the ethical climate will have an increasing feeling of "fit" and will be less likely to consider leaving the firm. It would take some other factors, such as the necessity of a family move, for this type of employee to leave the organization. Economic conditions may also lead to a tight job market that makes it difficult or impossible for a salesperson to leave his or her present position (Mobley, 1982). Lucas, Parasuraman, Davis, and Enis (1987) noted the effect of economic conditions and other job opportunities on a salesperson's propensity to leave. Thus, turnover could be affected by external environmental conditions as well as the internal environment of the firm.

The model fit in this study provides new insights into the importance of ethical climate in a sales organization. Based on the results, it is important to have a positive association between individual moral values and the ethical climate. Without this fit, a decrease in job satisfaction and organizational commitment may lead to a decrease in organizational performance. The positive relationship between ethical climate, job satisfaction, and organizational commitment provides evidence that ethical climate contributes to positive organizational outcomes.

Managerial Implications

The managerial and practical implications of this study relate to the importance of establishing a strong ethical climate in a sales organization. First, this ethical climate is a part of the organizational climate that is influenced by management, employees, industry, and other factors. In turn, the culture influences daily decision making and needs to be managed in a way that reduces ethical conflict. For example, during the recruiting process, organizations should communicate their expectations for inappropriate conduct and determine a candidate's ability and willingness to meet these standards. Trevino and Youngblood (1990) have written about the importance of eliminating "bad apples" from "good barrels." By the same reasoning, organizational recruiters have an obligation to hire individuals who are going to reinforce and strengthen ethical standards.

Another implication arises from the pressure that salespeople often feel in reaching organizational goals. Organizational strategy and objectives must be developed with respect to ethical standards. A code of ethics is useful if salespeople are not given full organizational support for achieving sales goals in a legal and ethical manner. Ethical conflict can arise for a sales manager who learns that a high achieving salesperson is reaching his or her goals with tactics that breach organizational ethical values. At this point, ethical standards and organizational goals may be in direct conflict. The organizational culture must be prepared to choose the higher ethical standard over short-term gains in sales and profitability.

The choice sends a clear message to other salespeople about the importance of ethics in the organization. In turn, employee's beliefs and perceptions will be reinforced and the culture will continue to improve its ethical standards.

The ethical climate needs to be consistently managed by communicating ethical standards and holding organizational members accountable for conformance. Because of their boundary-spanning role and responsibility for revenue, an organization needs to pay careful attention to the management of ethics in the sales force. This attention begins in the recruiting phase and continues through goal-setting, employee evaluation, and ongoing training and communication. Another benefit of taking care in dealing with salespeople comes through their contact with outside stakeholders (customers, suppliers, competitors, etc.). If diligence is not taken in dealing with training and communication with salespeople, not only does it send the wrong message to the stakeholder, but also to other organizational employees who operate under close organizational scrutiny due to the nature of their internal position. As this study indicates, the ethical climate is an important aspect of job-related outcomes that are well known to researchers and practitioners in the sales management field. A focus on organizational ethics should improve job satisfaction and organizational commitment. From these improvements, turnover intentions should decrease.

Limitations and Conclusions

Despite the contributions of this study, it is important to note several limitations. First, the study is limited in its generalizability because it was conducted within a single organization's sales force. The study must be interpreted with the understanding that other organizational cultures and marketing positions have unique characteristics that may alter the relationship between ethical climate and job-related outcomes. The specific type of industry, business environment, governmental regulation, or other organizational factor may influence the relationships found in this study.

A second limitation of this study relates to the possibility that individual moral values and ethical climate are second-order factors. This might suggest that there are several facets of individual moral values and ethical climate that affect the outcome variables. Third, the study was conducted at one point in time and does not reflect the possibility of organizational learning in the ethics area. It would be useful for future studies to utilize a longitudinal design to determine if these results are consistent over time. Today, many organizations are implementing ethical compliance programs that are designed to alter and solidify ethical climate (LeClair, Ferrell, & Ferrell, 1997). A longitudinal design could capture the extent to which ethics programs and ethics training change perceptions of ethical climate, and job satisfaction, commitment, and turnover.

Finally, a future study could also overcome a limitation associated with the practical and financial effects of ethical climate. The next logical extension of this research would be to link ethical climate to organizational performance and profitability. Multiple organizations' organizational cultures and job-related outcomes as related to performance and profitability could be compared. This research would not only benefit academics, but could also provide a powerful message to marketing managers and practitioners.

While these limitations are important considerations in interpreting the results, this study makes a contribution toward understanding the importance of individual moral values and ethical climate to organizational outcomes. This study does not specify a correct ethical climate, but rather demonstrates the importance of individual values and organizational climate to job-related outcomes. Managers should strive for creating a strong ethical climate if they want to reduce the potential for ethical conflict. This conflict can lead to less organizational commitment, lower job satisfaction, and possibly, increased turnover. Increased intentions to leave the organization have been associated with increased potential for illegal acts and more illegal acts encourage learning of these inappropriate behaviors by other sales force members (Ferrell & Gresham, 1985; Ferrell, Gresham, & Fraedrich, 1989). Conversely, a positive association between ethical climate and individual values can create a situation that benefits both employees and the organization.

The results of this study appear consistent with Maignan and Ferrell (1999) who found that specific organizational values are conducive of corporate citizenship, which in turn is associated with greater employee commitment and business performance (defined as return on investment, return on assets, and profit growth). This study, conducted in France, provides encouragement for additional studies on the relationship between ethical climate and satisfaction, as well as commitment and turnover in international settings. Evaluation of the link between ethical climate and business performance (related to profits) could strengthen support for ethics training in sales organizations (Maignan & Ferrell, 1999).

APPENDIX

Sample Construct Items

Individual Moral Values Scenario and Scale

Scenario: A young man, recently hired as a salesperson for a local retail store, has been working very hard to favorably impress his boss with his selling ability. At times, this young man, anxious for an order, has been a little overeager. To get the order, he exaggerates the value of the item or withholds relevant information concerning the product he is trying to sell. No fraud or deceit is intended by his actions, he is simply overeager.

Action: His boss, the owner of the retail store, is aware of the salesman's actions but he has done nothing to stop such practices.

Scale to Evaluate the Action:

Just	————	Unjust
Fair	————	Unfair
Morally Right	————	Not Morally Right
Acceptable to My Family	————	Not Acceptable to My Family
Culturally Acceptable	————	Not Culturally Acceptable
Traditionally Acceptable	————	Not Traditionally Acceptable
Violates an Unspoken Promise	————	Does Not Violate an Unspoken Promise
Violates an Unwritten Contract	————	Does Not Violate an Unwritten Contract

Ethical Climate

The most important concern is the good of all people in the organization as a whole.

In this organization, people are expected to strictly follow legal or professional standards.

Successful people in this organization go by the book.

In this organization, people protect their own interests above all else.

The most important concern in this company is each person's own sense of right and wrong.

Job Satisfaction

I feel I am happier in my work than most other people.

I feel real enjoyment in my work.

I feel fairly well satisfied with my present job.

Organizational Commitment

I would accept almost any type of job assignment in order to keep working for this organization.

I am proud to tell others that I am part of this organization.

I really care about the fate of this organization.

Turnover

How would you rate your chance of:

  Quitting in the next 3 months.
  Quitting in the next 6 months.
  Quitting sometime in the next year.
  Quitting sometime in the next 2 years.

REFERENCES

Abbey, A., & J.W. Dickson. (1983). R & D Work Climate and Innovation in Semiconductors. *Academy of Management Journal, 26*, 362-368.

Akaah, I.P., & Riordan, E.A. (1989). Judgments of marketing professionals about ethical issues in marketing research: A replication and extension. *Journal of Marketing Research, 26*(February), 112-120.

Anderson, J.C., & Gerbing, D.W. (1984). The effect of sampling error on convergence, improper solutions, and goodness-of-fit indices for maximum likelihood confirmatory factor analysis. *Psychometrika, 2*, 155-173.

Apasu, Y. (1986). Identifying the antecedents of salespersons' intention to leave. *Akron Business and Economic Review, 17*(Winter), 85-97.

Armstrong, J.S., & Overton, T.S. (1977). Estimating nonresponse bias in mail surveys. *Journal of Marketing Research, 14*(August), 396-402.

Ashforth, B.E. (1985). Climate formation: Issues and extensions. *Academy of Management Review, 10*, 837-847.

Bagozzi, R.P. (1980). *Causal models in marketing*. New York: Wiley.

Bagozzi, R.P., & Heatherton, T.F. (1994). A general approach to representing multifaceted personality constructs: Application to state self-esteem. *Structural Equation Modeling, 1*(1), 35-67.

Beauchamp, T.L., & Bowie, N.E. (1983). *Ethical theory and business*. Englewood Cliffs, NJ: Prentice-Hall.

Bellizzi, J.A., & Hite, R.E. (1989). Supervising unethical salesforce behavior. *Journal of Marketing, 53*(April), 36-47.

Bluedorn, A.C. (1982). A unified model of turnover from organizations. *Human Relations, 35*(February), 135-153.

Brayfield, A.H., & Rothe, H.F. (1951) An index of job satisfaction. *Journal of Applied Psychology, 35*(October), 307-311.

Brown, S.P., & Peterson, R.A. (1993). Antecedents and consequences of salesperson job satisfaction: meta-analysis and assessment of causal effects. *Journal of Marketing Research, 30*(February), 63-77.

Carr, A.Z. (1968). Is business bluffing ethical? *Harvard Business Review, 46*(January/February), 143-153.

Churchill, G.A., Ford, N.M., & Walker, O.C., Jr. (1974). Measuring the job satisfaction of industrial salesmen. *Journal of Marketing Research, 11*(August), 254-260.

Churchill, G.A., Ford, N.M., & Walker, O.C., Jr. (1976). Organizational climate and job satisfaction in the salesforce. *Journal of Marketing Research, 13*(November), 323-332.

Clinard, M.B. (1983). *Corporate ethics and crime*. Beverly Hills, CA: Sage.

Cotton, J.L., & Tuttle, J.M. (1986). Employee turnover: A meta-analysis and review with implications for research. *Academy of Management Review*, 11(January), 55-70.

DeCotiis, T.A., & Summers, T.P. (1987). A path analysis of a model of the antecedents and consequences of organizational commitment. *Human Relations, 40*(July), 445-470.

DeGeorge, R.T. (1995). *Business ethics* (4th ed.). Englewood Cliffs, NJ: Prentice-Hall.

Deshpande, R., Farley, J.U., & Webster, F.E., Jr. (1993). Corporate culture, customer orientation, and innovativeness in japanese firms: A quadrad analysis. *Journal of Marketing, 57*(January), 23-37.

Dillman, D.A. (1978). *Mail and telephone surveys: The total design method*. New York: John Wiley and Sons.

Donaldson, T., & Werhane, P.H. (1983). *Ethical issues in business*. Englewood Cliffs, NJ: Prentice-Hall.

Downey, H.K., Hellriegel, D., & Slocum, J.W. (1975). Congruence between individual needs, organizational climate, job satisfaction and performance. *Academy of Management Journal, 18*, 149-155.

Dubinsky, A.J., Berkowitz, E.N., & Rudelius, W. (1980). Ethical problems of field sales personnel. *MSU Business Topics, 28*(3), 11-16.

Dubinsky, A.J., & Gwin, J.M. (1981). Business ethics: Buyers and sellers. *Journal of Purchasing and Materials Management, 17*(Winter), 9-16.

Dubinsky, A.J., & Ingram, T.N. (1984). Correlates of salespeople's ethical conflict: An exploratory investigation. *Journal of Business Ethics, 3*(November), 343-353.

Dubinsky, A.J., & Skinner, S.J. (1984). Turnover tendencies among retail salespeople: Relationships with job satisfaction and demographic characteristics. In R.W. Belk et al. (Eds.), *1984 AMA educators' proceedings* (pp. 153-157). Chicago: American Marketing Association.

Dubinsky, A.J., & Loken, B. (1989). Analyzing ethical decision making in marketing. *Journal of Business Research, 19*(September), 83-107.

Dubinsky, A.J., Jolson, M.A., Michaels, R.E., Kotabe, M., & Lim, C.U. (1992). Ethical perceptions of field sales personnel: An empirical assessment. *Journal of Personal Selling and Sales Management, 12*(Fall), 9-21.

Ferrell, O.C., & Gresham, L.G. (1985). A contingency framework for understanding ethical decision making in marketing. *Journal of Marketing, 49*(Summer), 87-96.

Ferrell, O.C., Gresham, L.G., & Fraedrich, J. (1989). A synthesis of ethical decision models for marketing. *Journal of Macromarketing, 9*(Fall), 55-64.

Ferrell, O.C., & Skinner, S.J. (1988). Ethical behavior and bureaucratic structure in marketing research organizations. *Journal of Marketing Research, 25*(February), 103-109.

Fornell, C., & Larcker, D.F. (1981). Evaluating structural equation models with unobservable variables and measurement error. *Journal of Marketing Research, 18*(February), 39-50.

Fraedrich, J., & Ferrell, O.C. (1992). Cognitive consistency of marketing managers in ethical situations. *Journal of the Academy of Marketing Science, 20*(Summer), 245-252.

Futrell, C.M., & Parasuraman, A. (1984). The relationship of satisfaction and performance to salesforce turnover. *Journal of Marketing, 48*(Fall), 33-40.

Gatignon, H., & Robertson, T.S. (1989). Technology diffusion: An empirical test of competitive effects. *Journal of Marketing, 53*(January), 35-49.

Ghosh, A. (1990). *Retail management.* Chicago: The Dryden Press.

Goolsby, J., & Hunt, S.D. (1992). Cognitive moral development and marketing. *Journal of Marketing, 56*(January), 56-68.

Hair, J.F., Jr., Anderson, R.E., Tatham, R.L., & Black, W.C. (1992). *Multivariate data analysis* (3rd ed.). New York: Macmillan.

Harris, J.R. (1990). Ethical values of individuals at different levels in the organizational hierarchy of a single firm. *Journal of Business Ethics, 9*(September), 741-750.

Haughey, J.C. (1993). Does loyalty in the workplace have a future? *Business Ethics Quarterly, 3*(January), 1-16.

Henthorne, T.L., Robin, D.R., & Reidenbach, R.E. (1992). Identifying the gaps in ethical perceptions between managers and salespeople: A multidimensional approach. *Journal of Business Ethics, 11*(November), 849-856.

Hughes, M.A., Price, R.L., & Marrs, D.W. (1986). Linking theory construction and theory testing: Models with multiple indicators of latent variables. *Academy of Management Review, 11*(1), 128-144.

Hunt, S.D., & Vitell, S. (1986). A general theory of marketing ethics. *Journal of Macromarketing, 6*(Spring), 5-16.

Hunt, S.D., Wood, V.R., & Chonko, L.B. (1989). Corporate ethical values and organizational commitment in marketing. *Journal of Marketing, 53*(July), 79-90.

Hunt, S.D., & Vásquez-Párraga, A.Z. (1993). Organizational consequences, marketing ethics, and salesforce supervision. *Journal of Marketing Research, 30*(February), 78-90.

Ingram, T.N., Lee, K.S., & Lucas, G.H., Jr. (1991). Commitment and involvement: Assessing a salesforce typology, *Journal of the Academy of Marketing Science, 19*(Summer), 187-197.

Johnston, M.W., Varadarajan, P.R., Futrell, C.M., & Sager, J. (1987). The relationship between organizational commitment, job satisfaction, and turnover among new salespeople. *Journal of Personal Selling and Sales Management, 7*(November), 29-38.

Johnston, M.W., Parasuraman, A., Futrell, C.M., & Black, W.C. (1990). A longitudinal assessment of the impact of selected organizational influences on salespeople's organizational commitment during early employment. *Journal of Marketing Research, 27*(August), 333-344.

Jones, T.M. (1991). Ethical decision making by individuals in organizations: An issue-contingent model. *Academy of Management Review, 16*(April), 366-395.

Joreskog, K.G., & Sorbom, D. (1984). *LISREL: Analysis of linear structure relationships by the method of maximum likelihood.* Mooresville: Scientific Software.

Joreskog, K.G., & Sorbom, D. (1989). *LISREL VII, A guide to the program and application.* Chicago: SPSS, Inc.

Kelley, S.W., & Dorsch, M.J. (1991). Ethical climate, organizational commitment, and indebtedness among purchasing executives. *Journal of Personal Selling and Sales Management, 11*(Fall), 55-65.

Kenny, D.A. (1979). *Correlation and causality.* New York: Wiley.

Kim, J.-O., & Mueller, C.W. (1978). *Introduction to factor analysis.* New York: Sage.

Laczniak, G.R., & Murphy, P.E. (1993). *Ethical marketing decisions: The higher road.* Needham Heights: Allyn and Bacon.

LeClair, D.T., Ferrell, O.C., & Ferrell, L. (1997). The federal sentencing guidelines for organizations: Implications for international marketing strategy. *Journal of Public Policy & Marketing, 16*(Spring), 26-37.

Levy, M., & Dubinsky, A.J. (1983). Identifying and addressing retail salespeople's ethical problems: A method and application. *Journal of Retailing, 59*(Spring), 46-66.

Lucas, G.J., Jr., Parasuraman, A., Davis, R.A., & Enis, B.M. (1987). An empirical study of salesforce turnover. *Journal of Marketing, 51*(July), 34-59.

Maignan, I., & Ferrell, O.C. (1999). Antecedents and benefits of corporate citizenship: An investigation of French businesses. *Journal of Business Research.*

Marsh, H.W., Balla, J.R., & McDonald, R.P. (1988). Goodness-of-fit indexes in confirmatory factory analysis: The effects of sample size. *Psychological Bulletin, 103*(3), 391-410.

Martin, W.S., Duncan, W.J., Powers, T.L., & Sawyer, J.C. (1989). Costs and benefits of selected response inducement techniques in mail survey research. *Journal of Business Research, 19*(August), 67-79.

Michaels, R.E., Cron, W.L., Dubinsky, A.J., & Joachimsthaler, E.A. (1988). Influence of formalization on the organizational commitment and work alienation of salespeople and industrial buyers. *Journal of Marketing Research, 25*(November), 376-383.

Mobley, W.H. (1982). *Employee turnover: Causes, consequences, and control.* Reading, PA: Addison-Wesley.

Mowday, R.T., Steers, R.M., & Porter, L.W. (1979). The measure of organizational commitment. *Journal of Vocational Behavior, 14*(April), 224-247.

Murphy, P.E., & Laczniak, G.R. (1981). Marketing ethics: A review with implications for managers, educators and researchers. In B.M. Enish & K.J. Roering (Eds.), *Review of marketing 1981* (pp. 251-266). Chicago: American Marketing Association.

Nunnally, J.C. (1978). *Psychometric theory.* New York: McGraw-Hill.

Pervin, L.A. (1968). Performance and satisfaction as a function of individual environment fit. *Psychological Bulletin, 69*, 56-68.

Price, J.L., & Mueller, C.W. (1986). *Handbook of organizational measurement*. Marshfield: Pitman Publishing.

Reidenbach, R.E., & Robin, D.P. (1988). Some initial steps toward improving the measurement of ethical evaluations of marketing activities. *Journal of Business Ethics, 7*(November), 871-879.

Reidenbach, R.E., Robin, D.P., & Dawson, L. (1991). An application and extension of a multidimensional ethics scale to selected marketing practices and marketing groups. *Journal of the Academy of Marketing Science, 19*(Spring), 83-92.

Sager, J.K., Varadarajan, P.R., & Futrell, C.M. (1988). Understanding salesperson turnover: A partial evaluation of Mobley's turnover process model. *Journal of Personal Selling and Sales Management, 8*(May), 21-35.

Sager, J.K., Futrell, C.M., & Varadarajan, R. (1989). Exploring salesperson turnover: A causal model. *Journal of Business Research, 18*(June), 303-326.

Sager, J.K., & Johnston, M.W. (1989). Antecedents and outcomes of organizational commitment: A study of salespeople. *Journal of Personal Selling and Sales Management, 9*(Spring), 30-41.

Sathe, V. (1983). Implications of corporate culture: A manager's guide to action. *Organizational Dynamics, 12*, 5-23.

Schneider, B., & Rentsch, J. (1988). Managing climate and cultures: A futures perspective. In J. Hage (Ed.), *Futures of organizations* (pp. 181-200). Lexington, MA: Lexington Books.

Schwepker, C.H., Jr., Ferrell, O.C., & Ingram, T.H. (1997). The influence of ethical climate and ethical conflict on role stress in the sales force. *Journal of the Academy of Marketing Science, 25*(Spring), 99-107.

Trevino, L.K. (1986). Ethical decision-making in organizations: A person-situation interactionist model. *Academy of Management Review, 11*(3), 601-617.

Trevino, L.K., & Youngblood, S.A. (1990). Bad apples in bad barrels: A causal analysis of ethical decision-making behavior. *Journal of Applied Psychology, 75*(August), 378-385.

Victor, B., & Cullen, J.B. (1987). A theory and measure of ethical climate in organizations. In W.C. Frederick & L.E. Preston (Eds.), *Research in corporate social performance and policy* (pp. 51-71). Greenwich, CT: JAI Press.

Victor, B., & Cullen, J.B. (1988). The organizational bases for ethical work climates. *Administrative Science Quarterly, 33*(March), 101-125.

Vitell, S.J., & Davis, D.L. (1990). The relationship between ethics and job satisfaction: An empirical investigation. *Journal of Business Ethics, 9*(June), 489-494.

Vitell, S.J., & Hunt, S.D. (1990). The general theory of marketing ethics: A partial test of the model. In J.N. Sheth (Ed.), *Research in marketing* (Vol. 10, 237-265). Greenwich, CT: JAI Press.

Williams, L.J., & Hazer, J.T. (1986). Antecedents and consequences of satisfaction and commitment in turnover models: A reanalysis using latent variable structural equation models. *Journal of Applied Psychology, 17*(4), 219-231.

Wotruba, T.R. (1990). A comprehensive framework for the analysis of ethical behavior, with a focus on sales organizations. *Journal of Personal Selling and Sales Management, 10*(Spring), 29-42.

CURBING CORPORATE CRIME:
MANAGERIAL AND ETHICAL
IMPLICATIONS OF THE FEDERAL
SENTENCING GUIDELINES FOR ORGANIZATIONS

Gene R. Laczniak and Russ Roberson

ABSTRACT

This paper examines the 1991 federal sentencing guidelines with respect to organizations. These guidelines, only recently being applied in U.S. courts, require minimum fines and imprisonment terms for criminal acts by culpable executives and their organizations. The paper will examine the history of the federal sentencing guidelines for organizations (FSGOs), a synopsis of their workings, the strategic response of U.S. companies to the FSGOs, and the case for and against these guidelines. Finally, this paper will examine the managerial implications of the FSGOs with special attention provided to the ethical issues raised by the guidelines.

Research in Marketing, Volume 15, pages 49-67.
Copyright © 1999 by JAI Press Inc.
All rights of reproduction in any form reserved.
ISBN: 0-7623-566-5

Do you ever expect a corporation to have a conscience when it has no soul to be damned and no body to be kicked?

—Edward, First Baron, Thurlow (1731-1806)
Lord High Chancellor Of England

American business executives be advised. The United States Sentencing Commission (USSC), a relatively small government agency, has implemented the full force of its 1991 federal fines and sentencing guidelines for organizations (FSGOs). Over the next decade, it is likely that several senior executives will land in prison while organizations pay fines as high as $495 million (O'Donnell, 1997). Escaping executive jail time and associated organizational fines will not prevent the likelihood of higher, but ultimately beneficial, operating costs as businesses attempt to comply with the guidelines.The government has made it fairly easy to establish financial penalty levels and the length of time that senior management could be incarcerated. All of this is done with a relatively straightforward format that computes penalties based on the size of the business, the level of organizational cooperation in any criminal investigation, the effectiveness of the firm's internal compliance program, and the company's prior criminal history (U.S. Sentencing Commission, 1994a). The upshot of these regulations is that it appears to be in the best interests of organizations to institutionalize ethics controls into the corporation as rapidly as possible.

What exactly are the organizational fines and sentencing guidelines and how do they potentially effect U.S. organizations? The FSGOs are federal prescriptions, covering almost all corporate criminal violations, which place responsibility for organizational criminal actions squarely on the shoulders of executive management even if they had no awareness of their firm's criminal activity. Included within the purview of these guidelines are corporate convictions for crimes such as antitrust violations, bribery, bid-rigging, insider trading, tax fraud, counterfeiting trademarks, export duty evasion, product mislabeling, price fixing, and many more. Second, the FSGOs specify the level of punitive monetary fines against the offending organization. Finally, and most critically, the FSGOs take away substantial plea bargaining flexibility from the courts when dealing with organizational violations. The FSGOs set minimum fines and imprisonment times which, in the absence of mitigating circumstances, *must* be imposed by the court. For reasons explained below, these guidelines only now are beginning to have their full effect on U.S. business.

What is the genesis of the federal sentencing guidelines? The FSGOs derive from the 1987 *individual* sentencing guidelines which in turn can be traced to the formation of the USSC in 1984. Just as the individual sentencing guidelines have dramatically increased criminal prison sentences, expect the FSGOs to similarly affect the behavior of American businesses (Barrett, 1990). Richard Conaboy (1995), Chairman of the USSC, states "these guidelines (FSGOs) broke ground by codifying into law incentives for organizations to take crime-deterring actions, especially...to establish rigorous, effective, and internal compliance programs." This paper will focus on the current and future impact of the FSGOs on U.S. business. It is intended to supplement, amplify, and extend many of the excellent points made in a recent book, *Integrity Management* (LeClair, Ferrell, & Fraedrich, 1998), which utilizes the FSGOs as one of its focal themes. Specifically, this paper will succinctly cover:

- the history of the FSGOs;
- a brief synopsis of how the FSGOs work;
- the impact of the FSGOs on U.S. businesses;
- strategic responses of U.S. companies to the FSGOs;
- the case against and for the FSGOs; and
- managerial and research implications of the FSGOs.

HISTORY OF THE ORGANIZATIONAL FINES AND SENTENCING GUIDELINES

The history of the FSGOs is important because their evolution is controversial and may provide the basis for eventual modification of the law. In 1966, President Lyndon Johnson, believing federal criminal laws to be vague and applied inconsistently, commissioned then California Governor Edmund Brown to recommend reforms of the federal criminal law statutes. Five years later, the Brown Commission issued a final report to Congress, and two years after that, the Nixon Administration unsuccessfully sought to enact the Brown recommendations. In 1976, Senator Edward Kennedy, a long time advocate of criminal sentencing reform, introduced a comprehensive bill to establish sentencing guidelines, versions of which were introduced in the next three Congresses. None of the legislation debated through the 97th Congress made any mention of a national sentencing commission, or more importantly, was binding on federal judges. But in 1983, Congress sought to establish a consistent *and binding* set of sentences for federal crimes through the formation of a national sentencing commission (Breyer, 1988; Wilkins, 1988). In 1984, with President Reagan's approval of the Sentencing Reform Act, the United States Sentencing Commission (USSC) was born. The Sentencing Reform Act of 1984 delegated to the USSC the previously held authority of Congress to set sentencing for federal crimes (Fargason, 1993). The delegation of power, however, was not without direction. In part, Congress specifically mandated that the USSC must:

- take into account the circumstances of aggravation, the community view of the offense, and the deterrent effect of a particular sentence; and
- that the guidelines must correct for the fact that the current federal sentences did not accurately reflect the seriousness of some offenses (Nagel, 1990).

The delegation of sentencing reform to the USSC, and specifically the place-
ment of the USSC under the judicial branch, has been controversial from the
beginning. Challenged in the U.S. Supreme Court with *Mistretta* v. *United States*,
the high court voted 8-1 (Justice Scalia dissenting) for upholding the constitution-
ality of the act and demanded the USSC as an independent judicial branch agency.
Justice Scalia, in opposition, argued that the work of the commission involved the
application of governmental power against individuals and thus should be
restricted solely to the legislative branch where citizens could exercise their right
to remove from office those who vote for issues which the public opposes (Scalia,
1995). In other words, the public has typically supported case-by-case adjudica-
tion and, therefore, the FSGOs may violate due process because defendants are
not given individual sentences. In *Mistretta* v. *United States*, however, the
Supreme Court settled the issues of improper legislative delegation and the violation of the separation of powers doctrine, but they left open the question of due
process. None of the due process appeals have been accepted by the U.S. Supreme
Court to date (Siegal, 1994).

Frustration abounded in another area of law—*corporate* criminal law. Federal judges were struggling to find meaningful ways to sanction law-breaking
corporations after a spate of violations in the late 1970s and early 1980s
(Thornton & Vogel, 1981). Moreover, many court mandated punishments
seemed to be without strong logic or reason given the severity and/or pattern of
the violations. In very similar cases, involving corporate fraud, illegal sales of
drug samples, theft of trade secrets, and price fixing, punishments ranged from
prison time to community service for the persons involved and the fines levied
varied by millions of dollars (Swenson, 1995). There simply seemed to be little consistency in punishment and restitution in cases involving corporate misconduct.

Multiple USSC studies conducted from 1984 to 1990 that tracked thousands of
organizations found similar federal criminal cases were being treated differently,
and that in some instances, the fines given corporations were even substantially
less than the cost corporations would have to incur to obey the law (Swenson,
1995). Therefore, in 1991 the USSC attempted to bring uniformity to the area of
corporate criminal sentencing law by submitting the FSGOs to Congress. The
legislation which followed set *binding* requirements on federal judges that:

- restitution should not be considered part of any judgment, but rather the cost
  to make the victim(s) whole again should be primary;
- imposed fines should divest organizations of their assets if it is determined
  that the organization operated primarily for illegal purposes;
- larger organizations should pay more for similar crimes than smaller
  organizations; and
- higher fines be set for any organization that does not have a meaningful program to prevent and detect criminal violations or in which

top management was involved in the offense (U.S. Sentencing Commission, 1994b).

Perhaps the most important implication of this legislation was that the USSC set up criteria for having a meaningful program to prevent and detect criminal violations. This represented the core philosophy of the USSC in that the essential barriers to corporate crime were to be embodied in the corporate culture itself rather than in the black-letter law. The presence of these organizational characteristics, which promote legal and ethical behavior, mitigate the penalties that wrong-doing corporations received. These organizational recommendations are as follows:

- Corporations must establish compliance standards and procedures, and they must be effectively communicated.
- A high level individual(s) must have responsibility to oversee compliance.
- Organizations must take steps to achieve compliance (e.g., through the use of an auditing system).
- Organizations must take disciplinary actions against managers who are not compliant; this includes executives who should have detected a noncompliance.
- Organizations must take actions to assure the noncompliances, when they have occurred, will not happen again (U.S. Sentencing Commission, 1994b).

The FSGOs add some qualifiers with respect to the proposed corporate social auditing programs. Specifically:

- the failure not to detect a noncompliance does not, in itself, mean a compliance program is ineffective; and
- that no mitigation should be given to an organization that establishes a compliance program *after* the organization becomes aware of a noncompliance (U.S. Sentencing Commission, 1994b).

In response to all of this, the business community initially took a legalistic approach and argued against the FSGOs contending that Congress created the USSC to address the sentencing of individuals, and not corporations (Barrett, 1990). U.S. businesses now have two basic options available if they believe the FSGOs to be unfair. They can attempt to convince Congress to specifically reject the FSGOs, or they can attempt to persuade Congress to abolish the USSC. Although the abolishment of the USSC is very unlikely, the repeal or modification of the FSGOs may become an issue in the 2000 federal elections or beyond. It can be argued that former President Reagan, or most of the members of Congress in the early 1980s, never intended the application of the criminal guidelines in the Sentencing Reform Act to be applied to corporate America. A review of the literature by one of the authors has not brought forth even one reference to *orga-*

Table 1. Synopsis of FSGOs Point System

Corporate Violation	Points Assessed
• Base Points (i.e., each organization starts at a base level given a particular violation); for example:	+5
• Level of Authority and Size of Organization (e.g., a CEO of a business with less than 25 employees receives only 1 point while a CEO of a business with more than 10,000 employees receives 5 points), that is, larger organizations receive bigger punishments;	+1, +2, +3, +4, or +5
• Prior History of Criminal Activity (the more previous violations, the higher the point adjustment);	+1, +2, or more
• Violation of Court Order (the more previous violations, the higher the point assessment);	0, +1 or +2
• Obstruction of Justice;	+3
• Effective Program to Prevent and Detect Violations of the Law;	−3
• Other Self-Reporting, Cooperation, and Acceptance of Responsibility (based upon the organizational accommodations mentioned earlier).	−1, −2, −3, −4, or −5

nizational sentencing guidelines when the Sentencing Reform Act of 1984 was debated by Congress. With the various Republican proposals before Congress advocating limits on corporate liability, it is not unreasonable to expect that there will be continued calls for the modification of the FSGOs. This is especially likely if the Republicans sweep the 2000 elections in both the legislative and executive branches. Nevertheless, the USSC believed its directives allowed a broad application of federal sentencing reform. Thus, in 1987 federal sentencing guidelines became law for individuals, followed in 1991 by the sentencing guidelines becoming law *for organizations.*

The FSGOs are just now being widely applied in the federal courts because they regulate organizational actions taken after *the passage of the law.* As corporate criminal investigations are often lengthy, sometimes taking years to litigate, it is only recently that the true influence of the guidelines upon U.S. organizations is emerging in the federal courts.

A SYNOPSIS OF HOW THE FSGOS WORK

At this point an *abbreviated* explanation of the point system underlying the FSGOs is provided. The guidelines apply to all felonies and Class A misdemeanors for which organizations have been convicted. Basically, the FSGOs work on a point system which is then implemented by the court when an organization is found in violation of the law. For each proven criminal violation by a corporation, points are computed leading to a base fine which is then increased or decreased depending on the point amount. For instance, *insider trading* has a base load of 8 points while *price fixing* has a base level of 10. Thus, the perceived seriousness of the offense sets the initial point level. But this too, is adjusted for the amount of illegal gain, or the pecuniary loss to others, resulting from the situation at focus. The possible executive imprisonment range is also set by the point accumulation. As the points increase, so does the fine and the possible time of imprisonment. As a general reference, a hypothetical application of the FSGOs' point system is summarized in Table 1 (Burress & O'Sullivan, 1995).

With regard to Table 1, consider for example an organization with a base fine of $10 million. Adding the guideline points accumulated as described above, the actual fines become:

Guideline Points	Minimum Fine	Maximum Fine
• 10 or More	$20 million	$40 million
• 5	$10 million	$20 million
• 0	$2 million	$2 million

From such illustrations then, it should be obvious that having an effective compliance program, reporting noncompliance, cooperating during a criminal investigation, and accepting responsibility, can dramatically benefit an organization with respect to any sentence received. Each of these steps can result in the reduction of points associated with a particular violation. Cumulatively, these areas have the potential to remove eight points from the guideline point system, and could offset the points accumulated from the guaranteed base, penalties for top management involvement, as well as organizational size. All else being equal, in the hypothetical example listed above, *maximum* organizational safeguards could be worth $19.5 to $38 million in fine reductions *per violation*. The possible savings very likely justify the expenditures necessary to comply with the organizational guidelines. Based on such hypothetical calculations, it is fairly easy to understand why corporations have reacted so expediently to the FSGOs, even if the motivation is mostly financial.

IMPACT OF THE FSGOS ON U.S. BUSINESSES

To understand how significantly the FSGOs have affected the outcomes of court proceedings against corporations, managers need only to review several high profile cases that were settled shortly before and after the implementation of the guidelines (Barrett, 1990). Specifically,

- In 1990, First Bank of Georgia pleaded guilty to money laundering and was fined $82,500. If First Bank made the same plea under the organizational guidelines the fine would have been between $3-$10 million.
- Ashland Oil Company was convicted in 1988 of discharging 500,000 gallons of oil into the Monongahela River and was fined $2.5 million. Under the organizational sentencing guidelines the fine would have been $30-$50 million.

In contrast, under the FSGOs:

- C.R. Bard was charged in 1993 with RICO violations which included charges of illegal experimentation on subjects with unapproved catheters, changing the design without FDA approval, concealing from the FDA catheter malfunctions, and lying to FDA. In a 1994 plea agreement, Bard agreed to $30.5 million in criminal fines and $30.5 million in civil fines while some Bard executives are facing up to five years in prison and individual fines of $250,000 (Kahan, 1995).
- Honda had two former executives (West Coast Sales Manager and Senior Vice President) convicted of bribery in 1995. The executives were taking millions in payoffs in return for the award of dealerships and for the adequate re-stocking existing dealerships with Hondas. The West Coast Sales Manager faces up to 35 years in prison while the Senior Vice President faces up to 5 years in prison ("Former Executives for Honda," 1995).
- Tenet Healthcare was charged in 1993 with billing fraud, improper payments to induce referrals, and the improper waiver of co-payments and deductibles. In 1993, Tenet suspended dividends in order to pay an additional $360 million to conclude federal investigations and settle other claims (Meyers, 1995).

In all likelood, relatively small organizational fines and minimal prison terms for culpable executives will be less common in the future. Corporate critics, consumer activists, and most government regulators applaud this trend. As Richard P. Conaboy (1995, p. 1), Chairman of the USSC puts it: "A corporate crime is a problem in this country. It undermines the public's health, safety, financial security, as well as its confidence in our free market system." The trend, and the FSGOs are a big part of this, seems to be for the courts to treat corporations in a harsher manner. For example, from 1984 to 1988 the median corporate criminal fine collected was $10,000, jumping to $200,000 between 1989 to 1990. Still, according to Mark Cohen, an economist at Vanderbilt University and a former USSC staff member, with the full implementation of the organizational federal sentencing guidelines, executives should expect the collection of fines to increase "tenfold, twentyfold, or thirtyfold" (Barrett, 1990). Taking all this into consideration, unethical U.S. companies will face an even more litigious climate. U.S. attorneys now have a powerful incentive to turn civil cases into criminal cases because the fine level now makes them worth litigating.

A 1991 U.S. Sentencing Commission study compared previous corporate sentences to the predicted sentences if the FSGOs had been in effect. Just looking at broad categories of corporate crime and based on information in the 1991 study, most violations would result in substantially higher penalties (U.S. Sentencing Commission, 1991).

To take just two examples for antitrust violations, 85 percent of the judgments would have resulted in higher fines to the organization (with the most severe fine increasing $15.9 million); and for mislabeling of products, 67 percent of the judgments would have resulted in higher fines to the organization (with the most severe fine increasing $2.25 million). A review of corporate cases in federal courts (1984-1990) indicates that approximately 300 organizations are sentenced each year (Scalia, 1995). As of late 1995, there have only been 208 cases sentenced under the FSGOs because pre-guideline statutes applied. The numbers of cases sentenced under the FSGOs has been increasing each year, such that in 1994, 54 percent of organizations were sentenced under them. With the passing of each year the percentage of organizations sentenced under the FSGOs obviously will increase, eventually becoming 100 percent, because the FSGOs apply to all post-1991 violations. Using the cases sentenced to date as a basis, the financial impact on organizations of the FSGOs has been calculated by government sources. The analysis may be tentative because of the limited sample size; however, one point is clear—*the average organization can expect to pay about double the fine under the FSGOs than previously* (Scalia, 1995).

Key to the above discussion, however, is not the cases which have been sentenced under the FSGOs but instead the number of cases which have been settled under consent decrees. In other words, what is provocative is the number of organizations that agree to modify their future behavior rather than taking their chances under the new FSGOs. At least 28 organizations have settled their cases in this manner (Jordan, 1995). Some of the organizations that have signed consent decrees are the American Bar Association, Caremark, Denny's, El Paso Natural Gas, Food Lion, Grumman Corporation, Prudential Securities, Sara Lee Corporation, United Technologies, and the W.R. Grace Company.

STRATEGIC RESPONSE OF U.S. COMPANIES TO THE FSGOS

What steps can U.S. corporations take to avoid the increased legal jeopardy they face under the FSGOs? One answer is obvious: attempt to create a corporate climate that will mitigate the likelihood of illegal and unethical behavior by company managers (Paine, 1994). It seems apparent that one of the driving motivations behind the FSGOs is the desire by the public to legally compel ethical corporate behavior. The history of this legislation makes it clear that it is a product of a society fed up with illegal and improper corporate behavior that has often been met with minimal punishment. Now, in the event of organizational violations, the FSGOs allow for a reduction of fines and sentences *only if* organizations have taken preventative steps prior to and during criminal investigations. Thus, the FSGOs have become the watershed event of the past 25 years in *forcing* organizations to think about the implementation of legal and ethical compliance.

Under the organizational guidelines, these preventative steps are referred to as "due diligence." Steps include, but are not limited to, the establishment of an internal compliance program, the self-reporting of criminal violations, and substantial organizational cooperation during a criminal investigation. The point reduction incentives discussed above may help explain why over 200 large American businesses have appointed ethics officers since 1991 (Labrich, 1992). However, these actions by themselves may not be enough to lessen the impact of fines and sentences imposed under the guidelines unless the programs are judged to be effective. As of late 1995, only one organization's compliance program has actually been deemed by the court as meeting the requirements of the FSGOs (Scalia, 1995). Admittedly, few cases prosecuted thus far have had their organization's compliance programs as a central issue; and it may be as simple as not knowing how good a compliance program an organization has until a true test occurs. Dow Corning's (DC) chief ethics officer was asked why the DC ethics office did not insist upon product recall when the inherent safety issues with the infamous silicone breast implants were strongly questioned. He compared DC's compliance program to a cup of tea in that one just does not know how good a bag of tea is until it is placed in water. Dow did not know how lacking its compliance program was until it was tested, and failed (*National Public Radio*, 1995). Certain large health care firms like Johnson & Johnson have taken steps to have its compliance program reviewed by outside legal firms to assure that if the compliance program is ever tested, it will pass muster. Importantly, the FSGOs require (U.S. Sentencing Commission, 1994b) that for an internal compliance program to be effective such programs must:

- empower a high level individual(s) to oversee the organization's compliance program (typically, this involves charging someone at the corporate VP level or above to supervise these efforts such steps are consistent with long standing recommendations in the business ethics literature for organizations to appoint an ethical ombudsman or chief *ethics* officer [Murphy, 1988]);
- involve the board of directors. (This is most easily accomplished by having reports routed to a subcommittee of the board on all substantive findings concerning the compliance programs);
- enlist senior management in actively implementing the organization's compliance efforts (again, this step is consistent with the

Table 2. U.S. Corporate Response to FSGOs Calls for Organizational Change

Key Findings of the United States Sentencing Commission Study (1995)

- Ethics codes are in place for:
    - 95 percent of all *Fortune 500* companies,
    - 51 percent of German businesses,
    - 40 percent of United Kingdom organizations, and
    - 30 percent of French companies.

- Of all the organizations surveyed, the FSGOs influenced:
    - 45 percent to enhance current compliance efforts,
    - 20 percent to initiate a compliance program,
    - 63 percent to modify training programs,
    - 49 percent to modify compliance materials,
    - 43 percent to retain outside counsel, and
    - 43 percent to modify the compliance auditing system.

- In order to prevent retaliation against individuals who report the noncompliance:
    - 82 percent of organizations have procedures to protect employees who have reported a noncompliance, yet
    - only 28 percent of organizations have taken steps to assure individuals who have reported a noncompliance were not the victim of retaliation (e.g., employee follow-up or examining an employee's performance appraisal over time for [unwarranted] poor performance ratings, etc.).
    - 38 percent of the respondents indicted they would fear retaliation for reporting a noncompliance.

Key Findings of the Price Waterhouse LLP Study (1994)

- Of the organizations surveyed, the FSGOs influenced:
    - 41 percent to issue or reissue employee codes of conduct,
    - 66 percent to formally vest responsibility for the corporate compliance programs in a board of directors committee,
    - 78 percent to have employees sign acknowledgments of having read and understood their organization's code of business conduct, and
    - 87 percent to ask employees to confirm annually, in writing, that they have not violated any section of the code of business conduct.

- Internationally, however:
    - Only 6 percent of the organizations assess corruption risks in their foreign operations.

resounding theme of the business ethics literature that the morality of the organization begins at the top [Murphy, 1989]);
- discipline and respond appropriately to problems (e.g., voluntary product warnings or recalls) based on internal compliance assessments;
- establish independent reporting relationships for individuals who are involved in the internal compliance assessment program; and
- do not retaliate against individuals who are involved in the internal compliance assessment.

What have some organizations already done to respond to the guidelines? The Bank of Tokyo Trust, Ltd. (North American Operations) is one example of an organization that has taken steps to comply with the due diligence clauses of the FSGOs although they have had no court imposed experiences which would require it (Thornhill, 1995). Herbert Thornhill, Jr., Deputy Counsel for Tokyo Trust, believes that if programs are developed around the organization guidelines "you will already have a structure in place for employee training, auditing, supervision, and the creation written policy statements" and that "all you have to do is update your program each time you receive a new directive (from the USSC)." Thornhill (1995) further states, "the reality of sustaining huge fines and the related injury to the Bank's reputation is a great incentive to follow the guidelines." Thornhill is probably right in both speculations, because numerous organizations are taking steps to respond to the guidelines.

To date, two studies have been conducted that illustrate the American business current response to the federal guidelines. One study was commissioned by the USSC and the other was performed by Price Waterhouse LLP (Counters, 1995). The USSC study was administered by the Minnesota Association for Applied Ethics, the Bentley College Center for Business Ethics, and the Wharton School of Business. In that investigation, 330 organizations of varying size and type were surveyed. The Price Waterhouse (1994) research was based on a less comprehensive sample, but nevertheless included a wide cross-section of industries (e.g., health care, beverage, energy and chemical, and defense contractors). Major findings from the studies are presented in Table 2.

It is also important to understand that the FSGOs technically apply only to U.S. markets. Obviously, they also apply to foreign corporations operating in the United States. From the data it appears that many U.S. businesses have made a good faith attempt to comply. However, the associated cost burden of compliance on U.S. organizations may provide a competitive advantage to foreign organizations. The USSC study clearly shows foreign corporations are lagging U.S. businesses in compliance to the FSGO specifications (Counters, 1995). Because the FSGOs do not bind overseas organizations in their international markets, perhaps this should not be surprising.

Nevertheless, in an excellent and comprehensive paper, LeClair, Ferrell, and Ferrell (1997) contend that FSGOs provide the foundation for creating an ethical, *international* business culture as well. As an increasing global economy drives the need for a "level economic playing field" for all competitors, these authors see the FSGOs, along with international codes of conduct such as the Caux Principles (Skelly, 1995), as the proactive benchmarks for creating the rules of competitive strategy that will protect the common good.

Collectively, the most compelling implication of these two studies is that the FSGOs have forced organizations to speed up the institutionalization of programs to monitor and impel legal and ethical behavior. Specific corporate adjustments, such as increased enforcement of codes of conduct, enhanced employee training regarding socially responsible behavior, and social audits reviewed at the board of directors level, have been strongly recommended by business ethicists for many years (Laczniak & Murphy, 1993). For those organizations that have not yet undertaken this organizational restructuring, the time of procrastination is over. One rationale for such changes is that proactive steps that institutionalize ethical concerns are the best way to create an ethical *and legal* organizational climate that promotes responsible behavior and avoids litigation (Travino & Nelson, 1995). The institutionalization of compliance programs also provides the corporate infra-structure for organizations to oversee not only their legal obligations but also all aspects of their promulgated codes of corporate conduct. The FSGO program spe-cifically helps managers make the ethical decision more often and in an expedient manner. If certain firms are perceived as operating on an ethical plane far above their required responsibilities according to the law, they are much more likely to be judged as having a corporate climate conducive to compliance during any future violation investigations.

THE CASE AGAINST AND FOR THE FSGOS

The FSGOs have not been well received in all sectors of the business community. For this reason, we begin with the disadvantages of the guidelines from a business standpoint.

Cons

There are several perceived negatives inherent in the accommodation of the FSGOs by corporations. From a pure operating cost standpoint, the FSGOs will create substantial short-term expenses (e.g., due diligence systems, ethical audits, potential legal fines, and possible executive incarceration) for U.S. businesses. The most obvious cost is that of additional staff to administer and respond to an independent, internal compliance program. These costs must either be absorbed by the business itself, via its stockholders, or passed along to its customers. These high compliance costs and the *potentially* astronomical legal judgment costs of the guidelines may actually bankrupt a few dubious companies.

Less obvious are the costs of potential delays of new products and services entering markets as American businesses shy away from risk as a result of poten-tially high fines and the possible imprisonment required by the guidelines. Specif-ically, U.S. organizations *might* avoid various markets because certain strategic alliances might be perceived as collusive. Product introductions *may* be halted for fear of charges stemming from inadequate product testing. International markets *could* be abdicated because of the demands for "extra payments" (i.e., bribes) from distributors that will now be policed and punished even more severely. These market delays could eventually impact the quality of life for the worldwide consumer. For example, medical innovations and other products might have delayed entry into various markets. With reference to foreign markets, the due diligence requirements of the FSGOs will certainly add to relative costs of U.S. produced products. Because the stockholders of the business must typically absorb the cost of compliance, if the rate of return on their investments decline due to the FSGOs, investors could be more likely to look outside the United States for their financial opportunities. The FSGOs might be the catalyst that sends some domestic investors to foreign markets, or even closer to home, sends additional American jobs to foreign countries due to a higher U.S. cost structure.

Finally, because of the greater sanctions associated with the FSGOs, there will be a greater incentive for the government to prosecute corporate crime. If more organizations select litigation to oppose possible penalties, corporate legal costs may substantially increase. In summary, it should be recognized that most of the objections voiced by the business community are economic and utilitarian in nature.

Pros

Worldwide consumers and U.S. organizations will also be likely to derive palpable benefits from the FSGOs. First, consumers will have greater assurance that the products and services they purchase are produced and delivered in a way which fully complies with U.S. laws. Moreover, any noncompliances that might affect product performance will be detected more quickly than under previous law, and appropriate responsive action will more likely be taken in a resolute manner. In the long term, even on the worldwide playing field, the FSGOs could offer real competitive advantages to U.S. businesses even if foreign competitors do not abide by the same rules. It is conceivable that the FSGOs could benefit U.S. businesses through *decreased* litigation activities and more rigorously evaluated products and services that reach worldwide consumers on an ongoing basis. Litigation expenses are likely to decrease in the long run because when violations are evident, the outcome (in terms of penalty) is specified and known. Moreover, proactive attention to rigorous compliance programs are cost effective because they modify the entire schedule of possible violations and sanctions in favor of the ethical, compliance-oriented organization.

Additionally, U.S. consumers might realize the reduced use of tax revenues for organizational criminal investigations due to the self-reporting incentives of the FSGOs. Therefore, more public monies may be available for areas of greater concern to the American public. Finally, over time, organizations that are serious about their ethical behavior, should be able to better determine key areas of noncompliance and subsequently discover, resolve, and prevent noncompliances such that the impact of the FSGOs may be kept minimal.

MANAGERIAL AND RESEARCH
IMPLICATIONS OF THE FSGOS

Recognizing that the FSGOs cut both ways, certain managerial implications of the guidelines are fairly clear-cut. First, top management should direct their corporate legal counsel to become familiar with the details of the FSGOs if they have not already done so. Beyond the black-letter law, substantial information is available from the USSC which provides commentary on the guidelines based on commission sponsored conferences and evaluative, research studies (Conaboy, 1995). Second, all corporations should initiate a compliance program that conforms to the FSGOs (Swenson, 1994). If such a compliance program is already in place, it should be audited for conformance. As noted earlier, the presence of a compliance program, if it is implemented *after* a violation has already occurred, does not serve as a mitigating factor for possible FSGO penalties for that violation. The responsibility for compliance oversight should be vested at the board of director's level. The ethics committee of the board (if it exists) or a designated director should review the compliance program at least annually and be informed on a management-by-exception basis of any "nonconformance" situations which could place the organization in legal jeopardy.

Third, corporations should use the USSC mandated compliance program as an opportunity to institutionalize formal ethical audit mechanisms. Again, the business and marketing literature contain detailed recommendations concerning the nature and scope of such programs and how they best can be implemented (Ferrell & Fraedrich, 1997; Laczniak & Murphy, 1993). These efforts should not only be used to monitor that organizational performance is congruent with the law, but also to assure that all company strategy is consistent with the spirit of its corporate code of ethics. The point here is that the vast majority of large U.S. corporations have codes of ethics that lay out corporate desirata which go beyond the law (Murphy, 1998). Audits which give testimony to the spirit of such ethical climate in the organization verify the intent of the corporation to execute its operations in a socially responsible manner. While most large corporations have corporate codes of ethics, the centrality of these codes in guiding corporate decisions and shaping corporate culture varies greatly from firm to firm (Lancaster, 1997). Clearly, public frustration with illegal *and unethical* corporate behavior led to the mandated behavioral requirements of the FSGOs. Therefore, businesses should view the presence of compliance programs as an opportunity to ensure that they operate in the public interest as well as to alleviate further citizen backlash that could stimulate additional business regulations (Laczniak et al., 1995). Finally, organizations should monitor the external environment for public policy and academic studies involving the FSGOs. Certainly macro-studies will soon emerge which will analyze the specific programmatic effects of FSGOs on various industries. In addition, the subjective nature of the FSGO point system will likely stimulate academic researchers to operationally define graduations of corporate misbehavior (Laufer, 1994).

The FSGOs also provide academic *researchers* with a golden opportunity to explore various aspects of corporate compliance programs, the penalties associated with differing organizational violations, and the effectiveness of sundry ethics improvement plans. Consider, for example, the following research questions that necessitate considered investigation and commentary in the academic literature.

- Does the existing point system used by the USSC appropriately capture the severity and possible attendant managerial culpability of the various corporate violations covered by the guidelines?
- How should the effectiveness of corporate compliance systems be evaluated? What mechanics exist to disseminate the "best" compliance systems within and across industries?
- What has been the legal and ethical track record of organizations with comprehensive compliance programs when compared to similar companies without them?
- Have foreign competitors with ethical compliance programs for U.S. operations utilized these in their other international divisions?
- Do U.S. companies feel competitively disadvantaged by the FSGOs when operating in international markets? How has their attitude and reaction parallelled U.S. corporate response to previous legislation such as the Foreign Corrupt Practices Act (1977)?
- Have corporate compliance systems and ethical audits contributed to a climate of *distrust* among employees?

The litmus test for judging effective compliance programs may not emerge for a few years. Organizations are modifying their internal operations to account for the FSGOs' requirements based on their own internal analysis and the initial rulings of U.S. courts. But a few simple questions, asked right now, however, may help businesses quickly judge the adequacy of their compliance programs before the courts get a chance to do it for them. The questions that must immediately be asked and answered are as follows.

- Does one's organization's compliance program have the ability to detect substantive areas of legal and ethical violations in a reasonable time frame? (A reasonable time frame might be derived from a risk analysis of the industry in which the organization operates. For example, if the organization has been experiencing increased regulatory citations in some aspect of their operations, this might be an area of focus.)
- Does the top management respond correctly and expediently with respect to known legal or ethical violations once they become aware of them?

- Are the individuals who bring forth the awareness of legal or ethical violations still employed by the organization in a meaningful capacity?

CONCLUSION

In our judgment, the temporary increase in operating costs because of due diligence will not significantly hamper most U.S. businesses. Such expenditures can be planned for and paid for without significant impact on the business's bottom line and may even improve it by helping to ensure safer, higher quality products. In the short term, it is possible that the costs of due diligence as well as potential fines could damage a few, especially smaller, U.S. businesses. Even though FSGO penalties are adjusted for company size, not many small organizations can suffer the magnitude of the full fineage limit imposed by the guidelines without threat to their survival.

But all things considered, the federal sentencing guidelines are an idea whose time has come. U.S. businesses should have probably conceived of and implemented strong ethical compliance programs long ago. Regrettably, it has once again taken U.S. government regulation to force long advocated ethical business practices and good common sense. Corporate crime and unethical management behavior is a problem. Anything that is done to assure that U.S. corporations obey existing law is hard to oppose. Future public policy analysis will definitively establish whether the relatively rapid switch to the FSGOs was a good idea. Perhaps the organizational guidelines should have been instituted over a longer period of time allowing for a longer phasing in of compliance programs, and a gradual increase in the organizational fines and executive imprisonment times. Perhaps modifications need to be made in the penalty schedules and typical USSC guideline interpretations. Only time and careful research will tell if the FSGOs have truly benefited U.S. businesses, and in turn, worldwide consumers. But, given the advent of the FSGOs, there is no question that some U.S. businesses must amend their past behaviors and prepare to operate on a higher ethical plane if only because a new and significant law has forced them to do the right thing.

REFERENCES

Barrett, P.M. (1990, November 11). Corporate criminals face stiffer federal fines under sentencing guidelines expected for 1991. *Wall Street Journal*, p. A20.

Bradshaw, T., & Vogel, D. (1981). *Corporations and their critics.* New York: McGraw Hill.

Breyer, S. (1988). The federal sentencing guidelines and the key compromises upon which they rest. *Hofstra Law Review, 17*(1).

Burress, L.R., & O'Sullivan, J.R. (1995, September 7). How the federal sentencing guidelines for organizations work: An overview. In *Corporate crime in America: Strengthening the "good citizen corporation"* (pp. 5-16). United States Sentencing Commission Symposium.

Conaboy, R. (1995, September 7). *Corporate crime in America: Strengthening the "good citizen corporation."* United States Sentencing Commission Symposium. Washington, DC.

Counters, C. (1995, September 7). A presentation of empirical research on compliance practices: What companies say they are doing—what employees hear. In *Corporate crime in America: Strengthening the "good citizen corporation"* (pp. 105-120). United States Sentencing Commission Symposium.

Fargason, J.S. (1993). *Legal compliance auditing and the federal sentencing guidelines.* Altamonte Springs, FL: Institute of Internal Auditors.

Ferrell, O.C., & Fraedrich, J. (1997). *Business ethics: Ethical decision making and cases* (3rd ed.). Boston: Houghton Mifflin Co.

Jordon, K.S. (1995, September 7). Compliance criteria in consent decrees. *Corporate crime in America: Strengthening the "good citizen corporation"* (pp. 279-281). United States Sentencing Commission Symposium.

Kahan, J.S. (1995). DA criminal prosecution: New trends and old problems. *Medical Device and Diagnostic Industry* (January), 101-106.

Labrich, K. (1992, April 20). The new crisis in business ethics. *Business Week*, pp. 167-176.

Former executives for Honda guilty in bribery case. (1995, June 2). *Milwaukee Journal Sentinel*, p. 8A.

Laczniak, G.R., & Murphy, P.E. (1993). *Ethical marketing decisions the higher road.* Boston, MA: Allyn & Bacon.

Laczniak, G.R., Berkowitz, M.W., Brooker, R.G., & Hale, J.P. (1995). The ethics of business: improving of deteriorating? *Business Horizons* (January-February), 39-47.

Lancaster, H. (1997, April 8). You have your values, how do you identify your employers? *The Wall Street Journal*, p. B1.

Laufer, W.S. (1994). Corporate bodies and guilty minds. *Emory Law Journal*, 43(Spring), 647-730.

LeClair, D.T., Ferrell, O.C., & Ferrell, L. (1997). Federal sentencing guidelines for organizations: Legal, ethical and public policy issues for international marketing. *Journal of Public Policy & Marketing*, 16(1), 26-37.

LeClair, D.T., Ferrell, O.C., & Fraedrich, J. (1998). *Integrity management: A guide for legal and ethical issues.* Tampa, FL: University of Tampa Press.

Meyers, J.A. (1995, September 7). When theory and reality converge: Three corporate experiences in developing effective compliance programs. In *Corporate crime in America: Strengthening the "good citizen corporation."* United States Sentencing Commission Symposium. Washington, DC.

Murphy, P.E. (1988). Implementing business ethics. *Journal of Business Ethics* (December), 907-915.

Murphy, P.E. (1989). Creating ethical corporate structures. *Sloan Management Review* (Winter), 81-87.

Murphy, P.E. (1998). *Eighty exemplary ethics statements.* Notre Dame, IN: University of Notre Dame Press.

Nagel, I.H. (1990). Structuring sentencing discretion: The new federal sentencing guidelines. *The Journal of Criminal Law and Criminology*, 80(4), 905-910.

National Public Radio. (1995, November 11). Weekend edition. (November 11).

O'Donnell, J. (1997, November 10). White-collar crooks getting more jail time. *USA Today*, p. B1.

Paine, L.S. (1994). Managing for organizational integrity. *Harvard Business Review* (March/April), 106-117.

Price Waterhouse. (1994). *Corporate compliance programs: Leading edge practices.* Price Waterhouse LLP.

Scalia, J., Jr. (1995, September 7). Cases Sentenced Under The Guidelines,"In *Corporate crime in America: Strengthening the "good citizen corporation"* (p. 260). United States Sentencing Commission Symposium. Washington, DC.

Siegel, R. (1994). *The NPR interviews.* Houghton Mifflin.

Skelly, J. (1995). The rise of international ethics. *Journal of Business Ethics* (May/June), 24ff.

Swenson, W. (1994). An effective program to prevent and detect violations of law. In J.M. Kaplan, J.E. Murphy, & W.M. Swenson (Eds.), *Compliance programs—Preventing civil and criminal liability*. Deerfield, IL: Clark, Boardmand Callaghan.

Swenson, W. (1995, September 7). The organizational guidelines' carrot and stick philosophy, and their focus on effective compliance. In *Corporate crime in America: Strengthening the "Good Citizen Corporation"* (pp. 17-26). United States Sentencing Commission Symposium.

Thornhill, H.L., Jr. (1995). When theory and reality converge: Three corporate experiences in developing effective compliance programs. In *Corporate crime in America: Strengthening the "good citizen corporation"* (pp. 49-53). United States Sentencing Commission Symposium.

Thornton, B., & Vogel, D. (1981). *Corporations and their critics*. New York: McGraw Hill Book Company.

Travino, L.K., & Nelson, K.A. (1995). *Managing business ethics: Straight talk about how to do it right*. New York: John Wiley.

United States Sentencing Commission. (1991). *Supplemental report on sentencing guidelines for organizations*. Washington, DC: United States Government Printing Office.

United States Sentencing Commission. (1994a). *United States Sentencing Commission 1994 annual report*. Washington, DC: United States Government Printing Office.

United States Sentencing Commission. (1994b). *Guidelines manual*. Washington, DC: United States Government Printing Office.

Wilkins, W. (1988). Plea negotiations, acceptance of responsibility, role of the offender, and departures: Policy decisions in the promulgation of federal sentencing guidelines. *Wake Forest Law Review*, 23(2).

THE ROLE OF FORMAL POLICIES AND INFORMAL CULTURE ON ETHICAL DECISION MAKING BY MARKETING MANAGERS

James H. Leigh and Patrick E. Murphy

ABSTRACT

The processes by which formal corporate ethics policies and associated informal cultural manifestations relate to ethical decision making were investigated using a cross-sectional sample of marketing executives. Informal culture was found to have a direct relationship with ethical decision making. The relationship of formal policies, however, was largely an indirect one, operating through the corporate culture. Implications and future research directions are provided.

What factors promote ethical decision making by marketing managers? This question is not an easy one to answer. As criticisms continue to appear in the press of the transgressions by marketers in several industries whose products raise ethical questions (e.g., tobacco) and those where practices have been called into question (e.g., advertising and athletic shoes), marketing executives are paying

Research in Marketing, Volume 15, pages 69-99.
ISBN: 0-7623-566-5

closer attention to how ethical decisions can be fostered. It is certainly true that the educational, family, and religious backgrounds of individuals serve to influence their ethical predispositions. At the same time, each manager makes decisions in the context of the organization and its values and procedures. Because most business decisions occur within an organizational setting, there is a need to develop a better understanding of the nature of organizational influences on ethics in marketing.

One approach in the area of ethics is to stress formal corporate policies that are distributed to all employees. Promulgating and publicizing a code of ethics is one such method. Written codes have been hailed as important documents to set the ethical tone of a firm (Benson, 1989; Molander, 1987; Murphy, 1995). Another formal mechanism is a clear delineation of the sanctions that will be applied for violation of company policy or provisions of the code. The necessity for enforcement procedures and penalties for noncompliance are recognized as being essential for monitoring the code and discouraging unethical action (Mathews, 1987; Murphy, 1998).

Another set of organizational factors—the informal corporate culture—is viewed as essential to ethical decision making. Informal culture is characterized by an emphasis on the social fabric of the organization and is transmitted by stories about corporate heroes, the founder's favorite sayings, and discussion of the implicit norms (and counternorms). A number of researchers in marketing (Ferrell, Gresham, & Fraedrich, 1989; Hunt, Wood, & Chonko, 1989), and in management (Deetz, 1985; Fleming, 1984), have recognized that corporate culture does affect ethical decisions. The purpose of this research is to determine how these formal and informal organizational factors influence ethical decision making in marketing. Specifically, the relative importance and relationship among these factors will be ascertained.

This paper is divided into five major parts. First, a brief synopsis of the conceptual and empirical research regarding ethics in marketing management is provided. Second, a model of ethical decision making in marketing linked specifically to formal corporate policies and informal corporate culture is proposed and research hypotheses offered. The third section outlines the methodology used in the study. Then, the results are examined. Finally, conclusions, implications, and research directions emanating from the project are discussed.

ETHICS AND MARKETING MANAGEMENT

The first articles on ethical issues in marketing appeared in the 1960s and were, for the most part, philosophical essays (see Murphy & Laczniak, 1981). The early empirical work dealing with the decision-making process tended to be lacking in theoretical foundations (Laczniak, 1983). The research tradition in marketing ethics continued in the 1970s with modest work on the subject. In the 1980s, a major research thrust was devoted to examining ethics in marketing (for a summary, see Murphy & Pridgen, 1991; Tsalkis & Fritzche, 1989). The 1990s have seen a growing emphasis on ethics associated with such emerging topics as infomercials, slotting allowances required by retail grocers, and privacy concerns stemming from database and internet marketing as well as the use of competitive intelligence gathering techniques in both domestic and international arenas.

Several comprehensive models of ethical decision making in business and marketing have been developed. Bommer, Gratto, Gravander, and Tuttle (1987) and Trevino (1986) formulated models of business ethics. Ferrell and Gresham (1985), Ferrell, Gresham, and Fraedrich (1989), and Hunt and Vitell (1986) proposed general theories of marketing ethics. Although these five models differ in approach, they all suggest that ethical decision making is influenced by three categories of factors: individual characteristics, organizational characteristics, and environmental factors. Because of the difficulty in testing all model inputs within the context of a single study, one set of factors should be examined initially. The decision was made for this research to focus exclusively on organizational characteristics given that these factors are the only ones over which an organization possesses some degree of control.

Several survey-based studies have been published that focus on ethics in marketing management (Akaah & Lund, 1994; Baumhart, 1961; Brenner & Molander, 1977; Chonko & Hunt, 1985; Ferrell & Weaver, 1978; Fritzsche, 1988; Goolsby & Hunt, 1992; Hunt & Chonko, 1984; Laczniak, Lusch, & Murphy, 1979; Lincoln, Pressley, & Little, 1982). One common thrust of these articles concerned the identification of managerial perceptions regarding particular ethical problems and appropriate conduct. Of relevance to the present study is the finding that the corporate context plays a major role in determining the ethical standards of marketing managers (Akaah & Lund, 1994; Chonko & Hunt, 1985; Ferrell & Weaver, 1978; Lincoln, Pressley, & Little, 1982). None of these articles, however, examined the relationship between ethics and an assessment of a firm's cultural dimension.

To date, Robin and Reidenbach (1987) are the only authors that have explicitly linked ethics and culture to marketing's strategic planning function. They indicated that core ethical values "should become part of the marketing mission and part of the organization's culture" (p. 49). In their book, Robin and Reidenbach (1989) devoted a chapter to examining the linkage between culture and ethics.

The research examined here extends both the conceptual work on models of marketing ethics and earlier empirical studies by employing a survey research methodology that allows for the influence of internal corporate factors (i.e., formal corporate policies and informal corporate culture) upon the perceptions of marketing managers toward a range of ethical issues. This project employs the contingency management approach noted by Deshpande and Webster (1989) to study organizational culture. Corporate culture is treated here as an endogenous, independent variable studied through cross-sectional survey research.

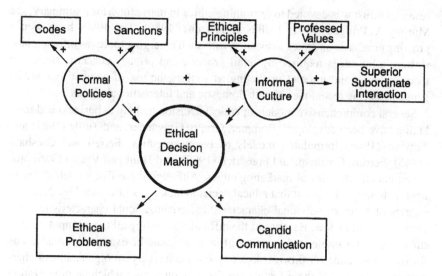

Figure 1.   Organization Factors Influencing Ethical Decision Making

A MODEL OF ORGANIZATIONAL FACTORS INFLUENCING ETHICAL DECISION MAKING

The comprehensive models of business and marketing ethics all include reference to organizational constructs as inputs into ethical decision making. These constructs are: (1) corporate goals, stated policies, and corporate culture (Bommer et al., 1987); (2) interaction between the person and situation-job context, organizational culture, and work characteristics (Trevino, 1986); (3) pressures within the firm (Ferrell & Gresham, 1985); and (4) the organizational environment (Hunt & Vitell, 1986). Taken together, it is clear that these authors feel that organizational factors represent very important influences on ethics.

The present conceptualization isolates two primary groups of organizational factors: formal corporate policies and informal corporate culture. Figure 1 provides a diagram of their proposed impact on an individual manager's ethical decision making. The model only includes those policy and culture factors that are specifically related to ethical considerations.

Figure 1 suggests that informal corporate culture influences ethical decision making in a direct manner. The model stipulates that ethical decisions result in part from a positive corporate culture. Moreover, clear signals about what is valued and expected through the use of formal policies should result in behavior consistent with managerial expectations. Thus, beyond having a strong culture, management must also promulgate formal policies conducive to fostering an ethical tone. For example, developing a written ethics statement, communicating it broadly, and enforcing violations of it are all formal actions that can positively impact corporate culture. The model posits that formal policies and procedures exhibit a direct effect on ethical decision making and, more importantly, have an indirect effect through their impact on the informal culture of an organization. That is, these policies are necessary, but not sufficient to create an ethical climate.

Formal Corporate Policies

The initial dimension of analysis relating to ethics is that of formal organizational policies. It has long been advocated that companies "institutionalize" ethics through codes (Austin, 1961; Harris, 1978) and committees (Purcell, 1978; Weber, 1981). More recent work calls for detailed and useful codes (Benson, 1989; Murphy, 1988, 1995) and extensive corporate training programs in ethics (Murphy, 1989, 1998; Sims, 1991).

Major corporate policies associated with ethical behavior are labeled code and sanctions in Figure 1.[1] The presence of a specific and useful written code appears to be the most frequent way that ethical policies are formally disseminated within a firm. The sanctions employed by the corporation to discourage unethical behavior can be interpreted as an ethical control system. The presence of appropriate sanctions adds an enforcement component and stresses to the employee that the firm takes its ethical posture seriously, while at the same time protects the company legally. Companies that communicate their codes to outsiders are also signalling to stakeholders (i.e., customers, suppliers, competitors, etc.) their commitment both to establishing and enforcing ethical behavior. It should be added that the role of top management leadership is critical in both developing the code and making certain that others in the organization (i.e., compliance or legal office) enforce it (Laczniak & Murphy, 1993; Schlegelmilch, 1998).

Corporate codes are in place at most large companies as a vehicle to foster ethical sensitivity (Center for Business Ethics, 1992). The existence of a written code of conduct is generally thought to enhance ethics within the firm. However, codes have come under criticism for being too general, platitudinous and legalistic, and not being substantive (Berenbeim, 1987; Cressy & Moore, 1983; Hite, Bellizzi, & Fraser, 1988; Molander, 1987; Robin, Giallourakis, David, and Moritz, 1989). Therefore, codes that offer specific guidance (e.g., containing a question and answer section or giving concrete examples) useful to the marketing manager help overcome some of these criticisms.

Having suitable sanctions for ethical violations are thought to be a prerequisite for improving an organization's ethics. Several researchers have sounded this call: the absence of meaningful enforcement of a code contributes to poor ethical choices by managers (Gellerman, 1986, 1989), codes are ineffective if not enforced (Laczniak & Inderreiden, 1987), and procedures for monitoring compliance with ethical policies are a necessity (Bommer et al., 1987). Eighty percent of large companies have sanctions for code violations, and firms where the legal department administers the code are "somewhat more likely to include sanctions" (Murphy, 1995, p. 734). Company managers might apply a number of possible sanctions, ranging from none to loss of job. In her empirical work on codes, Mathews (1987) identified four sanctions (reprimand, fine, demotion, and dismissal/firing). She found only the firing sanction was explicitly discussed in one third of the codes. It should be noted that sanctions and written codes of ethics are complementary; either may exist on its own. More recently, Nwachukwa and Vitell (1997) found mixed results regarding the impact of codes and their enforcement on managerial judgments.

These formal organizational policies are usually viewed as necessary, but not sufficient mechanisms for enhancing the ethical posture of an organization. They relate more to the procedures for dealing with ethics. Most observers believe that they must be reinforced by a culture that not only espouses a commitment to ethics, but practices it daily. Therefore, it is essential that the cultural dimensions of a firm also be studied.

Informal Corporate Culture

The second dimension of organizational analysis of interest is corporate culture. The study of culture emerged from the management literature and has been applied to marketing (Deshpande & Webster, 1989). Culture concerns the organization's informal value and belief system, which is distinct from its formal mandates. This frame of reference guides the behavior of individuals within the firm and shapes the company's identity. Cultural norms influence the actions of employees toward all stakeholders of the organization.

The impact of corporate culture on organizational performance has received widespread attention by academicians and practitioners (Deal & Kennedy, 1982; Fombrun, 1983; Gordon, 1991; O'Reilly, 1989; Pascale, 1984; Peters & Waterman, 1982; Schein, 1985). Furthermore, the central role culture plays in personal selling (Weitz, Sujan, & Sujan, 1986), marketing decision making (Parasuraman & Deshpande, 1984), and strategic planning (Deshpande & Parasuraman, 1986; Mahajan, Varadarajan, & Kerin, 1987) is widely accepted.

About the same time that marketing scholars were recognizing the link between culture and strategy implementation, researchers examining management ethics began to take note of culture's importance on corporate ethical behavior (Butcher, 1985; Deetz, 1985; Hoffman, Moore, & Fedo, 1984; Jones, 1985; McCoy, 1985). Specific proposals have been advanced tying ethics and culture: "management must create candid corporate cultures—cultures that are characterized by open and honest communication" (Serpa, 1985, p. 425); managers should articulate and communicate their ideology and discuss ethical questions to reduce "moral stress" (Waters & Bird, 1987); and a fit should exist between organizational climate and the means to control ethical behaviors (Victor & Cullen, 1988).

A number of formulations have been forwarded that attempt to reflect the elusive corporate culture construct (Deal & Kennedy, 1982; Peters & Waterman, 1982). Several other writers have explicitly recognized the role of ethics in their study of corporate culture. An early application of the McKinsey 7S framework (Pascale & Athos, 1981) labeled the shared values variable as "spiritual values," noting an implicit moral dimension. In empirical work on the same construct, Posner and his colleagues (Posner, Kouzes, & Schmidt, 1985; Posner & Schmidt, 1984) and Frederick and Weber (1987) indicated that shared values are related to ethical behavior. Furthermore, strong cultures are ones where "behavior is guided by innate senses of right and wrong and of moral obligation largely independent of any particular rewards or penalties" (Reimann & Wiener, 1988, p. 37). Finally, Sinclair (1993) advocates that a subcultural approach to understanding the link between ethics and corporate culture is superior to one where management tries to create a unitary and cohesive culture throughout the firm.

Corporate culture has an informal focus that relates to the social fabric of an organization. Peters and Waterman (1982) contrast it with the formal policy variables, calling culture the "software" of the firm. They contend that relevant culture variables include staff, skills, and shared values. Values have been specified as part of the informal corporate culture from the earliest conceptions of the construct. Based on these perspectives, Figure 1 shows that professed values are viewed as central in tying culture to ethics. In the 1990s, ethics and corporate culture has been extended to focus on the role of ethics in total quality management (Chen, Sawyers, & Williams, 1997).

Honesty or openness in interaction when superiors and subordinates communicate with one another is a second hallmark of an ethical corporate culture (see Figure 1). This position was persuasively argued by Serpa (1985) who stated:

The perceived threat or fear of embarrassment of the past must be removed and replaced by the belief that sincerity and forthright communication will be encouraged and rewarded. Once this belief is accepted by members of an organization, the new norms of behavior will be reinforced and a candid culture will be created (p. 429).

Bommer and his colleagues (1987) also indicated that communication within an organization needs to be "timely, clear and accurate, as well as open and frank," if the corporate culture is to reduce unethical activity (p. 272).

The third variable—ethical principles—is instrumental in setting the informal climate of the organization. Some companies like Champion International and United Technologies have such a corporate credo or statement of guiding principles. For most firms, however, the ethical principles are implicit and part of the informal culture rather than of formal policies. Pastin (1986) studied a number of companies and developed a set of propositions pertaining to their ethical posture. He notes that an ethical firm fosters individuality as opposed to suppression. A high level of ethical conduct is a natural product of an emphasis on individual responsibility, with the cultural climate serving to disseminate the guiding ethical principles.

In summary, these corporate culture variables are not intended to represent an exhaustive list of factors that make up this construct. Rather, they were chosen because they are firmly grounded in the literature and can be operationalized. As Figure 1 depicts, both formal corporate policies and informal corporate culture (operationalized as ethical principles, professed values, and superior-subordinate interaction) influence ethical decision making. The presumed linkage is stronger for culture, but formal policies (operationalized in Figure 1 as structure—presence of code—and systems—sanctions for enforcement) should also have an impact on marketing managers' views toward ethical decision making.

Research Hypotheses

The proposed relationships are grounded in past studies and theoretical development in business and marketing ethics. Codes of ethics are important because they provide a clarity of expectations (Keogh, 1988), set out the rules of the game (Molander, 1987), and are believed to foster employee ethical values and increase organizational commitment (Hunt, Wood, & Chonko, 1989). However, Hunt and Vásquez-Párraga (1993) found that corporate culture is a stronger determinant of ethical action than corporate codes. Ferrell and Gresham (1985) included professional codes, corporate policy, and reward/punishment as influences to the "opportunity" variable of their model. In their integrated model (Ferrell, Gresham, & Fraedrich, 1989), organizational culture was added to the set, and the following was proposed: "Even if there is a formal policy on ethical behavior, informal understanding of enforcement and appropriate behavior for success will affect opportunity and behavior" (p. 61).

Based on our model and the published research in this area, it appears that the presence of formal policies and a strong corporate culture enhance ethical decision making compared to organizations where this thrust is lacking. A Business Roundtable publication (Keogh, 1988) argues that to make their ethics effective, companies must recognize that an ethical corporate culture is "a vital strategic key to survival and profitability in a highly competitive era" (p. 6). Berenbeim (1992) notes that "senior managers now recognize that dealing with ethics issues is part of nearly every employee's job" (p. 21). However, no prior research has addressed the joint roles of formal and informal culture in ethical decision making. It is clear that such research is relevant and important to managerial decision making in marketing. Based on the literature reviewed, the following hypotheses can be offered.

Informal corporate culture is more important than formal corporate policies in influencing the perceptions of ethical decision making by marketing managers.

The influence of formal policies on perceptions of ethical decision making by marketing managers is both direct and indirect, operating through the informal culture of an organization.

METHOD

Instrument

Because a large amount of information was to be requested from respondents in a national sample, a mail survey was the only viable alternative. A six-page questionnaire was developed and pretested with a random sample of marketing practitioners. The survey contained a combination of multiple choice, scaled, and open-ended questions. They provided factual (e.g., existence of corporate code, sanctions dealing with ethical violations), attitudinal (e.g., perceptions of ethical problems facing the individual using seven-point agree-disagree scales), and demographic (e.g., age, gender, company size) information.

Sample

The sample was drawn from practitioner members of the American Marketing Association. A systematic sampling of every fifth name from the AMA membership file of executive members was undertaken, and gummed labels with names and addresses were provided to the researchers by AMA. A total of 5,200 AMA members were sent the survey, cover letter, and postage-paid reply envelope. Twenty-six were returned as undeliverable. The number of respondents totaled 773.

The 15 percent response rate was lower than desired, but it likely resulted due to at least three identifiable causes. The sensitivity of the topic to some respondents and the length of the survey were no doubt factors that had an impact on the response rate (Gaedeke & Tootelian, 1976). Also, for cost reasons, no response enhancing techniques, such as precontacts or reminders, were used. Nonetheless, the response rate to this study is comparable to other national surveys of executives on business ethics (Berenbeim, 1987, 1992; McFeeley, Wackerle, & Jett, 1987; Touche Ross, 1988), comparable to the pretest response rates in the ethics survey of AMA practitioners undertaken by Goolsby and Hunt (1992), and is even better than the most recently published article on ethics in marketing by Sparks and Hunt (1998).

An extensive nonresponse bias test was conducted. From the original list of AMA members, every 25th name was held out from the initial mailing. These 200 individuals (hold-out sample) and 200 nonrespondents who had received the actual survey were sent a one-page questionnaire. Fifty-four percent of the hold-out sample and 45.5 percent of the nonrespondent sample completed the short

Table 1. Demographic Comparisons Between Survey
Respondents, Nonrespondents, and Hold-out Sample

	Sample Respondents	Nonrespondents	Hold-out Sample
Age:			
<35	42.4%	41.0%	39.8%
35-44	34.4	25.3	37.1
45-54	16.3	16.8	16.7
≥55	8.0	16.8	6.5
(N)	(762)	(95)	(108)
Gender			
Male	64.0%	53.5%	56.0%
Female	36.0	46.5	44.0
(N)	(764)	(86)	(104)
Managerial Position			
Lower mgmt.	8.3%	8.8%	6.0%
Middle mgmt.	56.3	60.4	53.0
Upper mgmt.	35.4	30.8	39.0
(N)	(748)	(91)	(106)
Salary			
<$20,000	3.2%	6.7%	3.8%
$20,000-34,999	22.6	22.5	27.9
$35,000-49,999	27.8	30.3	25.0
$50,000-74,999	26.2	29.2	25.0
$75,000-99,999	11.3	6.7	7.7
≥$100,000	8.8	4.5	10.8
(N)	(751)	(89)	(104)
Company Sales			
<$1 million	12.6%	13.6%	12.0%
$1-10 million	14.5	17.0	17.0
$11-25 million	8.3	10.2	7.0
$26-50 million	9.2	10.2	4.0
$51-100 million	9.8	6.8	11.8
$101-500 million	15.7	13.6	13.7
$501-999 million	6.7	5.7	3.9
$1-10 billion	16.5	17.0	24.5
>$10 billion	6.8	5.7	2.9
(N)	(747)	(88)	(102)
Company Code of Ethics?			
Yes	46.9%	48.4%	35.2%
No	43.2	43.1	53.7
Don't Know	9.9	43.1	11.1
(N)	(768)	(95)	(108)

Table 2. Variance-Covariance and Correlation Matrices of Construct Indicators

Variance-Covariance Matrix

Formal Policies

		[1]	[2]	[3]	[4]	[5]	[6]	[7]
Code	[1]	40.46						
Sanctions	[2]	3.36	2.54					

Informal Culture

		[1]	[2]	[3]	[4]	[5]	[6]	[7]
Ethical principles	[3]	5.05	1.09	22.58				
Professed values	[4]	7.01	0.75	13.71	60.31			
Superior-subordinate interaction	[5]	10.37	1.88	21.27	29.99	92.63		

Ethical Decision Making

		[1]	[2]	[3]	[4]	[5]	[6]	[7]
Ethical problems	[6]	8.53	2.16	23.83	37.96	44.85	72.13	
Candid communication	[7]	4.13	1.09	13.62	21.66	30.43	33.88	35.18
		[1]	[2]	[3]	[4]	[5]	[6]	[7]

Correlation Matrix

Formal Policies

		[1]	[2]	[3]	[4]	[5]	[6]	[7]
Code	[1]	1.00						
Sanctions	[2]	.33	1.00					

Informal Culture

		[1]	[2]	[3]	[4]	[5]	[6]	[7]
Ethical principles	[3]	.17	.14	1.00				
Professed values	[4]	.14	.06	.37	1.00			
Superior-subordinate Interaction	[5]	.17	.12	.47	.40	1.00		

Ethical Decision Making

		[1]	[2]	[3]	[4]	[5]	[6]	[7]
Ethical problems	[6]	.16	.16	.59	.58	.55	1.00	
Candid communication	[7]	.11	.12	.48	.47	.53	.67	1.00
		[1]	[2]	[3]	[4]	[5]	[6]	[7]

instrument. These rates of response support the idea that the low response rate in the main survey was related to its length.

Table 1 shows the percentages of responses on several characteristics for the three groups. The responses of the nonrespondent and hold-out groups did not differ significantly from the respondents on any of the four demographic (age, gender, salary, and position) variables (all $p > .05$). The percentages of respondents stating that their company had a written code of ethics in place was also not significantly different among the three groups ($p > .05$), nor was the reported total company sales data ($p > .05$). Therefore, the respondent group does not appear to be different from the AMA marketing practitioner population in terms of general characteristics. A further indication that the respondents in this study come from a representative group of companies is the finding that 55% of the companies here (vs. 52% nationally; Berenbeim, 1987) will terminate employees for violating their code of ethics. Moreover, it appears that on the basis of this comparison, problems of social desirability response biases do not seem to be evident.

Other relevant characteristics are that respondents come from a range of industries: industrial products (24%), consumer durables (15%), consumer packaged goods (12%), research firms (10%), advertising agencies (8%), and health care (7%). In addition, almost all respondents (98%) have bachelor's degrees and over one-half hold advanced degrees.

Measurement of Organization-related Constructs

Measurement of the model inputs shown in Figure 1 was accomplished by using a number of questions and scaled responses. Details of the manner in which scale item coding was accomplished and the assessment of measurement quality are given in detail in Appendix A. Specific scale content for the multi-item scales used as indicators for the informal culture and ethical decision making constructs is given in Appendix B.

Analysis Approach

LISREL was used to examine the substantive relationships. Summated scales were constructed for each dimension of the three constructs, based on the reliability results obtained. Item scale values for the ethical problems and candid communication indicators were reversed prior to summation to facilitate interpretation of construct relationships. Thus, all dimensions should be positively, as opposed to negatively related. The variance-covariance matrix using listwise deletion ($n = 541$), which is shown in Table 2, was used as input.

RESULTS

Preliminary Measurement Tests

The correlation matrix of the formal policies and informal culture construct indicators shown in Table 2 was used as input for a confirmatory factor analysis to assess the convergent and discriminant validity of the two antecedent constructs. Results of the LISREL analysis provided strong support that the two constructs differ from one another and that the indicators of each one relate closely ($\chi^2 = 1.31$, df = 4, $p = .86$; TCD = .853; AGFI = .99; RMSR = .012). All other internal fit indicators easily surpassed the minimum levels outlined by Bagozzi and Yi (1988). Of particular note, the construct loadings were in the .6 to .8 range. The correlation between the two constructs of .36 is supportive of discriminant validity, which was substantiated by testing the two-dimension solution against a unidimensional model ($\Delta\chi^2 = 33.71$, df = 1, $p < .001$).

It was not possible to analyze in conclusive fashion the construct validity of the ethical decision-making construct. Nevertheless, the correlation of .67 among the two indicators (see Table 2) is suggestive of convergence. Moreover, this correlation is larger than the correlations of the two ethical decision-making indicators with the informal culture dimensions (range of .47 to .59), which provides evidence of the separateness and thus the discriminant validity of each construct. Taken together, it can be concluded that none of the preliminary tests revealed substantive data problems.

Structural Model Testing

The variance-covariance matrix was used for all structural model testing of the relationships shown in Figure 1 in order to obtain unbiased estimates of parameter standard errors (Bagozzi & Yi, 1988). Based on Jöreskog and Sörbom (1982), the loading of one indicator on each construct was fixed at 1.00 to set the scaling metric for each unobservable construct. As this procedure has been criticized for being arbitrary and not providing standard error estimates for the fixed parameters (see Dillon & Kumar, 1987), all model tests were run several times, using a different variable as the reference indicator for each construct. This approach enabled assessment of the significance of all indicators and provided a rough gauge of the stability of structural parameters.

Preliminary structural model tests indicated a Heywood case existed on the error parameter associated with the ethical decision-making construct. Negative error estimates are believed to be common in practice, being due to either sampling fluctuations, inappropriate model fitting, or model indefiniteness (Dillon, Kumar, & Mulani, 1987). Anderson and Gerbing (1984) conducted a Monte Carlo simulation which revealed that improper solutions, such as Heywood cases, occurred more frequently for models with only two or three indicators of each construct, as is the case here. Confidence intervals constructed for the offensive parameter value consistently included zero, all with a reasonably sized standard error estimate, which indicates that the likely basis for the negative error was due to sampling fluctuations. The appropriate remedy recommended by these authors is to fix the parameter at a small positive number and re-estimate the model. All subsequent model tests incorporated this modification.

The results of model tests revealed that a good fit was obtained. Although the obtained chi-square of 26.95 with 12 degrees of freedom is significant ($p = .008$), the AGFI (.981), TCD (.994), and RMSR (.852) are suggestive of a close fit. The largest normalized residual of only 1.35 and a roughly linear Q-Q

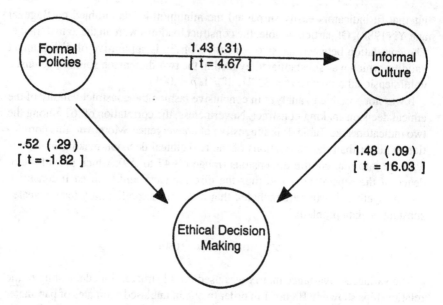

Note: Unstandardized parameter values shown, with standard errors given in parentheses and t-values in brackets.

Figure 2.   Structural Model Relationships of Ethical Decision Making

plot with slope greater than 1 provide supportive evidence. The *t*-values for all estimated parameters, except for the structural parameter directly connecting formal policies with ethical decision making, were highly significant ($p <$ .001). Moreover, indicator loadings and reliabilities were reasonable. These results held irrespective of which indicator were used as the referent for a particular construct. Although the parameter values and associated standard errors varied to an extent across solutions, the *t*-values did not vary more than 5 percent in magnitude.

A partial assessment of the extent to which the structural relationships are affected by measurement-structure interaction (Kumar & Dillon, 1987) was conducted by fixing the loadings for the indicators of each construct at the values obtained from the separate analyses of construct measurement properties. As two of the constructs are each represented by only two indicators, it was not possible to fix both the loading and error terms of each indicator, as was suggested by Dillon and Kumar (1987), but the procedure followed does allow for partial assessment. The difference in fit between this restricted model and the hypothesized model ($\Delta\chi^2 = 38.24$, df = 4, $p < .001$) suggests the presence of some measurement-structure interaction. However, the structural relationships are basically equivalent among the two models,[8] indicating that measurement properties do not

Table 3. Structural Model Results of Analyses Using Alternative Measures of the Formal Policies Construct Indicators

Model	χ^2	df	p	AGFI	RMSR	TCD	Direction of Structural Relationships [t-value]		
							FP-IC	FP-EDM	IC-EDM
8 FP items as one construct	1285	63	.000	.648	.460	.993	+ [5.97]	− [−2.53]	+ [17.14]
Presence of code item as code dimension	31.02	12	.002	.970	.795	.971	+ [2.51]	− [−0.85]	+ [16.30]
Sum of 2 code evaluative items as code dimension	26.14	12	.010	.975	.781	.997	+ [4.57]	− [−2.23]	+ [16.13]
Sum of 4 sanctions a sanctions dimension	27.16	12	.007	.974	.775	.994	+ [4.75]	− [−2.27]	+ [16.82]
Sums of 2 code evaluative tems as code and 4 sanctions as sanctions dimensions	26.68	12	.009	.974	.766	.994	+ [4.96]	− [−2.25]	+ [16.77]

Key:

FP = Formal Policies construct
IC = Informal Culture construct
EDM = Ethical Decision Making construct

account for the structural relationships of interest and the hypothesized model results can be interpreted.

The structural relationships for the hypothesized model are shown in Figure 2. The informal culture construct is strongly and positively related to ethical decision making ($p < .001$). The relationship of formal policies with ethical decision making is primarily an indirect one, operating through informal culture in a positive direction ($p < .001$). In contrast, the direct relationship is not quite significant ($p < .075$), and is negative in sign, which is counter to the hypothesized direction. The standardized parameter values reveal that the informal culture-ethical decision-making linkage is quite strong (.92), the formal policies-informal culture parameter is weaker, but still important (.36), and the formal policies-ethical decision-making direct relationship is weak (−.11). Except for the negative direct relationship of the formal policies construct, the hypothesized structure is supported.

Additional Structural Model Tests

A series of additional analyses were conducted using different formulations of the code and sanction indicators of the formal policies construct in light of the possibility that the structural relationships uncovered could have been the result of the manner in which the indicator measurements were constructed. In particular, analyses were conducted where (1) the eight items used in the construction of the formal policies indicators were specified as being separate representations of the construct, (2) the single item pertaining to the presence of a code of ethics was specified as the code dimension indicator, (3) the sum of the two evaluative aspects of the code (i.e., perceived usefulness and degree of specificity) was used as the code indicator, (4) the sum of the four sanctions as representing the sanctions dimension (i.e., deleting the no sanctions item from the scale), and (5) the combination of models 3 and 4. The summary results of these analyses are given in Table 3.

As can be seen, the fit of the models are quite good and comparable to the fit of the core structural model formulation. The model specifying the eight items used to develop the formal policies indicators as forming one construct is an exception, but that is to be expected. Of interest here is the direction and relative size of the structural relationships. Although the magnitudes of the particular relationships differed to an extent across the model formulations, it can be concluded that the structural relationships shown in Figure 2 are not the result of the manner in which the formal policies indicators were operationalized.

The first research proposition posits that informal culture is more important than formal policies in explaining perceptions of ethical decision making. The structural results shown in Figure 2 provide general support for this premise, but a more direct test is warranted. An analysis was conducted in which formal policies and informal culture were specified as separate exogenous constructs uncorrelated with one another to isolate their direct relative importance. The chi-square

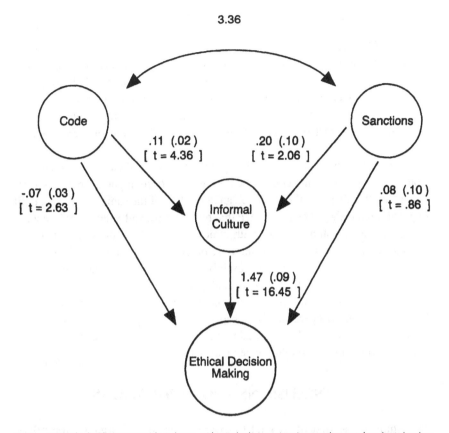

Note: Unstandardized parameter values shown, with standard errors given in parentheses and *t-value* in brackets.

Figure 3. Disaggregated Structural Relationships of Formal Policies Indicators

for this model is much larger ($\chi^2 = 55.95$, df = 13, $p = .000$) than for the model formulation specifying the indirect linkage of formal policies through informal culture ($\Delta\chi^2 = 29.00$, df = 1, $p < .001$). Of relevance here is the comparison of the two parameters. The unstandardized value of the parameter linking informal culture with ethical decision making is sizable (1.45, se = .09, $t = 16.44$, $p < .001$), compared to the one for formal policies (.120, se = .06, $t = 1.94$, $p < .06$), providing strong support for the research proposition. It is noteworthy that the sign of the formal policies parameter is positive if indirect effects through informal culture are not estimated.

Additional analyses were conducted to isolate the underlying basis for the negative direct relationship of formal policies with ethical decision making found in the first structural analysis. The two formal policies indicators were treated as separate exogenous constructs as shown in Figure 3. The fit of this model was comparable to the primary structural model test (χ^2 = 23.08, df = 11, p = .017; AGFI = .981, TCD = .994; RMSR = .824). As can be seen in the figure, the negative direct relationship of formal policies with ethical decision making can be traced to the code indicator having a negative direct relationship ($p <$ .01) and the sanctions indicator having a positive, but nonsignificant ($p > .30$) direct relationship with ethical decision making. In contrast, both indicators have positive indirect relationships through informal culture ($p < .001$ and .05, respectively).

Given that the negative direct relationship of formal policies with ethical decision making is due to the code indicator and not to the inputs of both construct indicators, this result could simply be an aberration of the sample or of model fitting, although it should be mentioned that Nwachukwa and Vitell (1997) reported a negative relationship of codes with ethical judgments. It does seem plausible that such results could emanate from those organizations where there is not a supportive informal culture in place. Possibly, they lack official sanctions for noncompliance. As discussed in the formal policies section of Appendix A, 30 percent of the respondents reported that there are no sanctions for noncompliance. More importantly, 15 percent of the respondents who reported their company has a formal code of ethics also reported that no sanctions exist. Under such circumstances, formal policies might not be taken seriously.

CONCLUSIONS AND IMPLICATIONS

This study is the first of its kind to examine the role of organization-related processes on ethical decision making in marketing. In particular, the manner in which formal corporate policies and the informal culture of organizations serve to affect ethical decision making were examined using a cross-sectional sample of marketing managers from U.S.-based corporations. Results of the structural model tests indicated that the informal corporate culture has a very strong direct influence on ethical decision making. In contrast, formal policies were found to have an indirect relationship with ethical decision making, operating through informal culture, and a weak, negative direct relationship. Although the low response rate is a definite limitation of the study, the strong direct and indirect relationships of informal culture and formal policies, respectively, with ethical decision making appear to be generalizable to other samples and study contexts. It should also be mentioned that social desirability responding by study participants cannot be ruled out as a basis for the patterns of results. However, such biases are believed to be minimal based on the comparisons made between respondents and nonrespondents.

Implications

The implications of these findings are straightforward and important. A positive informal corporate culture is a necessary prerequisite to supporting and sustaining the integrity of formal codes and sanctions. Without such a culture, the effects of formal policies are less clear, and may even have negative outcomes on ethical decision making. Lip service alone is clearly insufficient; there must be a commitment and example provided by top management that filters throughout the entire organization if ethical decision making is to be the standard for proper behavior. For example, individuals who pad their expense accounts must be reprimanded while employees who "walk away from business" when bribery is a prerequisite must be rewarded.

The strongest implication from the results of this study appears to be that too much emphasis placed on written codes of conduct may not produce the intended effects. Recent statistics indicate that 80-90 percent of large U.S.-based corporations with codes in place (Berenbeim, 1992; Center for Business Ethics, 1992; Murphy, 1995) periodically revise them. The fact that ethical decision making could be influenced negatively by codes means that just having one is not enough. In fact, a code of ethics may operate in a negative fashion if it is viewed as a top-down mandate without adequate support, discussion, and enforcement across the organization.

The finding that codes have a negative impact is understandable in the light of the current environment in some companies. For example, many firms have downsized, there is pressure by management to perform and employees are disgruntled with compensation levels of senior management. Insight into the limitations of codes can be gained from recent criticisms of corporate values statements that received substantial emphasis in the 1990s (Nash, 1995; Stewart, 1996). These writers see a "disconnect" in many organizations between the professed values and day-to-day operations. Only 60 percent of employees believe that their companies meant what they said in their values statements. In other instances, companies spend much time and money on "packaging" their values with use of coffee mugs, brochures, and slick PR programs without also focusing on the substance of the values. According to these writers, and consistent with our findings, culture rather than values statements should be the central thrust: "They (values) have to be compatible with the culture that's already there; pretty words won't bloom in the wrong soil" (Stewart, 1996, p. 138), and "programs seeking to change cultures and values carry a special vulnerability to becoming a self-defeating exercise" (Nash, 1995, p. 13).

Marketing firms who are seriously attempting to influence ethical decision making in a positive direction should use codes and training programs in ethics as vehicles to reinforce the culture so that managers feel comfortable in making the "right" decision from an ethical standpoint. Paying special attention to principles, values, and superior-subordinate interactions all represent methods to enhance the ethical sensitivity of marketing managers. Companies should strive for integrity-based, rather than compliance-based, programs (Paine, 1994).

Future Research Directions

There are several directions for future research that emanate from the present study. First, the nature of organizational processes in ethical decision making would benefit from further study. In particular, emphasis should be placed on a more detailed examination that would allow for the determination of the basis for the negative direct relationship of formal policies on ethical decision making. It may be possible that a more novel and complete analysis of the influence of codes would provide additional insights. Companies which promulgate and promote values statements or corporate credos instead of codes might operate differently (Murphy, 1998). In addition, there is a need to investigate how other organizational constructs, such as other aspects of organizational culture, relate to the factors and their relationships investigated in this study.

Second, there is a need for identifying and testing additional formal policies constructs. The nature and scope of ethics training programs may be another critical component both to setting an ethical culture and the process of ethical decision making. These programs are currently offered in two-thirds of the largest companies in the United States, and about one-half of them have specific modules on marketing and selling (Murphy, 1992). A recent study (Sparks & Hunt, 1998) found that ethical sensitivity is learned and marketers are socialized into their organizations and professional societies by training.

Third, a more complete delineation of informal corporate culture is warranted. Senior management directives provide a major input into the corporate culture. The actions of top management (Chonko & Hunt, 1985; Hunt, Chonko, & Wilcox, 1984) have been found to be a significant input into the climate for ethical decision making. Because the behavior of top management sets the "tone" for the entire firm, the behavior of the CEO and top marketing executives need to be explicitly studied in more detail. Managerial leadership in marketing needs to be examined so that both ethical and economic performance criteria can be studied. Depth interviews of these managers examining the importance of personal characteristics relative to organizational ones could help illuminate the amorphous culture variable. Alternately, the presence of "subcultures" within the overall corporate culture should be investigated. Sinclair (1993) posits that a subculture which is bottom-up driven and relies on the individual, and not institutional processes, produces better ethics. Her hypothesis needs to be tested.

Fourth, additional cross-sectional studies of marketing managers are necessary. One avenue for future research would be to focus on marketing executives in a few organizations with a strong commitment to ethical behavior and contrast their responses to organization-related constructs with individuals working in firms with a questionable or unknown ethical posture. This type of analysis could be conducted both domestically and internationally and would help to isolate exactly which organizational factors lead to ethical decision making.

Promulgating and revising corporate codes and placing sanctions on violation of the code are relatively short-term (and some would say easy) approaches to instilling ethics into an organization. Rules (codes) and regulations (sanctions) can be developed; the question remains as to their impact. However, the results of this study indicate that the longer term and more difficult avenue of nurturing the corporate culture is a superior method of bringing about ethical decision making. An emphasis on creating a principles- and values-based candid corporate culture represents a continuing challenge to marketing executives.

APPENDIX A

Scale Item Coding and Measurement Properties

Organization-related Measures

Measurement of the model inputs shown in Figure 1 was accomplished by using a number of questions and scaled responses.

Formal Policies. For the code dimension, the existence or absence of a formal, written company code of ethics was one item used to measure this component. Although codes are controversial, they are viewed as one of the major structural mechanisms for incorporating ethics into the firm (Bennett, 1988; Touche Ross, 1988). For this measure, yes responses (47% of the sample) were coded 2, and no (44%) and don't know (9%) were coded 0 and 1, respectively, based on the finding that measurement error is minimized by treating don't know as an intermediate response option, as opposed to assigning "don't know" and "no" the same code. The two additional code-related questions addressed the perceived usefulness (i.e., "My company's code of ethics is useful in dealing with day-to-day activities"), and degree of specificity the code is for the respondent (i.e., "My company's code of ethics is specific enough to deal with ethical issues facing me"), using a seven-point, strongly disagree (1) to strongly agree (7) response format. The dimensions of usefulness (Benson, 1989) and specificity (Murphy, 1988, 1989) have been noted as essential characteristics of codes. For these two questions, respondents were assigned the score of 0 if they reported on the first question that their company does not have a formal code of ethics, or they don't know, based on the premise that if an employee has no company code of ethics to use as a benchmark, it is not at all useful or specific for providing them with guidance in handling everyday activities. This scaling approach enabled the use of data from all respondents—those with and without a formal written code of ethics.

The three items were subjected to reliability analysis using both coefficient alpha and LISREL VI (Jöreskog & Sörbom, 1982). In both analyses, these items were found to be internally consistent (.90 and .98, respectively). However, given that the 44 percent of the respondents who reported their firm has no formal code of ethics and the 9 percent who did not know were assigned a score of 0 to the two evaluative questions regarding perceived usefulness and degree of specificity, these reliability estimates are inflated due to the inherent internal consistency created through this scaling approach. The magnitude of the inflation is not substantial, though, because the coefficient alpha for the two evaluative questions is .81 for the subgroup of respondents reporting their organization has a formal code of ethics.

The *sanctions* dimension was measured by determining what procedures the respondent feels are in place to deal with ethical violations of the code or company policies. Based on Mathews (1987), the response options that were given (and sample results) are: no sanctions (30%), reprimand by superior (48%), loss of pay (12%), suspension (20%), and loss of job (55%). As respondents were instructed to check all that apply, each option was treated as a separate variable, with 0-1 response options. Of those respondents reporting one or more sanctions, 20 percent checked only the job loss option, 33 percent checked both the superior reprimand and the job loss options, and the remaining 47 percent reported other combinations of two, three, or all four sanctions. It was determined that the pattern of responses to the five categories are internally consistent, based on the KR-20 formula for coefficient alpha $(.79)^2$ and LISREL (.81).

The items measuring each of the two dimensions were subjected to a confirmatory factor analysis using LISREL in which two dimensions were specified. In that analysis the loadings of the items on their respective dimension all exceeded .60 and were in the .7-.9 range. The *t*-values for all estimated parameters were sizeable (all exceeding 8.0), and the total coefficient of determination (TCD = .994), the root mean square residual (RMSR = .079), and the adjusted goodness of fit index (AGFI = .91) indicated a satisfactory fit. These results meet or exceed guidelines outlined by Bagozzi and Yi (1988) for measurement model testing. The correlation among the two dimensions of .41 indicates that the two dimensions are indeed separate and do not form a unidimensional construct. To test this issue directly, a second confirmatory factor analysis was conducted that assumed the eight items form a unidimensional construct. The difference in chi-square values between the two model tests of 912 ($p < .0001$, df = 1) leads to the conclusion that the two dimensions should be considered as separate indicators of the construct.

Informal Culture. Measurement of the informal corporate culture of an organization is traditionally accomplished by employing attitudinal batteries of statements that span the relevant domains of concern. This approach was followed here (see Appendix B for scale items). The ethical principles dimension was measured using four statements offered by Pastin (1986) to describe firms where ethics is emphasized in managerial decision making. The four items were determined to be reasonably internally consistent using both coefficient alpha (.73)[3] and LISREL (.76). The professed values dimension pertains to both the organization and its employees. An existing eleven-item scale developed by Lincoln, Pressley, and Little (1982) was used to measure these values. Reliability analysis indicated that one item was not consistent with the others. After elimination of that item from further consideration, the coefficient alpha and LISREL-determined reliability estimates of the remaining ten items are .91[4] and .89, respectively. The superior-subordinate interaction dimension is derived from Serpa's (1985) description of a culture that is characterized by open communication. The seven-item semantic differential scale items were found to be internally consistent, based on both coefficient alpha (.84)[5] and LISREL (.83).

The twenty-one items measuring the three dimensions of the informal culture construct were assessed in a confirmatory factor analysis with LISREL in the same manner as that done with the formal policies one. Results of the analysis were generally congruent with Bagozzi and Yi's (1988) recommendations. The loadings were in the .60 to .83 range, with the exception of one superior-subordinate interaction item (.46), and the t-values for all estimated parameters were sizeable (all greater than 11.7). The TCD (.991), the RMSR (.041), and the AGFI (.92) are indicative of a reasonable fit. The correlations among the three dimensions of ethical principles, superior-subordinate interaction, and professed values were found to be .55, .43, and .42, respectively, providing indirect evidence that the informal culture construct should be treated as multidimensional. A direct test of the hypothesis was done by comparing the model with one that assumes the items load on one dimension. The difference in chi-square between the two models of 1942 ($p < .0001$, df = 3) leads to the conclusion that the construct should be treated as being multidimensional.

Ethical Decision Making Measures

As the extent of ethical decision making by marketing managers is difficult to measure directly, an indirect approach comparable to the one for assessing informal corporate culture was used. Two dimensions—ethical problems and candid communication—are posited to constitute the ethical decision making construct (items shown in Appendix B).

The first dimension, *ethical problems*, was measured using seven of the eight items in the scale developed by Hunt and Chonko (1984; Chonko & Hunt, 1985). One item was not included because it dealt with opportunities to engage in unethical behavior rather than with behavior per se. The seven-item scale was found to be internally consistent, based on coefficient alpha and LISREL analyses (both .85)[6]. The second dimension, *candid communication*, is based on the work of Serpa (1985), who stipulated that candor in communication within an organization is a key component in ethical decision making. As he noted later, "truthfulness and honesty in communicating is the biggest ethical dilemma managers face today" (quoted in *Chief Executive*, 1988). Five statements were developed by the authors to represent this dimension. Reliability analyses using coefficient alpha (.80)[7] and LISREL (.81) suggest that the measures are internally consistent.

The twelve items used to measure the two dimensions were analyzed in a confirmatory factor analysis using LISREL with two dimensions specified. As with the formal policies and informal culture constructs, the results of this analysis indicate that the ethical decision-making construct is multidimensional. The item loadings were generally sizeable (> .60), with one exception. The item pertaining to the ethical posture of successful and unsuccessful managers on the ethical problems dimension had a loading of .41. Nevertheless, all *t*-values were large (all greater than 11.3). The TCD (.932), the RMSR (.047), and the AGFI (.93) suggest the fit is reasonable. The correlation among the two dimensions is .82. The difference in chi-square between the two dimension solution and one that assumes the construct is unidimensional is 176 ($p < .0001$, df = 1), indicating that the construct should be treated as multidimensional.

APPENDIX B

Scale Content of Informal Corporate Culture and Ethical Decision-making Construct Indicators

I.   Informal Corporate Culture

    A.   Ethical Principles

        a.   My company is obsessed with fairness.

        b.   In my company, individuals assume personal responsibility for actions of the company.

        c.   In my company, individuals are at ease interacting with diverse internal and external stakeholder groups.

        d.   My company sees its activities in terms of a purpose that members of the company value.

Measured on a seven-point scale where 1 = "strongly disagree" to 7 = "strongly agree."

B. Professed Values

   a. To progress, one has to develop the philosophy that winning is everything.

   b. The career pressures of advancing leave one with an overdeveloped head and underdeveloped heart.

   c. One can succeed even if one's work is not the most important thing in one's life.

   d. Even though one might say and believe that something like "customer satisfaction" is the primary goal of the organization, one has to develop an attitude that making money is the single most important objective.

   e. One just about has to "sell their soul" to the organization to get ahead.

   f. To progress, one will occasionally have to indulge in "dirty tactics." (For example, taking credit for work done by someone else or insinuating that someone else did not do something they were supposed to do.)

   g. To advance, the corporation has to come first, even before one's family.

   h. One cannot progress without "stepping on a few people." All personal values have to be set aside in order for one to advance. To advance, one has to develop the philosophy that what does not relate to winning and career advancement, including one's family, does not really matter.

   i. To climb the ladder, one must not only be prepared to aggressively move past those who stand in the way, but may find it necessary to "clear the path."

Measured on a five-point scale where 1 = "almost never the case" to 5 = "almost always the case."

C. Superior-Subordinate Interaction

   a. Limited Communication—Open Communication

   b. Instills Fear—Instills Confidence

   c. Discourages Differing Views—Encourages Differing Views

   d. Avoids Confrontation—Supportive of Confrontation

   e. Rewards "Good News" Only—Rewards Truthfulness

    f.   Best to Agree and Not Question—Disagreement and Questioning Welcome

    g.   Defensive, Deceptive Communication—Truthful, Candid Communication

Measured by a seven-point semantic differential scale labeled (1) totally; (2) somewhat; (3) slightly; (4) neither; (5) slightly; (6) somewhat; (7) totally.

II.   Ethical Decision Making

    A.   Ethical Problems

        a.   Marketing managers in my company often engage in behaviors that I consider unethical.

        b.   Successful marketing managers in my company are generally more ethical than unsuccessful managers. (Reversed)

        c.   In order to succeed in my company, it is necessary to compromise one's ethics.

        d.   Successful managers in my company withhold information that is detrimental to their self-interests.

        e.   Successful managers in my company make rivals look bad in the eyes of important people in my company.

        f.   Successful managers in my company look for a "scapegoat" when they feel they may be associated with failure.

        g.   Successful managers in my company take credit for the ideas and accomplishments of others.

Measured on a seven-point scale where 1 = "strongly disagree" to 7 = "strongly agree."

    B.   Candid Communication

        a.   Employees in my company try to find out what management thinks and wants before expressing themselves.

        b.   Employees in my company are reluctant to provide negative information or bad news.

        c.   There is recurrent agreement (lack of any dissenting views) among managers in my organization on various issues.

        d.   The same information is provided over a period of time to justify a previous action.

e. Many informal one-on-one meetings follow group management meetings because it is safe to talk then.

Measured on a seven-point scale where 1 = "strongly disagree" to 7 = "strongly agree."

ACKNOWLEDGMENTS

The authors would like to thank the Special Issue Editors and the anonymous reviewers for their helpful comments and suggestions, Mark G. Dunn for his assistance in the data collection phase, and Notre Dame's College of Business Administration for its financial support. Preparation of the article was completed while the first author was on a Faculty Development Leave provided by the Lowry Mays College & Graduate School of Business at Texas A&M University.

NOTES

1. Another way of labeling these variables is structure (for code) and systems (for sanctions). These descriptors are used in the McKinsey 7S framework (Pascale & Athos, 1981; Peters & Waterman, 1982).

2. The coefficient alphas for the subgroups of respondents reporting their company has a formal code of ethics (Code group) and their company does not have a code or they don't know (No Code group) are .72 and .83, respectively. For the four sanctions options, the respective coefficient alphas are .66 and .76, and .71 for the overall sample. T-tests of the scale differences among the subgroups indicate those reporting their company has a code also report a greater number of sanctions for ethical violations ($p < .001$).

3. The respective coefficient alphas for the Code and No Code groups are .65 and .77. The average scale response for the Code group is higher than for the No Code group ($p < .03$).

4. The respective coefficient alphas for the two groups are .91 and .90. T-test results indicate the average scale response for the Code group is higher than the No Code group ($p < .02$).

5. The respective coefficient alphas for the Code and No Code groups are .83 and .85. The average scale response for the Code group is higher than the No Code groups ($p < .001$)

6. Coefficient alphas for both subgroups are .85. The mean difference among the groups is not significant ($p > .10$), although the average for the Code group exceeds the No Code group.

7. The respective coefficient alphas for the Code and No Code groups are .81 and .78. The groups do not differ in their average scale response ($p > .40$).

8. For the fixed loadings model, the Formal Policies-Informal Culture and Informal Culture-Ethical Decision Making relationships are positive and significant ($t = 4.67, 25.58$, respectively, both $p < .001$), and the Formal Policies-Ethical Decision Making relationship is negative and statistically significant ($t = -2.45, p < .02$). See Figure 2 for the hypothesized model results.

REFERENCES

Akaah, I.P., & Lund, D. (1994). The influence of personal and organizational values on marketing professionals' ethical behavior. *Journal of Business Ethics, 13*(June), 417-430.

Anderson, J.C., & Gerbing, D.W. (1984). The effect of sampling error on convergence, improper solutions, and goodness-of-fit indices for maximum likelihood confirmatory factor analysis. *Psychometrika, 49*(June), 155-173.

Austin, R.W. (1961). Code of conduct for executives. *Harvard Business Review, 39*(September-October), 53-61.

Bagozzi, R.P., & Yi, Y. (1988). On the evaluation of structural equation models. *Journal of the Academy of Marketing Science, 16*(Spring), 74-94.

Baumhart, R.C. (1961). How ethical are businessmen? *Harvard Business Review* (July-August), 6-19, 156-176.

Bennett, A. (1988, July 15). Ethics codes spread despite skepticism. *The Wall Street Journal*, p. 13.

Benson, G.C.S. (1989). Code of ethics. *Journal of Business Ethics, 8*, 305-320.

Berenbeim, R.E. (1987). *Corporate ethics.* New York: The Conference Board, Report No. 900.

Berenbeim, R.E. (1992). *Corporate ethics practices.* New York: The Conference Board, Report No. 986.

Bommer, M., Gratto, C., Gravander, J., & Tuttle, M. (1987). A behavioral model of ethical and unethical decision-making. *Journal of Business Ethics, 6*, 265-280.

Brenner, S.N., & Molander, E.A. (1977). Is the ethics of business changing? *Harvard Business Review, 55*(January-February), 57-71.

Butcher, C. (1985). Unethical business behavior must be understood. In P.J. Frost, L.F. Moore, M.R. Louis, C.C. Lundberg, & J. Martin (Eds.), *Organizational culture* (pp. 271-280). Beverly Hills, CA: Sage

Center for Business Ethics. (1992). Instilling ethical values in large corporations. *Journal of Business Ethics, 11*, 863-867.

Chen, A.Y.S., Sawyers, R.B., & Williams, P.F. (1997). Reinforcing ethical decision making through corporate culture. *Journal of Businness Ethics, 16*, 855-865.

Chief Executive. (1988, July/August). What to do about ethics? *CE Roundtable*, p. 46.

Chonko, L.B., & Hunt, S.D. (1985). Ethics and marketing management: An empirical investigation. *Journal of Business Research, 13*, 339-359.

Cressey, D.R., & Moore, C.A. (1983). Managerial values and corporate codes of ethics. *California Management Review, 25*(Summer), 53-77.

Deal, T.E., & Kennedy, A.A. (1982). *Corporate culture.* Reading, MA: Addison-Wesley.

Deetz, S. (1985). Ethical considerations in cultural research in organizations. In P.J. Frost, L.F. Moore, M.R. Louis, C.C. Lundberg, & J. Martin (Eds.), *Organizational culture* (pp. 253-269). Beverly Hills, CA: Sage.

Deshpande, T., & Parasuraman, A. (1986). Linking corporate culture to strategic planning. *Business Horizons, 29*(May-June), 28-37.

Deshpande, T., & Webster, F.E., Jr. (1989). Organizational culture and marketing: Defining the research agenda. *Journal of Marketing, 53*(January), 3-15.

Dillon, W.R., & Kumar, A. (1987). *A discussion of selected issues in covariance structure analysis: An amplification and reevaluation.* Unpublished working paper, University of South Carolina.

Dillon, W.R., Kumar, A., & Mulani, N. (1987). Offending estimates in covariance structure analysis: Comments on the causes of and solutions to heywood cases. *Psychological Bulletin, 101*(January), 126-135.

Ferrell, O.C., & Gresham, L.G. (1985). A contingency framework for understanding ethical decision making in marketing. *Journal of Marketing, 49*(Summer), 87-96.

Ferrell, O.C., & Fraedrich, J. (1989). A synthesis of ethical decision models for marketing. *Journal of Macromarketing, 9*(Fall), 55-64.

Ferrell, O.C., & Weaver, K.M. (1978). Ethical beliefs of marketing managers. *Journal of Marketing, 42*(July), 69-73.

Fleming, J.E. (1984). Managing the corporate ethical climate. In W.M. Hoffman, J.M. Moore, & D.A. Fedo (Eds.), *Corporate governance and institutionalizing ethics* (pp. 217-226). Lexington, MA: Lexington Books.

Fombrun, C.J. (1983). Corporate culture, environment and strategy. *Human Resource Management, 22*(Spring-Summer), 139-152.

Frederick, W.C., & Weber, J. (1987). The values of corporate managers and their critics: An empirical description and normative implications. In W.C. Frederick & L.E. Preston (Eds.), *Research in corporate social performance and policy* (Vol. 9, pp. 131-152). Greenwich, CT: JAI Press.

Fritzsche, D.J. (1988). An examination of marketing ethics: Role of the decision maker, consequences of the decision, management position and sex of the respondent. *Journal of Macromarketing, 8*(Fall), 29-39.

Gaedeke, R.M., & Tootelian, D.H. (1976). The Fortune 500 list: An endangered species for academic research. *Journal of Business Research, 4*(August), 283-288.

Gellerman, S.W. (1986). Why "good" managers make bad ethical choices. *Harvard Business Review, 64*(July-August), 85-90.

Gellerman, S.W. (1989). Managing ethics from the top down. *Sloan Management Review, 30*(Winter), 73-79.

Goolsby, J.R., & Hunt, S.D. (1992). Cognitive moral development. *Journal of Marketing, 56*(January), 55-68.

Gordon, G.G. (1991). Industry determinants of organizational culture. *Academy of Management Review, 16*(April), 396-415.

Harris, C.E. (1978). Structuring a workable business code of ethics. *University of Florida Law Review, 30,* 310-382.

Hite, R.E., Bellizzi, J.A., & Fraser, C. (1988). A content analysis of ethical policy statements regarding marketing activities. *Journal of Business Ethics, 7,* 771-776.

Hoffman, W.M., Moore, J.M., & Fedo, D.A. (Eds.). (1984). *Corporate governance and institutionalizing ethics.* Lexington, MA: Lexington Books.

Hunt, S.D., & Chonko, L.B. (1984). Marketing and machiavellianism. *Journal of Marketing, 48*(Summer), 30-42.

Hunt, S.D., Chonko, L.B., & Wilcox, J.B. (1984). Ethical problems of marketing researchers. *Journal of Marketing Research, 21*(August), 309-324.

Hunt, S.D., & Vásquez-Párraga, A.Z. (1993). Organizational consequences, marketing ethics, and salesforce supervision. *Journal of Marketing Research, 30*(February), 78-90.

Hunt, S.D., & Vitell, S. (1986). A general theory of marketing ethics. *Journal of Macromarketing* (Spring), 5-16.

Hunt, S.D., Wood, V.R., & Chonko, L.B. (1989). Corporate ethical values and organizational commitment in marketing. *Journal of Marketing, 53*(July), 79-90.

Jones, M.O. (1985). Is ethics the issue? In P.J. Frost, L.F. Moore, M.R. Louis, C.C. Lundberg, & J. Martin (Eds.), *Organizational culture* (pp. 235-252).Beverly Hills, CA: Sage.

Jöreskog, K.G., & Sörbom, D. (1982). *LISREL VI: Analysis of linear structural relations by the method of maximum likelihood.* Mooresville, IN: Scientific Software.

Keogh, J. (Ed.). (1988). *Corporate ethics: A prime business asset.* New York: The Business Roundtable.

Kumar, A., & Dillon, W.R. (1987). The interaction of measurement and structure in simultaneous equation models with unobservable variables. *Journal of Marketing Research, 24*(February), 98-105.

Laczniak, G.R. (1983). Frameworks for analyzing marketing ethics. *Journal of Macromarketing, 3*(Spring), 7-18.

Laczniak, G.R., & Inderrieden, E.J. (1987). The influence of stated organizational concern upon ethical decison making. *Journal of Business Ethics, 6*(May), 297-307.

Laczniak, G.R., Lusch, R.F., & Murphy, P.E. (1979). Social marketing: Its ethical dimensions. *Journal of Marketing, 43*(Spring), 29-36.

Laczniak, G.R., & Murphy, P.E. (1993). *Ethical marketing decisions: The higher road.* Englewood Cliffs, NJ: Prentice-Hall.

Lincoln, D.J., Pressley, M.M., & Little, T. (1982). Ethical beliefs and personal values of top level executives. *Journal of Business Research, 10*(December), 475-487.

Mahajan, V., Varadarajan, P.R., & Kerin, R.A. (1987). Metamorphosis in strategic market planning. In J. Sheth & G L. Frazier (Eds.), *Contemporary views on marketing practice* (pp. 67-110). Lexington, MA: Lexington Books.

Mathews, M.C. (1987). Codes of ethics: Organizational behavior and misbehavior. In W.C. Frederick & L.E. Preston (Eds.), *Research in corporate social performance and policy* (Vol. 9, pp. 107-130). Greenwich, CT: JAI Press.

McCoy, C.S. (1985). *Management of values: The ethical difference in corporate policy and performance.* Boston, MA: Pitman.

McFeeley, C.E., Wackerle, F.W., & Jett, C.C. (1987). *Survey on ethics: Results.* Chicago: McFeeley, Wackerle and Jett.

Molander, E.A. (1987). A paradigm for design, promulgation and enforcement of ethical codes, *Journal of Business Ethics, 6*, 619-632.

Murphy, P.E. (1988). Implementing business ethics. *Journal of Business Ethics, 7*, 907-916.

Murphy, P.E. (1989). Creating ethical corporate structures. *Sloan Management Review, 30*(Winter), 61-67.

Murphy, P.E. (1992). *Corporate training programs in business ethics: An empirical assessment.* Working paper, University of Notre Dame.

Murphy, P.E. (1995). Corporate ethics statements: Current status and future prospects. *Journal of Business Ethics, 14*, 727-740.

Murphy, P.E. (1998). *Eighty exemplary ethics statements.* Notre Dame, IN: University of Notre Dame Press.

Murphy, P.E., & Laczniak, G.R. (1981). Marketing ethics: A review with implications for managers, educators and researchers. In B.M. Enis & K.J. Roering (Eds.), *Review of marketing 1981* (pp. 251-266). Chicago: American Marketing Association.

Murphy, P.E., & Pridgen, D. (1991). Ethical and legal issues in marketing. In P.N. Bloom (Ed.), *Advances in marketing and public policy* (Vol. 2, pp. 185-244). Greenwich, CT: JAI Press.

Nash, L. (1995). The real truth about corporate 'values.' *The Public Relations Strategist* (Summer), 7-13.

Nwachukwa, S.L.S., & Vitell, S.J., Jr. (1997). The influence of corporate culture on managerial ethical judgments. *Journal of Business Ethics, 16*(June), 757-776.

O'Reilly, C. (1989). Corporations, culture and commitment: Motivational and social control in organizations. *California Management Review, 31*(Summer), 9-25.

Paine, L.S. (1994). Managing for organizational integrity. *Harvard Business Review* (March/April), 106-117.

Parasuraman, A., & Deshpande, R. (1984). The cultural context of marketing management. In R.W. Belk et al. (Eds.), *AMA Educators' Proceedings* (pp. 176-179). Chicago: American Marketing Association.

Pascale, R.T. (1984). Fitting new employees into the company culture. *Fortune* (May 28), 28-41.

Pascale, R.T., & Athos, A.G. (1981). *The art of Japanese management.* New York: Simon and Schuster.

Pastin, M. (1986). *The hard problems of management.* San Fransisco, CA: Jossey-Bass.

Peters, T.J., & Waterman, R.H. (1982). *In search of excellence.* New York: Harper and Row.

Posner, B.Z., Kouzes, J.M., & Schmidt, W.H. (1985). Shared values make a difference: An empirical test of corporate culture. *Human Resource Management, 24*(Fall), 293-309.

Posner, B.Z., & Schmidt, W.H. (1984). Values and the American manager: An update. *California Management Review, 26*(Spring), 202-216.

Purcell, T.V., S.J. (1978). Institutionalizing ethics on corporate boards. *Review of Social Economy, 36*(December), 41-53.

Reimann, B.C., & Wiener, Y. (1988). Corporate culture: Avoiding the Elitist trap. *Business Horizons, 31*(March/April), 36-44.

Robin, D.P., & Reidenbach, R.E. (1987). Social responsibility, ethics, and marketing strategy: Closing the gap between concept and application. *Journal of Marketing, 51*(January), 44-58.

Robin, D.P., & Reidenbach, R.E. (1989). *Business ethics: Where profits meet value systems.* Englewood Cliffs, NJ: Prentice-Hall.

Robin, D.P., Giallourakis, M., David, F.R., & Moritz, T.E. (1989). A different look at codes of ethics. *Business Horizons, 32*(January-February), 66-73.

Schein, E.H. (1985). *Organizational culture and leadership.* San Francisco, CA: Jossey-Bass.

Schlegelmilch, B. (1998). *Marketing ethics: An international perspective.* London: Thomson Business Press.

Serpa, R. (1985). Creating a candid culture. *Journal of Business Ethics, 4,* 425-430.

Sims, R.R. (1991). The institutionalization of organizational ethics. *Journal of Business Ethics, 10,* 493-506.

Sinclair, A. (1993). Approaches to organizational culture and ethics. *Journal of Business Ethics, 12,* 63-73.

Sparks, J.R., & Hunt, S.D. (1998). Marketing researcher ethical sensitivity: Conceptualization, measurement, and exploratory investigation. *Journal of Marketing, 62*(April), 92-109.

Stewart, T.A. (1996, June 10). Why value statements don't work. *Fortune,* pp., 137-138.

Touche Ross. (1988, January). *Ethics in American business.* New York: Author.

Trevino, L.K. (1986). Ethical decision making in organizations: A person-situation interactionist model. *Academy of Management Review, 11*(July), 601-617.

Tsalikis, J., & Fritzsche, D.J. (1989). Business ethics: A literature review with a focus on marketing ethics. *Journal of Business Ethics, 8,* 695-743.

Victor, B., & Cullen, J.B. (1988). The organizational bases of ethical work climate. *Administrative Science Quarterly, 33*(March), 101-124.

Waters, J.A., & Bird, F. (1987). The moral dimension of organizational culture. *Journal of Business Ethics, 6*(January), 15-20.

Weber, J. (1981). Institutionalizing ethics into the corporation. *MSU Business Topics, 29*(Spring), 47-52.

Weitz, B.A., Sujan, H., & Sujan, M. (1986). Knowledge, motivation, and adaptive behavior: A framework for improving selling effectiveness. *Journal of Marketing, 50*(October), 174-191.

AN EMPIRICALLY-BASED, INTEGRATIVE FRAMEWORK OF CORPORATE MORAL DEVELOPMENT

Katharina J. Srnka

ABSTRACT

This article presents the results of an exploratory study on moral reasoning and moral behavior conducted among Austrian marketing managers. Essentially, it introduces three distinctive manager types discovered in the Austrian market: The "Law-Alone" (type A) manager, the "Ethics-is-Good-Business" (type B) manager, and the "Case-by-Case" (type C) manager. Based on this typology a three-dimensional framework of social responsibility is developed. This framework integrates four theoretical concepts found in the marketing ethics literature: Smith's ethics continuum of moral behavior, Filios's four levels of social responsibility, Goodpaster's four ways of thinking about ethics in business, and Kohlberg's cognitive moral development. The framework presented comprises three different levels of social responsibility on which organizations can operate. It suggests that, in a growing company, corporate social responsibility evolves in a hierarchical manner, starting from a minimum level (i.e., adherence to existing laws and norms), continuing on a second level (i.e., active consideration of stakeholders' interests), ending at the high-

Research in Marketing, Volume 15, pages 101-137.
ISBN: 0-7623-566-5

est level (i.e., deliberately doing good for stakeholder groups or society as a whole). Although behavior on all three levels is driven by self-interest, the motives stated for choosing a socially responsible alternative gradually shift from a short-sighted self-centered position to a more strategic and socially oriented one.

INTRODUCTION

Much has been written on marketing ethics theory throughout the last two decades, and empirical studies in this field are proliferating, not only in the United States but increasingly in western Europe as well. Not much, however, has been done until now to reconcile different theoretical concepts and models with each other, and to link these to empirical results in the field of marketing ethics. Here, the author will discuss relevant ethical theories, then present a study conducted among Austrian marketing managers and introduce the three-manager typology based on the empirical findings and, finally, develop a new framework of corporate moral development combining normative and descriptive theoretical concepts of the marketing ethics literature and bringing them together with empirical findings. In the "Literature Review" section, an overview of ethical theories and a short description of selected theories is given. Furthermore, the concepts of Smith's ethics continuum, Filios's four levels of social responsibility, Goodpaster's four ways of thinking about ethics in business, and models based on Kohlberg's cognitive moral development, which have been discussed in the marketing ethics literature, are introduced. In the "Empirical Study" section, a qualitative study conducted among Austrian marketers and its results are presented. In "The Framework" section, the results are compared to the four theoretical concepts discussed before. Based on the findings, a three-dimensional framework of corporate moral development integrating Smith's, Filios's, Goodpaster's, and Kohlberg's concepts is developed. Then, the framework is extended by an ethical reflection of the developmental stages and it is demonstrated that management differentiates between moral and economic rationality. Finally, the framework is compared to an earlier conceptual model of corporate moral development proposed by Reidenbach and Robin.

LITERATURE REVIEW

Ethics Theory

Marketing ethics is concerned with the ethical reflection of marketing practices. Ethics can be described as a *science of norms* (Steinmann & Zerfass, 1993). Normative ethical theories in the marketing ethics literature are very often reduced to two fundamental positions: deontology and teleology (e.g., see Akaah & Riodan,

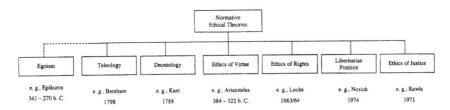

Figure 1. Normative Ethical Theories

1989; Ferrell & Gresham, 1985; Hunt & Vitell, 1986, 1993; Robin & Reidenbach, 1987). In fact, the field of ethical normative theory is much more diverse. An overview—which certainly cannot be an exhaustive one—of the most influential theories and their proponents or best-known advocates is given in Figure 1.

Although a discussion of the different theories would be interesting and insightful, this is beyond the scope of this manuscript. However, selected philosophical theories that are necessary to discuss the subsequently presented theoretical concepts and empirical findings will be introduced here. Readers interested in a more general overview are referred to Anzenbacher (1992), Chryssides and Kaler (1993, pp. 79-142), or Pieper (1994).

Normative Ethical Theories

Egoism can be regarded as the historically first "theory" in moral philosophy. The proponents of this approach (e.g., Epikur) believe that anything that maximizes individual pleasure is moral. Many philosophers do *not* consider egoism as an ethical principle, because they hold that only behavior, which considers social implications, can be morally approved. Although also based on pleasure maximization, *teleological theories* take into consideration not only the *consequences* for the actor himself but for *all* individuals or groups affected. Bentham has made the common good the sole arbiter of right and wrong. According to him and other proponents of the teleological approach, a certain action is seen as morally good if it, in sum, results in more good than evil for the stakeholders.[1] Deontological theories, on the other hand, do not evaluate behavior by judging its consequences but rather classify the act itself as ethically correct or not. According to Kant, human behavior is morally good if it is done out of a feeling of *duty* (justice, love, truth, etc.), moderated by reason. Human practice, which is motivated by profit orientation, even if it benefits society, is regarded as amoral.

The *Ethics of Virtue* interprets human behavior not as the sum of isolated actions but sees it as an integral life-process. Proponents of this theory suggest that not what an individual does but the individual him/herself should be judged. According to Aristotle, the virtuous man will, per se, act in a moral way. The *Ethics of Rights,* as proposed by Locke, can be seen as complimentary to Kant's

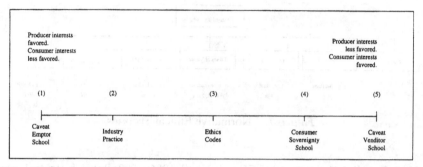

Note: Numbers in parentheses inserted by the author.
Source: Smith (1993, p. 21).

Figure 2. Ethics Continuum

deontologism. Its basic idea is that above any human law there is an objective moral order, the "natural law." This natural law declares that there are things all human beings have a right to, which are life and liberty. The *Libertarian Position* starts from the assumption that human rights are absolute. Nozick, a representative of this theory, makes the possession and enjoyment of private property an inviolable human right (besides life and liberty) which other people have an obligation not to interfere in. Finally, Rawls, in his *Theory of Justice*, believes that all free and rational persons in an initial position of equality would accept the principles of fairness and justice as the basic structure of society.

The theories presented here, as has been already pointed out, are strictly *normative*. However, ethical theory has also a descriptive component. One of the most relevant *descriptive* concepts is Kohlberg's theory of cognitive moral development. The Kohlbergian model describes, referring to the normative theories, how individual morality develops through time. Before turning to Kohlberg's theory, though, the concept of corporate social responsibility will be discussed here.

Corporate Social Responsibility

A company's social responsibility follows from a "set of generally accepted relationships, obligations and duties defined between the major institutions and the people" (Steiner, 1972, p. 18) through a social contract. As compared to the ethical concepts described above, social responsibility has the advantage of being much more specific. Essentially, it reflects a society's expectation of what a company must, should, must not, and should not do. Corporate social responsibility and business ethics are two essentially different concepts. Although their criteria often lead to the same conclusion, they do not necessarily have to (Robin & Reidenbach, 1987, p. 45). Actions that any given society defines as "responsible" in its social contract with business may be evaluated as amoral or even immoral by ethical standards. Similarly, actions dictated by moral philosophy could be seen as socially unacceptable within a certain social contract (Robin & Reidenbach, 1987, p. 45).

Following from its very definition, corporate social responsibility should be—at least for a given society—clear and universally accepted. There exist, though, within the American literature alone, many different positions as to how exactly a company's social responsibility is to be defined, ranging from a minimum to a maximum position. Friedman (1970), perhaps the most often cited proponent of the minimum-alternative, argues that the manager's only responsibility is "to increase...profits as long as it stays within the rules of the game" (p. 126), while other authors require managers to actively do good, even if this is not at all or only minimally related to the business activity. Smith's (1993, pp. 20ff) ethics continuum shows several typical positions proposed in the literature (Figure 2).

As can be seen in Figure 2, the various positions on the continuum reflect different conceptions of the firm's obligations toward its customers. They range from one extreme (1) where producer interests (e.g., profits) are most and consumer interests (e.g., safety) are least favored, to the other extreme (5) where producer interests are least and consumer interests are most favored. Between these, there can be found three other positions that all basically accept the profit goal, but in pursuing this, require management either (2) to follow industrial custom, or (3) to adhere to some ethics code (either that of the individual firm, of the industry, or a professional body such as the American Marketing Association), or, finally, (4) to respect individual sovereignty, which means that management should adapt its actions to the stakeholders *capabilities, information,* and *choice possibilities* (Smith, 1993, p. 30).

Approaching the concept from a slightly different perspective, Filios (1984, p. 307) differentiates four levels of social responsibility. The first level, which he calls the "minimum level," corresponds to the minimum position described by Friedman or Smith (see above) and is simply the meeting of legal requirements (e.g., payment of taxes). At a second level, public expectations determine the minimum corporate social activism, which is usually in part beyond what the law prescribes (e.g., health care programs). Level three requires businesses to take actions that *anticipate future public expectations* (e.g., product safety). The fourth level, finally, involves the *creation of public expectations* by setting new standards at the highest level of moral and social responsibility (promoting community development or taking a position on war, on racism, etc.).

Even if we have defined what socially responsible behavior is, we still do not know much about the moral reasoning on which this behavior is based. Goodpaster (1989) describes four ways of thinking about ethics in business,

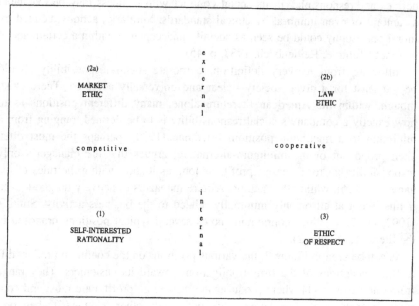

Source: Goodpaster (1989, p. 220).

Figure 3.   Motivations for Acting Socially Responsible

which can be interpreted as different forms of corporate moral reasoning. These are presented in Figure 3 and described below.

Goodpaster (1989, 218ff) characterizes ethics in business[2] as either (1) a guide to self-interest, a systemic constraint in the form of (2a) the "invisible hand" or (2b) the "hand-of-the-law," or (3) as securing respect for others.[3] While corporate self-interest and the respect for the individual are *internal* action guides, law and market forces are *external*. The manager following self-interest or market ethic regards concern for stakeholders to be built into the *competitive* market system, whereas law ethic and the ethic of respect do not make this presumption but rest on interpersonal *cooperation.*

Corporate Moral Development

Drawing on the work of Piaget (1932), Kohlberg (1969, 1973) contends that human moral reasoning develops in a progressive way from an egoistic to a teleological orientation and possibly further to a deontological position. Following Kohlberg individuals acquire, as their cognitive abilities develop through time, an increasingly accurate understanding of moral obligations. This *cognitive moral*

Table 1. Stages of Cognitive Moral Development

Stage	What Is "Right" and Why
Level 1: Preconventional	
Stage 1 Heteronomous morality	Avoiding the breaking of rules that are backed by punishment. Superior power of authority determines "right."
Stage 2 Instrumental purpose and exchange	Following one's own interest and letting others do the same. Following rules only when it is in one's self-interest. "Right" defined by equal exchange, a fair deal.
Level 2: Conventional	
Stage 3 Mutual interpersonal expectations, relationships and interpersonal conformity	Exhibition of stereotypical good behavior. Living up to what is expected in a person's role. Respect for trust, loyalty, gratitude. Belief in the Golden Rule, putting yourself in the other person's shoes.
Stage 4 Social accord and system maintenance	Making a contribution to society, group, or institution. Fulfilling duties to which you have agreed. Point of view of the system is maintained. Avoid breakdown of the system.
Level 3: Postconventional	
Stage 5 Social contract and individual rights	Rules are upheld because they are a social contract; however, nonrelative values are upheld regardless of majority opinion. Concern for laws and duties is based on rational determination of overall utility. Welfare and rights are protected.
Stage 6 Universal ethical principles	Self-chosen ethical principles determine right. Laws and social duties are valid only because they are based on such principles. Individual respects the dignity of all human beings in a decision and has personal commitment to beliefs.

Source: Goolsby and Hunt (1992, p. 57).

development can be characterized as a progression through as many as six stages, which are classified into three levels. At the *preconventional level* (stages 1 and 2), moral decisions arise on the basis of immediate punishments or rewards to the individual. At the *conventional level* (stages 3 and 4), reasoning emphasizes adhering to the group's rules and norms. Finally, at the *postconventional level* (stages 5 and 6), the individual feels committed to self-selected universal principles (Goolsby & Hunt, 1992, p. 56). Table 1 gives a summary of the six stages of moral development.

Inspired by the model of cognitive moral development, some authors contend that the concept of cognitive moral development might also be applicable to organizations. In essence, they argue that "it is the organization's culture that undergoes moral development" (Reidenbach & Robin, 1991, p. 273). Goodpaster and Matthews (1989, p. 159) expect "to find stages of development in organizational character that show significant patterns." Reidenbach and Robin (1991) hold that corporations exhibit specific behaviors that signal their level of moral development. Accordingly, they identify five levels of moral development and discuss the dynamics that move corporations from one level to another. Similarly, Sridhar and Camburn (1993) as well as Logsdon and Yuthas (1997) propose that organizations, like individuals, develop over time into collectivities of shared cognitions and rationale.

Most authors, however, qualify their concepts of corporate moral development by stating that direct application of Kohlberg's model is not possible. "Organizations simply do not develop in the same manner and under the same circumstances as individuals" (Reidenbach & Robin, 1991, p. 274). Kohlberg's model has characteristics not found or not to be expected in organizations. Kohlberg (1973) defines cognitive moral development and levels of moral development as follows.

1. The various levels of moral development are *qualitatively different ways of reasoning* rather than increasing knowledge or internalizing moral standards.
2. The levels represent an *invariant sequence* in the development.
3. Each level represents a *structured whole*.
4. The levels are *hierarchically integrated*. Individuals always prefer the highest level they understand (p. 94, translated, no italics in the original).

Another problem not even mentioned by most proponents of corporate moral development, are the premises for moral development: *cognitive maturity*, that is, the increasing capability to reflect on a more abstract level, and *moral experience*, that is, a number of conflicts faced earlier which stimulated cognitive-moral reflection (Kohlberg, 1973, pp. 102ff). In the following section, a study on management's ethical attitudes and behavior conducted among Austrian marketers is described and the results are presented. Based on the findings, a conceptual framework of socially responsible management behavior will be developed which integrates the four theoretical concepts discussed above: Smith's ethics continuum, Filios's four levels of social responsibility, Goodpaster's four ways of thinking about ethics in business, and Kohlberg's model of cognitive moral development.

EMPIRICAL STUDY

Methodology

Design

Within a more comprehensive project, an extensive study of the meaning and application of business ethics among Austrian marketers was planned and executed. As there existed little empirical evidence on business ethics in Austria, we decided to conduct an exploratory study on ethical attitudes and moral behavior of Austrian marketing managers. Given the lack of prior data, we resolved to make the study qualitative in nature. In particular, we intended to conduct in-depth interviews with a limited number of Austrian managers. To get a deeper understanding of managers' perceptions and feelings, and in order to better address these in the interviews, *preliminary telephone contacts* were made with managers chosen to participate in the study (for sample selection see below).

One of the many problems which became evident from the telephone contacts was that just a minority of managers were prepared to conduct the planned in-depth interviews. The only way to get the desired information from the remaining part of the sample was to compose a questionnaire, which managers were prepared to fill out and return, if sent to them by mail. Therefore, the design was modified. The procedure finally adopted was a combination of *in-depth interviews* with those prepared to speak to the interviewer personally and a *mail survey followed by a telephone interview* with the remaining part of the sample.

After the questionnaires (for details on the questionnaire see below) had been sent out, the personal interviews were conducted while waiting for response to the mailing. Interviews took place in the managers' offices in order to get an impression of their position and working conditions. This was believed to be helpful in the evaluation and interpretation of the responses. To be able to better interpret the responses to the mailed questionnaires and to assure comparability of results, the same form was also used during the personal interviews.

After the deadline indicated in the cover letter accompanying the mailed questionnaires had expired, almost 40 percent of the forms sent out had been received back. They were scanned to get an overall impression of managers' attitudes and to check item nonresponse. Two questionnaires were found unusable for analysis as they contained too many missing items. After this first scanning, all managers were contacted by telephone. Although it was quite obvious from the envelopes who had sent back the questionnaire (most companies print their logo on every piece of outgoing mail), it was conducted in this manner to avoid the impression of not respecting the respondents anonymity. Therefore each manager was asked whether she/he had filled out and returned the questionnaire.[4] If she/he had done so, the questions in the questionnaire were discussed to get a deeper understanding of the manager's ethical attitude. If the questionnaire had not been returned, the respective manager was asked to give reasons for not answering. The explanations given most often were (in the order indicated) "lack of time," "of no importance to my company," and "corporate policy not to give information." Altogether, it was felt that nonrespondents had only minor interest in ethical issues and seemed morally far less sensitive than respondents.

Sample

In this study the idea of quota sampling was followed. Subjects were selected by industry, company size (measured by number of employees), and market power (in terms of turnover). Companies from as many different industries as possible were included. Respondents were selected from such diverse industries as automobile production, banking, construction, dairy production, energy, food processing, gastronomy, health services, and jewelry. As a sampling frame the federal Austrian industry directory was used.[5]

Intuitively it seemed reasonable to consider only large companies that were organizationally structured enough to have an official ethics policy. However, as about 90 percent of the Austrian companies are small- or medium-sized, it was thought impossible to ignore this group in the study if the findings were to be meaningful. On the other hand, it is quite evident that it is the remaining 10 percent of the companies operating in the Austrian market which have the most influence on their environment due to their economic and political power. Particularly among these are multinational companies. Therefore, we decided to compose the sample of one-third small-sized, one-third medium-sized, and one-third large or multinational corporations. This rather rough selection criterion seems justified in view of the qualitative nature of the study.[6]

A problem we had to cope with was the fact that in Austria in most small-sized as well as some medium-sized companies no official marketing management position exists. This might be primarily due to the negative associations Austrians have with this job title. It is quite obvious that marketing activities are directed and executed in every company by someone. However, in Austrian firms these persons mostly have different, highly varying job titles. Therefore, the person "in charge of customer acquisition, communication and public relations" was addressed in the companies contacted.[7] The number of managers agreeing to cooperate ultimately came to 64, 12 of whom were prepared to be involved in personal interviews. Most subjects were located either in Vienna or in one of the other major cities in Austria.

Questionnaire

The main purpose of this study was exploratory and the questionnaire had to be formulated in a way which would allow one to get an understanding of management's perceptions of and reasoning behind acting in a socially responsible way.

Therefore, *open-ended questions* on these topics were included. The questions were formulated in the following way: "What is your opinion on social responsibility in Marketing?," "How are socially problematic situations handled in your company?", and "Explain the relationship between socially responsible behavior and profitability." Additionally, fixed alternative questions concerning the existence and the importance of social responsibility, as well as the determinants of socially responsible management behavior, were included. After each question, free space was left to provide reasons and *explanations* for the answers given. In general, most respondents elaborated in depth on the open-ended questions and explained their answers very openly.

Moreover, as a high tendency of respondents to give socially desirable answers was expected, we decided to use the vignette approach combined with a projective response method. We believed that the *vignette technique* would not only reduce the social desirability problem but also allow managers—mostly unfamiliar with philosophical terminology and ethical theories—to express their moral attitudes and behavior. Vignettes are short scenarios describing ethically problematic "real life" situations which respondents are asked to evaluate. This method has been widely used in empirical studies on marketing ethics (e.g., see DeConinck & Good, 1989; Fritzsche & Becker, 1983; Norris & Gifford, 1988).

Twenty scenarios were composed based on real cases of irresponsible corporate conduct which had occurred in Austria shortly before the study was conducted. After two pretests, eight scenarios were left which were regarded as being meaningful to marketing managers. They were included in the questionnaire (see Appendix Table A1). Four of the scenarios (situations 5 to 8) describe incorrect organizational behavior representing a direct threat to human life (e.g., dangerous products), while the remaining vignettes (situations 1 to 4) deal with misconduct which results in no immediate harm to human beings but are regarded as being socially problematic (e.g., misrepresentation of facts, unfair pricing).

To evaluate the managerial behavior described, a *projective response method* developed by Ferrell and Weaver (1978) was used. Respondents were requested to indicate whether they themselves *evaluated* the decision described as ethical/ unethical, whether the other managers would rate it as ethical/unethical, and whether their superior would see it as ethical/unethical. Furthermore, managers were to indicate whether they, other managers, and their superior would *act* as described (see answer sheet in Appendix Table A2). Ferrell and Gresham (1985) propose that both *peers* and *top management* have a great influence on managerial behavior. In their study of marketing managers, Zey-Ferrell, Weaver, and Ferrell (1979) found peers to be better predictors of ethical/unethical behavior than the respondent's own ethical belief system. We, therefore, believed this method would better indicate how managers think or would act than simply asking if they regard the respective behavior as socially responsible or not.

Table 2. Characteristics of Respondents (in percentages)

Age		Gender	
Less than 40	37	Male	87
40-49	33	Female	13
50 and more	30		
Marital Status		**Educational Level**	
Single	17	Skilled	20
Married/widowed	77	Professional	20
Divorced	3	Graduated[a]	60
No answer	3		
Educated/Graduated in[b]		**Formal Knowledge of Ethics**	
Social and economic sciences	67	Yes (school, university)	40
Techniques	13	Yes (personal interest)	27
Philosophy	3	No	33
No specialization	17		
Position		**Company Size**	
Lower management	3	1-49 employees (small size)	17
Middle management	53	50-499 employees (medium size)	36
Top management[c]	44	500 and more employees (large)	47

Notes: [a] "Graduated" = holding master degree or Ph.D.
[b] The specialization indicated under the heading "Educated/graduated in" is not restricted to any specific educational level stated under "Educational level." It simply indicates the respondents main field of education.
[c] "Top management" includes company owners.

Results and Analysis

Characteristics of Respondents

Of the 52 questionnaires sent out, 20 were received back, representing a response rate of 38.5 percent. The total number of managers included in the analysis (i.e., adding the 12 interviews and deleting two questionnaires with too many missing items) comes to 30. This equals a *total response rate* of 46.9 percent. Table 2 summarizes respondents' demographics.

As can be seen, the typical respondent was male, married, and held a degree (master or PhD) in social and economic sciences. Although two-thirds of the managers indicated that they had some formal education in ethics, from answers to subsequent questions on social responsibility and ethics it could be concluded that most respondents did not have any formal knowledge of moral philosophy. This, together with the observed tendency of managers to evaluate others as less ethical than oneself (more details below), suggests that there was a rather *high tendency to give socially desirable answers.*

Table 3. Answers to Closed-ended Questions on
Socially Responsible Behavior (in percentages)

Company has a social responsibility		Compared to company goals consumer interests are	
Agreed	77	More important	23
Disagreed	23	Of same importance	67
		Less important	10
Corporate social responsibility is...[a]		A socially responsible manager's behavior takes into consideration...[a]	
Not recognized	23	Moral principles	40
Legal requirement	17	Stakeholders' interests	67
Economic necessity	40	Organizational interests	73
Moral duty	67	Manager's self-interest	17

Note: [a] Multiple answers allowed.

With regard to age, subjects were more or less evenly distributed between 30 and 60 years of age. About 50 percent of the managers rated their hierarchical position as being middle management and 50 percent in top management. With view to company size, the envisaged proportion of one-third of the total sample was only reached for medium-sized companies. Both for large and/or multinational corporations and small companies the goal of 33 percent was missed by a wide margin, although in the opposite direction. Almost 50 percent of those prepared to fill out the questionnaire or to take the time for an interview were managers of large corporations, while less than 20 percent were managers of small companies.

Attitudes Toward Social Responsibility

Managers' attitudes toward social responsibility were studied based on the answers given to open-ended and fixed alternative questions as well as the responses to the scenarios. The responses were analyzed *qualitatively*, the main focus being on the *explanations* provided for the answers in the questionnaires and the information given in the interviews, both in person and by telephone.

Table 3 displays managers' responses to fixed alternative questions. It shows that, overall, Austrian managers in this study tend to overwhelmingly (77%) agree with the assertion that their company has a social responsibility, while less than one-fourth do not recognize such a responsibility.[8] Social responsibility is, first of all, regarded as a moral duty (67%), and, in many cases, is also seen as an economic necessity (40%). A comparably low fraction of managers (17%) perceive social responsibility as a legal requirement. Two-thirds of those questioned affirm that company goals and consumer interests are of equal importance, while almost one-fourth regard company goals as more important and only a minor fraction

Table 4. Managers Responses to Vignettes[9] (in percentages)

Scenario	I Believe It Is Ethical	Other Managers Believe it Is Ethical	I Would Do It	Other Managers Would Do it
1	10	53	20	53
2	40	50	57	70
3	40	57	43	80
4	0	50	0	40
5	7	20	20	40
6	0	7	0	23
7	7	30	3	27
8	3	10	0	27

(10%) perceive them as less important than consumer interests. Almost three-fourths of the managers in this study indicate that socially responsible managers consider company interests in their decisions and two-thirds think that these managers take the interests of all stakeholders into consideration. Four out of ten believe that socially responsible managers follow moral principles and less than one out of five indicate that they follow self-interest.

From Table 4 displaying managers' reactions to the eight vignettes, it can be seen that in all cases managers rated themselves much more ethically critical than their peers. This suggests a high tendency of managers to answer in a socially desirable way. Therefore, in the analysis of the vignettes, the "other manager" category was looked at. This category was believed to mirror best managers' actual attitudes and behavioral tendencies, thus minimizing bias due to social desirability.

In the "belief" (as well as in the "do") category, differences in responses to distinctive scenarios can be seen. Scenarios 1 to 4 were evaluated by one-half or more of the respondents as ethical. This was explained by the fact that they were perceived as having only minor consequences for those affected. Contrarily, scenarios 5 to 8 were mostly regarded as being unethical. This was explained by the fact that they represented actions—directly or indirectly—threatening human life. Looking at the two "other manager" response categories, differences are visible between the "believe" and the "do" categories. This indicates that managers sometimes do things they actually perceive to be unethical. Altogether, it can be said that managers are aware of the questionability of morally problematic issues. For "minor" forms of incorrect marketing activities managers indicate they might take the action, referring to the *responsible consumer* who is educated and informed enough to protect her/himself from such management behavior. If, however, consequences for those affected are perceived to be overly threatening to human life, managers tend to take full responsibility for what they do and prefer the socially responsible alternative.

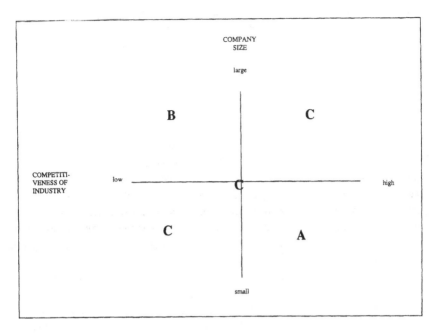

Figure 4. Manager Types in the Austrian Market

Manager Types

As has been already described in one of the preceding subsections, managers of smaller companies were by far less interested in participating in the study than those of large corporations. Managers of the smallest organizations persistently refused to participate because they felt that marketing ethics was something that concerned large and multinational corporations but not them. Managers of large companies, on the other hand, were almost enthusiastic to take part in the study and asked for the study results when available. These differences in ethical sensitivity and moral attitudes were observed also throughout the interviews and became even more visible from the analysis of the answers given in the questionnaires: Managers in large companies exhibited high ethical interest and sensitivity as compared to those in small companies. The differences between the two different manager groups became more clear-cut, when the industry was considered. Those managers interviewed who indicated extremely irresponsible attitudes and behaviors, also argued that the industry they were in was highly competitive.

In order to analyze the influence of company size and industry competition systematically, a post hoc grouping of managers along these dimensions was done. As *industry competition* had not, ex ante, been considered as a determinant of social responsibility; no measure of this variable had been included in

Table 5. Absolute and Relative Frequencies for Manager Types A, B, and C

Manager Type	Absolute Frequencies	Relative Frequencies
A	2	7%
B	4	13%
C	24	80%
All respondents	30	100%

the questionnaire. Therefore, managers were asked in the follow-up interviews to indicate *perceived competition in their industry* on a three-point scale ranging from *low* to *high*. Based on the two dimensions, *company size* and *industry competition*, the following classification was finally made: (1) on the one hand, there were managers in small companies (in most cases company *owners*) in very competitive industries, subsequently designated by the term *manager type A*; and (2) on the other hand, there was a manager group, subsequently denoted *manager type B*, composed of marketers (only *agent-managers*[10]) working in large corporations in industries with moderate competition. As certainly not all managers could be classified into one of the two groups described, a third intermediate manager type had to be defined. Managers who were allocated between the two poles A and B were called *manager type C*. This group represented the largest group of marketing managers. Figure 4 visualizes the three manager types along the two dimensions: company sizes and industry competition.

Absolute and relative frequencies for the distinctive manager types are given in Table 5. As can be seen, manager type A represents 7 percent, manager type B 13 percent, and manager type C 80 percent of the sample. Given that the majority of managers in Austria are small sized and in view of the fact that it was mostly managers of large companies who participated in the study, it is felt that type A managers in this study are underrepresented while type B managers are overrepresented.

Responses to Questions on Corporate Social Responsibility

The distinctive manager types pronounced different perceptions regarding the existence and importance of corporate social responsibility as well as the determinants of socially responsible management behavior. From Table 6 it can be seen that 50 percent of type A managers believe that companies do not have a social responsibility, while none of the type B managers and only 25 percent of type C managers think this way. Those 50 percent of type A managers who recognize a social responsibility of their organization believe it is a legal requirement (see Table 7). Compared to this, all type B managers recognize corporate social responsibility as a moral duty and one-half of them see it also as an economic

Table 6. Perceived Existence of Corporate Social
Responsibility for Different Manager Types (in percentages)

Corporate Social Responsibility Exists...	ManagerType		
	A	B	C
Yes	50	100	75
No	50	0	25

Table 7. Perception of Social Responsibility
for Different Manager Types [a] (in percentages)

Social Responsibility Is...	Manager Type		
	A	B	C
Not recognized	50	0	25
Legal requirement	50	0	17
Economic necessity	0	50	42
Moral duty	0	100	67

Note: [a] Multiple answers allowed.

Table 8. Importance of Organizational Goals versus
Consumer Interests for Different Manager Types (in percentages)

Compared to Organizational Goals Consumer Interests Are...	Manager Type		
	A	B	C
Less important	100	0	4
Equal	0	50	75
More important	0	50	21

necessity. Type C managers—those in-between—split between the various alternatives. Seventeen percent regard corporate social responsibility as a legal requirement, 42 percent as economic necessity, and 67 percent as moral duty.

Table 8 shows that all type A managers regard consumer interests as less important than organizational goals, whereas none of type B managers pronounce this opinion. They split half and half between seeing consumer interests as more important than or equal to organizational goals. Type C managers mostly (75%) regard consumer interests and organizational goals as equal in importance, while 21 percent believe consumers are more important and only 4 percent find them less important than organizational goals.

Table 9. Beliefs of Determinants of Management
Behavior for Different Manager Types (in percentages)

Management Behavior Follows...	Manager Type		
	A	B	C
Self-interest	50	0	17
Organizational interests	50	75	75
Stakeholder interests	0	75	71
Moral principles	0	50	42

In Table 9 we see that one-half of type A managers believe that managers follow self-interest in their decisions and one-half see organizational interests as a prevalent determinant of management conduct. None of them mention stakeholder interests or moral principles as relevant dimensions. In contrast, three-fourths of type B managers regard stakeholder interests as a major criterion for management actions and as many as that also believe that management has to consider organizational goals. Actually, they believe that it is imperative to consider stakeholder interests in order to achieve organizational goals. One-half of them mention moral rules as guiding principles for marketing managers, while none see self-interest as a relevant determinant. Again, type C managers split between the various alternatives. Seventeen percent mention self-interest, 75 percent organizational interest, 71 percent stakeholder interests, and 42 percent moral principles as determinants of managerial conduct.

Responses to Scenarios

Managers' responses to the different scenarios described in the questionnaire (see Table A3 in the Appendix) mirror the attitudes and perceptions pronounced in their responses to questions on corporate social responsibility. Again, the three manager groups show different moral tendencies. Comparing responses to the various scenarios it can be seen that, overall, type A managers regard the scenarios as least problematic. In contrast, type B managers show high ethical sensitivity and moral consciousness regarding the issues addressed. In their explanations they often indicate that the issues are problematic and have to be dealt with cautiously in order to act in the interest of society and the organization. Reactions of type C managers are highly dependent on the situation. Some actions (e.g., environmental issues: scenarios 4 and 5; product safety: scenarios 6 and 8, etc.) are perceived as less ethical and are less likely to be done by managers than other issues (e.g., fair pricing: scenario 3). As became evident from the interviews and the explanations given in the questionnaires, this

Table 10. Characteristics of Manager Types Found in the Austrian Market

Manager Type	Description	Company Size	Industry Competition	Management Behavior
A	"Law-Alone"	Small	High	Relatively low moral predisposition Higher tendency to act in a socially responsible way
B	"Good-Ethics-is-Good Business"	Large	Low	Relatively high moral predisposition Lower tendency to act in a socially irresponsible way
C	"Case-by-Case"	Between A and B		Between A and B

was a question of how sensitized managers were to the respective problem due to public discussion. The more an issue is debated publicly or in the media, the more it is condemned and the less likely it is to be done by managers.

Characteristics of Manager Types

Altogether, the analysis shows clear differences regarding moral attitudes and moral behavior between the three manager types identified. While managers classified as type A show relatively low moral predisposition and a comparatively high tendency to act socially irresponsibly,[11] type B managers are characterized by relatively high moral predisposition and a low readiness to be socially irresponsible, not only for moral but also for economic reasons. Type C managers fall somewhere in-between, usually, however, being in some way closer to one extreme than the other. They are less inclined to act socially irresponsibly in situations for which they have been *sensitized* (e.g., product safety, environmental issues) than in less controversial and threatening situations. Based on the findings, type A managers can be described as *"Law-Alone,"* type B managers as *"Ethics-Is-Good-Business,"* and type C managers as *"Case-by-Case"* ethical decision makers. Table 10 summarizes the findings.

In the following section the *three-manager typology* derived from the empirical data will be reconciled with existing theoretical marketing ethics concepts discussed in the first part of this paper. Furthermore, it will represent the basis for the development of a new framework of corporate moral development.

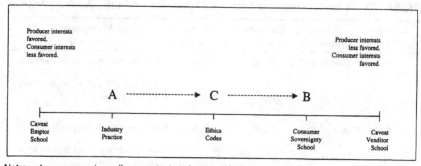

Notes: A = managers in small companies in industries with strong competition.
        B = managers in large companies in industries with moderate competition.
        C = managers in companies between extremes A and B.

Figure 5. Evaluation of Austrian Marketing
Management Behavior along the Ethics Continuum

THE FRAMEWORK

Reconciling Theory and the Three-Manager Typology

Smith's Ethics Continuum

In the interviews it was found that Austrian managers classified as type A in
many instances follow common *industry practices*, while the behavior of manager
type C is mostly in accordance with internal *ethics codes* (whether they be a formally written record or an evolved practice). Manager type B, on the other hand,
makes marketing practice dependent on the three criteria of the *consumer sovereignty* test (consumers' capability, information, and choice). A graphic classification of the different manager groups along the ethics continuum is presented in
Figure 5.

Goodpaster's Four Ways to Think About Ethics

Striking differences among manager types A, B, and C are also visible with
regard to the four types of thinking about responsible behavior as proposed by
Goodpaster. While type A managers are mostly driven by their (*immediate* and
egoistic) goal to "make the deal" and thereby regard the law as the only restriction
to their activities, type B managers in their marketing decisions show *respect* for
consumers—consumer satisfaction being their main goal—as well as for competitors and other stakeholder groups (*long-range market forces*). Managers falling
into the C category can again be found somewhere in-between the two extremes
A and B. Their behavior seems to follow *long-term* economic performance (*mar-*

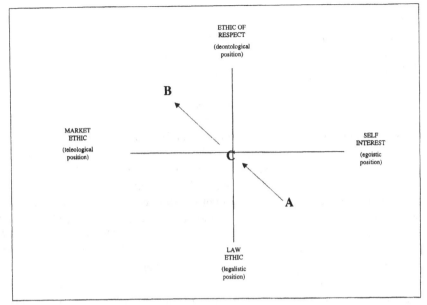

Source: Srnka (1997, p. 115).

Figure 6.   Austrian Managers' Moral Reasoning Behind Socially
Responsible Behavior/Cognitive Moral Development of Managers

ket forces) rather than *short-term* profits *(egoism)*. With view to respect for the
individual and law, type C managers cannot be clearly classified into one or the
other direction. Faced with situations perceived as extremely threatening to
human life or otherwise sensitive, they decide in accordance with the *ethics of
respect*, where they take a more *legalistic position* in less threatening and controversial issues. The classification according to Goodpaster's criteria is shown in
Figure 6.

Normative Ethical Theories

Assuming that Goodpaster's ways of thinking about socially responsible
behavior can be interpreted as forms of *moral reasoning* and considering the fact
that manager type A is to be found in the smaller companies and manager type B
in the larger companies, one could conclude that a pattern as shown in Figure 6
(see dotted arrows) exists: Management moves from an egoistic/legalistic position toward a teleological and probably further to a deontological position as the
company grows over time. A similar development from A to C and further to B
can be assumed with a view to *behavior*. As can be seen in the classification of

management behavior along the ethics continuum, managers in smaller companies tend to follow external industry practice; those in organizations of intermediate size mostly obey internally formulated ethics codes, whereas decision makers in the largest companies respect consumer sovereignty. Again, one can presume that when a company expands, management adapts its behavior accordingly as depicted in Figure 5 (see dotted arrows).

This pattern, in a way, corresponds to Kohlberg's scheme of cognitive moral development. Certainly the Kohlbergian scheme, as defined for individuals, cannot be directly applied to organizational behavior. Basically, though, it seems that *the idea of a stepwise evolution of morality* can be reasonably adopted for growing companies. In accordance with Goodpaster and Matthews' (1989) assumption and as suggested by the other proponents of organizational moral development, it might, therefore, be concluded that an organization passes from one stage of moral reasoning to the next as it grows and as it acquires more experience and more resources. This *corporate moral development* can be intuitively explained by the fact that managers of small companies—often being also their owners—feel that they need "every deal" to survive and earn their living, while marketers in larger corporations—mostly agent-managers—can (and are much more prepared to) afford to give up short-run profits in order to gain a good corporate reputation which, they believe, is a guarantee for good long-term performance. Marketing managers in the largest companies even express their readiness to *invest* in social responsibility. They are willing to spend money on social projects (employee programs, building homes for disabled citizens, etc.) expecting to create goodwill. A *socially responsible image* is believed to represent a *unique selling proposition* for the company differentiating it from competitors.

A Framework of Corporate Moral Development

Pulling the above arguments together, one can think of corporate social responsibility as emerging and developing in a certain hierarchical order with the resulting pyramid being composed of three levels. The first level represents mere obedience to existing laws and is the very basis of any managerial activity. Management practice at this level can be interpreted as being amoral, because it is prescribed by external forces (namely the law) and not the manager's morality. This stage corresponds to Goodpaster's law ethic and Kohlberg's' preconventional stage of cognitive moral development. We call this level *reactive corporate social responsibility*. If management has the capacity to pursue more than mere legality, it has the power to proceed to the next level, which we call the practice of *active social responsibility*. Being actively socially responsible means to consider the needs and interests of all stakeholders in management decisions. Being more or less equivalent to seeking the "greatest good for the greatest number" (see Bentham, 1966), moral reasoning at this stage can be classified as teleological. It

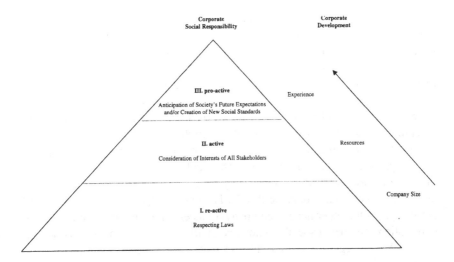

Figure 7. Levels of Corporate Social Responsibility

is in line with Goodpaster's market ethic and comparable to the Kohlbergian conventional stage. This level is the one which most marketing managers (namely type C managers) operate on.

When they can and want to afford it, however, managers may go even a step further and benefit society and its members by anticipating future social expectations or setting new social standards. As acting in anticipation of future societal needs or even setting new standards to benefit humanity seems very much to follow Kant's (1968) categorical imperative, it can be categorized as deontological. This highest level of corporate social responsibility is in accordance with Goodpaster's respect ethic and Kohlberg's postconventional stage and can be described as *proactive corporate social responsibility*. The distinction between reactive, active and proactive mentality is implicitly also made by Reidenbach and Robin (1991, p. 279). The pyramid and its various levels are illustrated in Figure 7.

Filios's Four Levels of Social Responsibility

As can be seen from the above, the three levels of social responsibility described are very similar to the four levels proposed by Filios (1984). Reactive social responsibility corresponds to Filios's minimum level; active social responsibility is equivalent to Filios's second level; and proactive social responsibility comprises both levels three and four as described by Filios. Combining these last two levels appears to be reasonable because it seems pointless from the manager's perspective to differentiate between the anticipation of future societal expectations and new standards set by a company's management. Facing a particular decision, it is unclear to management whether the action in question will be demanded by society at some time in the future or whether it never will come to people's minds, thus representing a new social standard.

Kohlberg's Model of Cognitive Moral Development

From what was said about the various levels of the pyramid, it follows that each level represents a *structured whole* and is *a qualitatively different way of reasoning and behaving*. Proceeding to a new level of social responsibility presupposes that the prior level(s) has/have been reached and the new level reached *integrates the/all prior level(s)*. One can reasonably expect a company respecting the interests of its stakeholders not prescribed by law to respect, in any case, those legally protected. On the other hand, a company, in its effort to anticipate future societal expectations and being socially innovative, will at the same time usually not only show behavior legally required but also meet current social expectations. This concept is also in accordance with Kohlberg's propositions. The movement from one level to the next (see arrow in Figure 7) usually follows an increase in company size, resources, and management experience. This, again, is in agreement with Kohlberg's model. We recall that Kohlberg names two premises for moral development: *cognitive maturity* (i.e., capacity of reasoning on a more abstract level) and *ethical conflicts* (i.e., situations which lead to ethical reflection). As cognitive maturity was found to be positively related to education (Trevino, 1992, p. 449), it can be argued that larger companies show a higher level of cognitive moral development because in larger organizations, there tend to be more managers with a higher education. This, actually, is the case in Austrian businesses. Also, an increase in company size will often coincide with more situations stimulating ethical reflection. This may also explain the higher tendency of big companies to act socially more responsible in that company growth usually brings about the institutionalization of ethics (e.g., through ethical training and education of personnel, codes of ethics, ethics committees, ethics audits, etc.). Actually, Robertson and Schlegelmilch's (1993, pp. 304ff) results of a study of 860 companies in the United Kingdom and the United States indicate that in both countries the most likely reasons for adopting a formal ethics policy were *growth* and *diversification*. It has been shown that the framework developed here integrates several theoretical concepts from the marketing ethics literature. Figure A1 in the Appendix gives a summarized overview of the various levels of the framework and how they correspond to the concepts suggested by Filios, Smith and Goodpaster, and Kohlberg.

The Extended Framework of Corporate Moral Development

The preceding description of the three pyramid levels is based on managers' responses to direct and indirect questions concerning *corporate* social responsi-

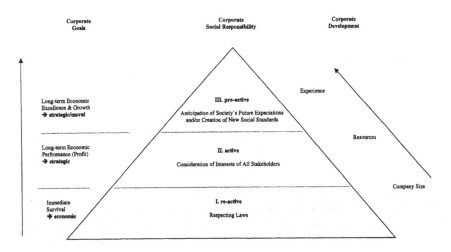

Figure 8. Extended Pyramid Framework of Corporate Social Responsibility

bility, which ranged from "we have to adhere to laws and nothing more than that" to "we have the moral mission to create a better world." The result—a framework supporting and integrating existing theoretical concepts—seems very appealing. However, when we turned in the interviews to questions of what the managers perceived to be *their own* obligations, they mentioned only one: profits. Managers not only react legally out of purely economic motives, but very much the same is true for active and proactive social responsible behavior.

On closer examination, one can conclude from the above that managers differentiate between two rationalities: moral (organization) and economic (manager). This is in line with Nijhof and Fisscher's findings that point to a tendency of management to distinguish between moral and economic arguments. According to Nijhof and Fisscher (1997), *economic arguments* refer exclusively to the instrumental goals (particularly short-run profitability assuring immediate survival). Managers on the reactive level (type A) were found to mostly revert to this kind of argumentation. Contrarily, managers on the proactive level (type B) occasionally mention purely moral reasons, which, as defined by Nijhof and Fisscher (1997), refer exclusively to ethical principles. Most marketers, however, on the active as well as on the proactive level (type C and B), combine both—moral and economic—arguments. Respecting the rights of stakeholders is seen as imperative if the company is not to vanish from the market in the long run due to negative reputation effects. Managers recognize that acting in a socially responsible way, even if costly at the moment—*when communicated to stakeholders!*—will benefit the organization in the long run. On the highest stage (type B), being socially innovative is understood as a way to show distinctiveness and therefore—again benefiting from reputation mechanisms—to become *excellent* in the sense of Peters and Watermann (1982) and to *grow*. This, in turn, corresponds to what Nijhof and Fisscher found and called strategic arguments. *Strategic arguments* consider economic as well as moral values (Nijhof & Fisscher, 1997). In view of these considerations, an extension of the pyramid framework seemed necessary. The adapted framework can be seen in Figure 8.

Clearly, managers on all three levels act *socially responsible* out of purely *economic* reasons. Managers, when explicitly asked, admit this very openly. Socially responsible corporate behavior is almost exclusively a "means to an end" (namely economic survival and/or performance) rather than as a "goal in itself" (Kant, 1968, p. 54). Thus, from an *ethical* point of view, management behavior on all levels is to be evaluated as *egoistic*. This egoism, however, should be interpreted as *enlighted self-interest* (see Derry, 1991) in the sense that managers understand that their economic goals can only be reached if present or future needs of society and its members are respected. This is not to deny that managers sometimes act out of a feeling of respect for the individual without looking primarily on economic consequences. They can, however, only do so if they can rationalize the activities dictated by personal moral feelings, when reporting to top management (thus making it a strategic argument), or if they have the final decision-making power (which is usually restricted to company owners).

The Framework and Other Models of Cognitive Moral Development

As has already been discussed earlier, several models of corporate moral development have been proposed in the marketing ethics literature (Logsdon & Yuthas, 1997; Reidenbach & Robin, 1991; Sridhar & Camburn, 1993). Only in rare cases, however (e.g., Logsdon & Yuthas, 1997[12]), have they been integrated with other concepts in the marketing ethics literature. Moreover, models of corporate moral development found in the literature either concentrate exclusively on the *justification* of corporate action or analyze *corporate behavior* only. The first alternative (i.e., looking to moral reasoning underlying management action) follows the Kohlbergian concept of progressive development of moral reasoning rather strictly, while the second alternative (i.e., looking to managerial action itself) is based on a much wider interpretation of Kohlberg's model. Kohlberg (1973, pp. 112, 117), however, calls for an integrated contemplation of moral reasoning and behavior. This paper extends existing theory in that the framework presented here integrates both aspects, the moral reasoning and the behavior of organizations, and it demonstrates parallels to the theoretical assumptions and premises of Kohlberg's model of (individual) cognitive moral development. Furthermore, the various stages of development are evaluated from an ethical point of view. Also, a distinction is made between a manager's moral and economic motives. Finally, the framework developed here is, to the author's knowledge, the first one based on ethical evaluations by managers themselves.

Table 11. Comparison of Stages of Corporate Moral Development

Reidenbach and Robin (1991)		Srnka (1998)	
Stage	Description	Stage	Description
5: Ethical	Decisions are made based on the inherent justness and fairness of the decision and fairness of the decision as well as the profitability of the decision. In this sense there is a balance between concerns for profits and ethics.	3: Pro-Active	Managers take a deontologically-oriented position and show respect for stakeholder groups and society. They strive for long-term economic prosperity and growth through socially responsible conduct and try to differentiate themselves from their competitors through anticipation of future public expectations or the creation of new social standards.
4: Emerging Ethical	Management actively seeks a greater balance between profits and ethics. There is an overt effort to manage the organization's culture to produce the desired ethical climate. Management approaches problem solving with an awareness of the ethical consequences of an action as well as its potential profitability.		
3: Responsive	Responsive organizations begin to strike a balance between profits and doing right. However, doing right is still more of an expediency rather than an end unto itself. Management responds to social pressures in order not to face censure or worse.	2: Active	Managers take a teleological position and follow long-term economic performance by considering stakeholder interests. They meet public expectations and show obedience to self-imposed ethical codes.
2: Legalistic	"If it's legal, it's O.K." mentality. Compliance with the letter of the law. Culture dictates obedience to laws, codes, and regulations. Management is principally concerned with adhering to the legality of an action rather than its morality.	1: Re-Active	Managers take an egoistic/legalistic position. They are driven by their immediate and egoistic goal to "survive." Law and common industry practices are regarded to be the sole restrictions to their activities.
1: Amora	"Winning-at-any-cost" attitude. Productivity and profitability are dominant values. Concern for ethics, if existent, is on an after-the-fact basis. Culture shaped by a strong belief in Adam Smith's invisible hand and the notion that the only social responsibility of business is to make a profit.		

This framework supports earlier works on corporate moral development. Particularly, it shows striking parallels to the conceptual model developed by Reidenbach and Robin (1991), the most significant model of corporate moral development found in the literature. Based on the study of a large number of cases of organizations, Reidenbach and Robin identify five levels of corporate moral development. Depending on the degree to which the social mission is recognized and blended with the economic mission, they distinguish *amoral, legalistic, responsive, emerging ethical,* and *ethical* stages of corporate moral development (Reidenbach & Robin, 1991). As is demonstrated in Table 11, these five stages correspond to a large extent to the three stages defined in the framework presented here. Reidenbach's and Robin's first two stages (amoral and legalistic) are comparable to the reactive level, the third level (responsive) equals the active level, and level four and five (emerging ethical and ethical) are comparable to the proactive level.

Our findings also lend support to the eight propositions made by Reidenbach and Robin (1991, pp. 274ff). Based on our results it can be assumed that *not all organizations pass through all stages of moral development* (proposition 1). This is true because corporate moral development is determined by company size and competition. If these dimensions do not change or change only to a limited extent, management may remain in one single stage all the time or move only from one stage to another one, but not any further. From our results it also follows that *an organization can begin its life in any stage of moral development* (proposition 2). This again can be explained by the two dimensions determining the level of corporate moral development, company size, and competition, which can come in any combination when a company is set up.

Whether or not *organizations in stage one predominantly do not leave this stage* (proposition 3) cannot be evaluated based on our empirical results. The same is true for the proposition that *organizations comprised of multiple departments, divisions, or SBUs can occupy different stages of moral development at the same time* (proposition 4). However, it might be assumed on the basis of our findings that if the various departments, divisions, or SBUs are small and exposed to high competition *within* their larger (type C, or even type B) organizations, their management can be classified as type A. This can be explained by the fact that these agent-managers face the same conditions as the classical type A owner-manager in small companies in highly competitive markets.

We also agree that *corporate moral development does not have to be a continuous process, but that stages can be skipped* (proposition 5) and that *organizations can regress to lower stages* (proposition 6). If there is a sudden change in industry competition (e.g., through the entrance of a large competitor or the acquisition of a competitor) or if the organization grows or shrinks in size (e.g., through merger or sale), corporate social responsibility might develop in one or the other direction. This contradicts Kohlberg's presumption that moral reasoning develops through an invariant sequence of stages with no regression taking place. It is, however, intuitively plausible and can be supported by Rest's (1979) alternative model of moral development. This model, basically accepting the sequence of Kohlberg's six stages, assumes that *subjects do not always use the highest level of moral reasoning* that has been attained to date.

As the study is cross-sectional, Reidenbach and Robin's proposition that *there is no time dimension associated with the moral development of an organization* (proposition 7) cannot be assessed. However, given that not all organizations pass through all stages of moral development (proposition 1), that organizations can begin their life in any stage (proposition 2), that stages can be skipped (proposition 5), and that organizations can regress to lower stages (proposition 6) it seems reasonable to assume that there is indeed *no time dimension* in the model. Future longitudinal studies will be required to investigate this point further. Finally, our results support the proposition that *two organizations can be in the same stage but one may be more advanced than the other* (proposition 8). This is particularly true if type C organizations are compared, because they are classified on a continuum somewhere between the two extremes A and B.

DISCUSSION

In this paper, an *exploratory study* conducted among Austrian marketing managers is reported and three manager types empirically found among Austrian marketers are described: "Law-Alone" type A managers found in small enterprises in highly competitive markets; "Ethics-Is-Good-Business" type B managers working in large organizations in moderately competitive markets; and "Case-By-Case" type C managers found in companies between extremes A and B. Based on this *three-manager typology* a three-level *framework of corporate moral development* is elaborated. The framework integrates *Kohlberg*'s cognitive moral development, *Smith*'s ethics continuum, *Filios*'s four levels of social responsibility, and *Goodpaster*'s motivations of corporate social responsibility.

According to the pyramid framework, corporate social responsibility increases when a company grows and acquires more financial resources and experience. It evolves from a minimum level (adherence to existing laws and norms), to a second level (active consideration of stakeholders' interests), and further to the highest level (deliberately doing good more or less unrelated to the organization's core business). While the *motivation* to act in a socially responsible way on all three levels is enlightened self-interest, the arguments stated for corporate conduct, however, evolve from purely economic (level I) to strategic (level II and III) in rare cases even reaching a purely moral position (level III). The framework developed here, and the empirical findings on which it is based, widely support earlier works on corporate moral development.

The three-manager typology and the framework presented in this paper can be used by researchers as well as practitioners as a means to understand how moral competence (reasoning) and moral performance (behavior) develop in organizations. It might be useful to build awareness among managers operating in firms on the lower levels to improve their practices (e.g., by means of industry guidelines). Furthermore, the framework also enables corporate managers on the intermediate level to identify changes needed in their organizations. Finally, it might be seen as a starting point for further theory building and empirical research.

Attention is drawn to the exploratory nature of the study on which the framework is based. Coupled with a limited sample size and the sensitive nature of the investigation, it suggests the need for a cautious interpretation and generalization of the results. Although a wide range of industries has been sampled, the findings may not be applicable to all industries. Also, marketing managers in Austria are not necessarily comparable to those in other countries. As has been explained before, an overwhelming majority of Austrian companies are small- or medium-sized, the family-run company being prevalent. Caution, therefore, is imperative when generalizing the results to other countries. Furthermore, the fact that only 13 percent of the respondents were female may have had distorting effect on results. Several studies have found women to be more ethical than men (e.g., Ferrell & Skinner, 1988; Goolsby & Hunt, 1992; Jones & Gautschi, 1988). Others, however, did not support this or found women even to be less ethical than men (e.g., Hunt & Chonko, 1984). The fact that the companies sampled were almost all from Vienna or other major cities in Austria can also be a major limitation. It may be argued that measuring management's perceptions, attitudes, and behavior may not be a valid method to assess organizational moral reasoning and conduct. The moral attitude and stage of cognitive development level of individual managers, however, are seen as predictors of corporate moral development (Logsdon & Yuthas, 1997, pp. 1218f; Reidenbach & Robin, 1991, p. 274; Trevino 1986). Also, a subjective measure of industry competition was used to classify managers. More objective indicators (e.g., concentration indices) might be used in future studies.

Another limitation is the fact, that a nonresponse error may have occurred which, given the exploratory design, could be assessed only qualitatively: Managers of small companies, while most reluctant to participate in the study, were also found to be least ethically sensitive and socially responsible. As this supports the findings and the framework developed, a nonresponse error is not regarded as overly problematic. It might be argued that the vignette approach is not an appropriate method for exploratory research. Coupled with projective response procedure and mostly concentrating on the explanations of the answers given, we believe the method permits good insights into managers' moral attitudes and behavior. Sridhar and Camburn (1993, p. 737) warn that a threat to validity may arise when using actual cases. The vignettes used may have received greater media exposure, which in turn may have resulted in greater severity in respondents' ratings and classification. This problem, however, was seen to be outweighed by the fact that real cases provide more relevance and credibility as compared to fictitious situations.

Another problem, which has already been mentioned, is the tendency of respondents to give socially desirable answers. Although we attempted to limit the extent of such influences through combining direct and indirect projective questions, asking several questions on the same topic, and concentrating on the "other managers" responses in the analysis, some distortion still may have resulted. This, however, "need not negate the relevance of the study findings, since the issue characterizes not only the present study but also others" (see Akaah & Riodan, 1990, p. 152). Hopefully, this article will stimulate conclusive research to evaluate the concept proposed. Essentially, longitudinal studies and case studies are proposed to investigate the temporal aspect implicit in the framework and to examine the probability of regression from a higher to a lower pyramid level. Also, further research may be necessary to evaluate gender bias within the framework of corporate moral development.

APPENDIX

Table A1. Vignettes

Situation 1	Situation 5
The manufacturer of small appliances advertises a three-year guarantee on all his products. The guarantee, however, is only valid if a coupon is filled out by the consumer and sent back to the manufacturer. This is not explicitly mentioned by the seller but indicated in small print in the instruction manual.	To reduce the creation of earth-near ozone it would be necessary for a certain company to install filters in its plants. As the high costs of installation are seen to represent a competitive disadvantage, management does not intend to install these filters as long there are no laws requiring it to do so.
Situation 2	**Situation 6**
A soft-drink producer has developed a new nonrefillable plastic bottle which is cheaper in production and handling than all reusable (and thus environmentally more friendly) bottles currently in use. As the test market has shown a high acceptance by the consumers, the company decides to introduce the new bottles.	A routine examination at the plant of a mineral water bottling factory reveals a slightly increased quantity of certain bacteria. The water, when used uncooked for the preparation of baby food, might have a laxative effect on the babies. In view of the high recall costs, management refuses to recall the water from the shelves.
Situation 3	**Situation 7**
Marketing research showed that consumers are willing to pay a higher price for safer products. Therefore, the manufacturer of electric appliances advertises the special safety precautions of one of his products. The advertised precautions, however, do not provide any additional security for the user.	Given the increasing limitations for advertising tobacco products, a producer of cigarettes has found a new way of promoting his products. Attractive teenage girls are recruited to go to bars and cafés mainly visited by teenagers and students to offer them a cigarette of the newly invented brand for a tasting.
Situation 4	**Situation 8**
A company in the chemical industry dumps chemical substances into a river nearby because the penalty for this practice is lower than the permit to secure disposal of the chemicals.	The manufacturer of cars refuses to inform the public that three cases of small explosions in the tank of a certain model had occurred when filling in petrol.

Table A2. Answer Sheet for Scenario Evaluation

Situation	Attitude			Behavior		
	Me	Others	My Superior	Me	Others	My Superior
1						
2						
3						
4						
5						
6						
7						
8						

Notes: Please insert "E" if you think the behavior is ethical, and "U" if you believe it is unethical.
Please insert "Y" if you think the person indicated below would act as described, and "N" if you think the person would not act as described.
Please give reasons for each answer (ad 1, ad 2, etc.)!

Table A3. A, B, and C Managers' Responses to Vignettes

Manager Type*	I Believe It Is Ethical	Other Managers Believe It Is Ethical	My Superior Believes It Is Ethical	I Would Do It	Other Managers Would Do It	My Superior Would Do It
Scenario 1						

The manufacturer of small appliances advertises a three-year guarantee on all his products. The guarantee, however, is only valid if a coupon is filled out by the consumer and sent back to the manufacturer. This is not explicitly mentioned by the seller but indicated in small print in the instruction manual.

	I Believe It Is Ethical	Other Managers Believe It Is Ethical	My Superior Believes It Is Ethical	I Would Do It	Other Managers Would Do It	My Superior Would Do It
A	50%	100%	—	50%	100%	—
B	0%	75%	0%	0%	25%	25%
C	8%	46%	21%	21%	54%	38%

Scenario 2

A soft drink producer has developed a new nonrefillable plastic bottle which is cheaper in production and handling than all reusable (and thus environmentally more friendly) bottles currently in use. As the test market has shown a high acceptance by the consumers the company decides to introduce the new bottles.

A	100%	—	50%	100%	—	50%
B	50%	25%	25%	50%	25%	0%
C	46%	46%	63%	71%	54%	46%

Scenario 3

Marketing research showed that consumers are willing to pay a higher price for safer products. Therefore, the manufacturer of electric appliances advertises the special safety precautions of one of his products. The advertised precautions, however, do not provide any additional security for the user.

A	50%	50%	—	50%	100%	—
B	0%	75%	0%	50%	100%	25%
C	46%	54%	54%	42%	75%	54%

(continued)

Table A3.   (Continued)

Manager Type*	I Believe It Is Ethical	Other Managers Believe It Is Ethical	My Superior Believes It Is Ethical	I Would Do It	Other Managers Would Do It	My Superior Would Do It
			Scenario 4			

A company in the chemical industry dumps chemical substances into a river nearby because the penalty for this practice is lower than the permit to secure disposal of the chemicals.

A	0%	100%	—	0%	100%	—
B	0%	0%	0%	0%	0%	0%
C	0%	54%	8%	0%	42%	13%

Scenario 5

To reduce the creation of earth-near ozone it would be necessary for a certain company to install filters in its plants. As the high costs of installation are seen to represent a competitive disadvantage, management does not intend to install these filters as long as there are no laws requiring to do so.

A	100%	—	100%	100%	—	50%
B	0%	0%	0%	0%	25%	0%
C	17%	0%	17%	42%	17%	4%

Scenario 6

A routine examination at the plant of a mineral water bottling factory reveals a slightly increased quantity of certain bacteria. The water, when used uncooked for the preparation of babyfood, might have a laxative effect on the babies. In view of the high recall costs, management refuses to recall the water from the shelves.

A	0%	50%	—	0%	100%	—
B	0%	0%	0%	0%	0%	0%
C	0%	4%	0%	0%	21%	4%

Scenario 7

Given the increasing limitations for advertising tobacco products, a producer of cigarettes has found a new way of promoting his products. Attractive teenage girls are recruited to go to bars and cafés mainly visited by teenagers and students to offer them a cigarette of the newly invented brand for a tasting.

A	100%	100%	—	50%	100%	—
B	0%	25%	0%	0%	0%	0%
C	0%	25%	4%	0%	25%	8%

Scenario 8

The manufacturer of cars refuses to inform the public that three cases of small explosions in the tank of a certain model had occurred when filling in petrol.

A	100%	—	0%	100%	—	0%
B	0%	0%	0%	0%	0%	0%
C	4%	0%	0%	25%	4%	4%

Notes: * As all type A managers were owner managers, the "My Superior" answer category was not meaningful to them. Four (17%) type C managers did not respond to the vignettes. Another 2 (8%) indicated that the "My Superior" category was not meaningful to them and that they, therefore, did not respond to this category.

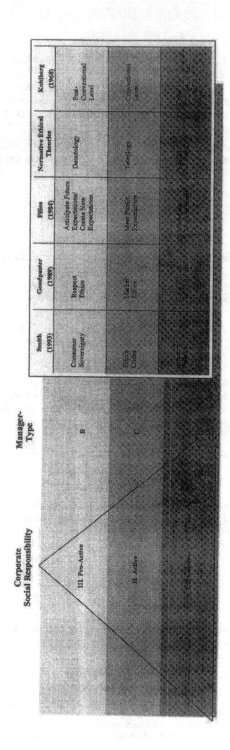

Figure A1. Levels of Corporate Social Responsibility

ACKNOWLEDGMENTS

The author would like to thank Dr. Udo Wagner and Dr. Eckehart Köhler for their critiques of earlier drafts of this manuscript. Also, I am very grateful to my colleagues Dr. Heribert Reisinger and Dr. Karl Krycha for their helpful remarks and comments.

NOTES

1. The term *stakeholder* denotes all parties—directly or indirectly—affected by the activities of an organization. Originally being a play on the word "stockholder," the term comprises all constituencies such as government, consumers, suppliers, employees, and so forth, but certainly also stockholders (see Goodpaster, 1989, 219ff).

2. "Ethics in business" can be interpreted here as *socially responsible behavior.*

3. Respecting rights and concerns of affected parties does, following Goodpaster (1989, p. 219), neither ignore corporate self-interest nor law or competition, but is an independent force in the manager's conscience.

4. No false indications were identified.

5. First, the industries were chosen alphabetically (the first three industries cited in the directory beginning with each letter A, B, etc.) Within the industries we again used alphabetical order to select subjects. Based on the information given in the industry directory (number of employees and annual turnover for 1994), we evaluated whether to include the company in the sample or to proceed to the next item listed in the directory.

6. In compliance with the Austrian Federal Census, small-sized companies were those having none to 49 employees, medium-sized those with 50-499, and large companies those with 500 or more employees.

7. In Austrian companies *marketing* is often presumed to be equal to *"selling," advertising, and/ or public relations.* Therefore, we chose this term to make clear who was to be contacted.

8. The term *corporate social responsibility* was defined neither in the questionnaire nor by the interviewer. The interviewee was explicitly told to think of her/his own conception of organizational responsibility toward society and people.

9. As positive and negative answer categories ("ethical"/"unethical" and "do"/"not do") sum up to 100 percent; only the "believe"/"do" responses are displayed in order to increase readability of the table. Given the fact that several managers indicated that the "my superior" category was not meaningful to them, no frequencies for this category are displayed here. Overall, responses to the "my superior" category were comparable to the "I" category (see Appendix Table A3).

10. The expression "agent-manager" is an allusion to the economic term "agent" who acts on the owner's behalf. It denotes the *employed manager* in a traditional corporation.

11. Several other studies found the management of smaller companies to be ethically less sensitive than other managers (e.g., Eynon, Hill, & Stevens, 1997).

12. Logsdon and Yuthas (1997) have tried to reconcile the levels of moral development with corporate social performance and stakeholder theories.

REFERENCES

Akaah, I.P. (1990). Attitudes of marketing professionals towards ethics in marketing research: A cross-national comparison. *Journal of Business Ethics, 9,* 45-53.

Akaah, I.P., & Riodan, E.A. (1989). Judgments of marketing professionals about ethical issues in marketing research: A replication and extension. *Journal of Marketing Research, 26*(February), 112-120.

Akaah, I.P., & Riodan, E.A. (1990). The incidence of unethical practices in marketing research: An empirical investigation *Journal of the Academy of Marketing Science, 18*(2), 143-152.

Anzenbacher, A. (1992). *Einführung in die ethik.* Düsseldorf: Patmos Verlag. Aristoteles. (repr. 1969). *Nikomachische ethik.* Stuttgart: Reclam Verlag.

Bentham, J. (1966). An introduction to the principles of morals and legislation. In E. Dumont (Ed.), *Einführung in die prinzipien der moral und gesetzgebung.*

Blasi, A. (1980). Bridging moral cognition and moral action: A critical review of the literature. *Psychological Bulleti,. 88,* 1-45.

Chryssides, G.D., & Kaler, J.H. (1993). *An introduction to business ethics.* London: Chapman & Hall.

DeConinck, J.B., & Good, D.J. (1989). Perceptual differences of sales practitioners and students concerning ethical behavior. *Journal of Business Ethics, 8,* 667-676.

Derry, R. (1991). Institutionalizing ethical motivation: Reflections on Goodpaster's agenda. In R.E. Freeman (Ed.), *Business ethics—The state of the art.* New York: Oxford University Press.

Dubinsky, A.J., & Levy, M. (1985). Ethics in retailing: Perceptions of retail salespeople. *Journal of the Academy of Marketing Science, 13*(Winter), 1-16.

Eynon, G., Hill, N.T., & Stevens, K.T. (1997). Factors that influence the moral reasoning abilities of accountants: Implications for universities and the profession. *Journal of Business Ethics, 16,* 1297-1309.

Ferrell, O.C., & Gresham, L.G. (1985). A contingency model for understanding ethical decision making in marketing. *Journal of Marketing, 49*(Summer), 87-96.

Ferrell, O.C., & Skinner, S.J. (1988). Ethical behavior and bureaucratic structure in marketing research organizations. *Journal of Marketing Research, 25*(February), 103-109. Ferrell, O.C., & Weaver, K.M. (1978). Ethical beliefs of marketing managers. *Journal of Marketing, 42*(July), 69-73.

Filios, V.P. (1984). Corporate social responsibility and public accountability. *Journal of Business Ethics, 3,* 305-314.

Friedman, M. (1970, September 13). The social responsibility of business is to increase its profits. *New York Times Magazine,* pp. 33, 122-126.

Fritzsche, D.J., & Becker, H. (1983). Ethical behavior of marketing managers. *Journal of Business Ethics, 2,* 291-299.

Gilligan, C. (1977). In a different voice: Woman's conceptions of the self and morality. *Harvard Educational Review, 49,* 431-446.

Goodpaster, K.E. (1989). Ethical imperatives and corporate leadership. In K.R. Andrews (Ed.), *Ethics in practice—Managing the moral corporation* (pp. 112-228). Boston: Harvard Business School Press.

Goodpaster, K.E., & Matthews, J.B., Jr. (1989). Can a corporation have a conscience? In K.R. Andrews (Ed.), *Ethics in practice—Managing the moral corporation* (pp. 155-167). Boston: Harvard Business School Press.

Goolsby, J.R., & Hunt, S.D. (1992). Cognitive moral development and marketing. *Journal of Marketing, 56*(January), 55-68.

Homann, K., & Blome-Drees, F. (1992). *Wirtschafts- und unternehmensethik.* Göttingen: Vandenhoek & Rupert.

Hunt, S.D., & Vitell, S.J. (1986). A general theory of marketing ethics. *Journal of Macromarketing, 6*(Spring), 5-16.

Hunt, S.D., & Vitell, S.J. (1993). The general theory of marketing ethics: A retrospective and revision. In N.C. Smith & J.A. Quelch (Eds.), *Ethics in marketing* (pp. 775-785). Homewood, IL: Irwin.

Izraeli, D. (1988). Ethical beliefs and behavior among managers: A cross-cultural perspective. *Journal of Business Ethics, 7,* 263-271.

Jones, T.M., &Gautschi, F.H., III. (1988). Will the ethics of business change? A survey of future executives. *Journal of Business Ethics, 7,* 231-248.

Kant, I. (1968). *Kritik der praktischen vernunft.* W. Weschedel (Ed.).

Kohlberg, L. (1969). Stage and sequence: The cognitive developmental approach in socialization. In D. Goslin (Ed.), *Handbook of socialization theory and research* (pp. 347-480). Chicago: Rand Mc Nally.

Kohlberg, L. (1997). Zusammenhänge zwischen der moralentwicklung in der kindheit und im erwachsenenalter—neu interpretiert. In W. Althof et al. (Eds.), *Die psychologie der moralentwicklung* (2nd ed.). Frankfurt/Main: Suhrkamp.

Kohlberg, L. (1981). *The philosophy of moral development.* New York: Harper & Row.

Logsdon, J.M., & Yuthas, K. (1997). Corporate social performance, stakeholder orientation, and organizational moral development. *Journal of Business Ethics, 16,* 1213-1226.

Maslow, A.H. (1943). A theory of human motivation. *Psychological Review,* 370-396.

Nijhof, A.H.J., & Fisscher, O. (1997). Dealing with ethical dilemmas in organizational change processes. *International Journal of Value Based Management, 10,* 173-192.

Norris, D.G., & Gifford, J.B. (1988). Retail store managers' and students' perceptions of ethical retail practices: A comparative and longitudinal analysis (1976-1986). *Journal of Business Ethics, 7,* 515-524.

Nozick, R. (1974). *Anarchy, state and utopia.* New York: Basic Books.

Peters, T.J., & Waterman, R.H., Jr. (1982). *In the search for excellence.* New York: Harper & Row.

Piaget, J. (1932). *Le jugement moral chez l'enfant.* München: Das moralische Urteil beim Kinde, DTV.

Pieper, A. (1994). *Einführung in die ethik* (3rd ed.). Franke Verlag: Tübingen and Basel.

Rawls, J. (1971). *A theory of justice.* Cambridge: The Belknap Press.

Reidenbach, R.E., & Robin, D.P. (1991). A conceptual model of corporate moral development. *Journal of Business Ethics, 10,* 273-284.

Rest, J. (1979). *Development in judging moral issues.* Minneapolis: University of Minnesota Press.

Robertson, D.C., & Schlegelmilch, B.B. (1993). Corporate institutionalization of ethics in the United States and Great Britain. *Journal of Business Ethics, 12,* 301-312.

Robin, D.P., & Reidenbach, R.E. (1987). Social responsibility, ethics, and marketing strategy: Closing the gap between concept and application. *Journal of Marketing, 51*(January), 44-58.

Smith, C.N. (1993). Ethics and the marketing manager. In N.C. Smith & J.A. Quelch (Eds.), *Ethics in marketing.* Homewood, IL: Irwin.

Sridhar, B.S., & Camburn, A. (1993). Stages of moral development of corporations. *Journal of Business Ethics, 12,* 727-739.

Srnka, K.J. (1997). Ethik im marketing—Einstellung und verhalten des managements. WUV: Wien.

Steiner, G.A. (1972). Social policies for business. *California Management Review* (Winter), 17-24.

Steinmann, H., & Löhr, A. (1989). Unternehmensethik, eine realistische Idee? In Seifert & Pfriem (Eds.), *Wirtschaftsethik und ökologische wirtschaftsforschung* (pp. 87-110).

Steinmann, H., & Zerfass, A. (1993). Unternehmensethik. In G. Enderle et al. (Eds.), *Lexikon der wirtschaftsethik* (co. 1117f). Herder Verlag: Freiburg im Breisgau, Basel und Wien.

Thoma, S.J. (1985). *On improving the relationship between moral reasoning and external criteria: The utilizer/nonutilizer dimension.* Unpublished doctoral dissertation, University of Minnesota.

Trevino, L.K. (1986). Ethical decision making in organizations: A person-situation interactionist model. *Academy of Management Review, 11*(3), 601-617.

Trevino, L.K. (1992). Moral reasoning and business ethics: Implications for research, education, and management. *Journal of Business Ethics, 11,* 445-459.

Tsalikis, J., & Fritzsche, D.J. (1989). Business ethics: A literature review with a focus on marketing ethics. *Journal of Business Ethics, 8,* 695-743.

Zey-Ferrell, M., Weaver, K.M., & Ferrell, O.C. (1979). Predicting unethical behavior among marketing practitioners. *Human Relations, 32*(7), 557-569.

ORGANIZATIONAL FRAMEWORK FOR SALES ETHICS MANAGEMENT

Arturo Z. Vásquez-Párraga and Lucette Comer

ABSTRACT

This study examines the role of organizational characteristics that tend to facilitate or inhibit ethical decision making within sales organizations. Sales organizations can and should offer predictable environments that facilitate salespeople's ethical behaviors. The presence and importance of key structural elements of the firm are discussed and evaluated in their collective role as facilitators or inhibitors of sales managers' ethical decision making. Based on a survey of sales managers in 480 American companies, moderately formalized organizations with large sales forces who are supervised closely by their managers, and who strictly enforce their codes of ethics, were found to be characterized by more desirable outcomes of the ethical decision-making process used by their sales managers.

A typical sales manager would like to understand what factors make sales organizations favorable or unfavorable environments for ethical behavior, both to induce individuals to behave ethically and groups to foster collective ethical

Research in Marketing, Volume 15, pages 139-174.

responsibility. Even without a code of ethics or any other written rule in place, sales organizations may predictably facilitate or inhibit individual ethical or unethical conduct, respectively, depending on key structural elements of the firm such as degree of formalization, span of control, enforcement of policies, size of the sales force, and size of the company.

Despite previous attempts to empirically identify the organizational variables that are relevant to individual ethical decision making in the context of the firm, a comprehensive, and at the same time, parsimonious organizational framework has not been offered. Different authors have arrived at different conclusions depending on which organizational variables they examined. For example, bureaucratic structure has been found to be positively related to ethical behavior (Ferrell & Skinner, 1988). Other research has found that the mere existence of a corporate code of ethics in the company has either (a) no effect on the employees' perceptions of ethical problems (Chonko & Hunt, 1985; Hunt, Chonko, & Wilcox, 1984) or (b) a very limited effect (Singhapakdi & Vitell, 1991). There is evidence that a proactive organizational approach (involving such things as top management actions, corporate ethical values, or organizational commitment), significantly influences ethical judgments (Akaah & Riordan, 1989; Hunt, Wood, & Chonko, 1989; Singhapakdi, Kraft, Vitell, & Rallapalli, 1995). Although such actions, values, and commitment reflect more than structural conditions of the firm, these findings underscore the importance of organizational factors in influencing individual ethical conduct.

One research stream pursued "proxy" measures of organizational involvement such as the firm's *ethical climate* (Kelley & Dorsch, 1991; Victor & Cullen, 1988). Ethical climate combines five dimensions (caring, laws and codes, rules, instrumental, and independence). In these studies, ethical climate was not linked to actual organizational variables, however, which substantially limits the usefulness of the approach.

The purpose of the present study is to investigate the impact of a structured set of organizational characteristics on the ethical decision making of sales managers in selling contexts. The facilitators-inhibitors approach (Guzzo & Gannett, 1988) is used to identify the intervening organizational characteristics and a theory of marketing ethics (Hunt & Vitell, 1986) is used to analyze the ethical decision making of sales managers regarding selling situations. First, background literature pertaining to organizational characteristics and to the theory of marketing ethics is reviewed. Then a set of research hypotheses are proposed based on the link between organizational framework and managers' ethical decision making. Finally, the results of the study are presented and discussed and managerial and research implications are addressed.

ORGANIZATIONAL FRAMEWORK

The present study has been developed in line with the ontological distinction that holds that organizations do not have moral status, while individual persons do (Collier, 1995; McMahon, 1995), and the resulting operational distinction between corporate moral responsibility and personal responsibility (Phillips, 1995). We examine the organization as a facilitator or inhibitor of individual ethical behavior (Brigley, 1995; Di Toro, 1995), not as an entity of moral status.

Facilitators and inhibitors are distinct features of a work environment that are in opposition only at times. Based on empirical research, Guzzo and Gannett (1988) concluded that facilitators affect several of the direct causes of performance effectiveness simultaneously, in addition to performance per se, and that they tend to push the performance of individuals and groups toward levels of maximal effectiveness. Confirming previous results (Steel & Mento, 1986), they further concluded (a) that inhibitors, for the most part, directly affect performance of individuals and groups; (b) that some of their effects are, in part, mediated by individual and organizational characteristics; and (c) that they tend to restrict performance toward minimally acceptable levels of effectiveness. As a result, they argued that the absence of an inhibitor could lead to higher performance than could the presence of an inhibitor, and that the absence of a facilitator could lead to lower performance than would the presence of a facilitator.

Katz and Kahn (1978) developed a general taxonomy of facilitators and inhibitors within an open-systems framework that classified the activities and events within organizations in terms of generic subsystems. The present research concerns the managerial subsystem that consists of the coordination of the other subsystems and the accomplishment of several management behaviors (e.g., planning, organizing, decision making, and controlling). Managerial behaviors directly relate to the creation of facilitators and inhibitors which, in turn, impact upon performance effectiveness. Specific examples of management behaviors include the policies and procedures specifying how things are to be done in the organization, leadership behaviors, personnel management, and reward-punishment policies.

Facilitating systems encourage individuals/groups to work at their maximum level of performance (Guzzo & Gannett, 1988). In these systems, salespeople and their managers focus their attention on the quality of performance. In particular, managers pay close attention to the way salespeople perform their jobs and the quality of their work. This approach makes ethical actions more visible, and hence more likely to impact the way salespeople arrive at their ethical decisions. Conversely, inhibiting systems implicitly encourage working at the lowest acceptable level (Guzzo & Gannett, 1988). In the sales force context, establishing quotas for sales performance may have the undesirable side effect of leveling output to the barest minimum, by encouraging salespeople to make only the minimum sales rather than to achieve the highest potential level. Once quota is achieved, these salespeople may cut corners with their work. Thus, better performance and higher ethical standards are likely to be found among those working within facilitating systems than among those working within inhibiting systems.

Indicators of Facilitators and Inhibitors within Organizations

We examine five indicators of facilitators and inhibitors that potentially impact upon the ethical climate within an organization: (1) the width of the span of control of individual sales managers, (2) the size of the sales force, (3) the size of the company, (4) the degree of "formalization" of policies and procedures, and (5) the likelihood of enforcement of stated policies and procedures. Managers in facilitating organizations tend to have narrow spans of control and work with relatively larger sales forces. Their organizations are relatively large in size, have formalized policies/procedures, and are perceived to have codes of ethics that are strictly enforced. Conversely, managers in inhibiting organizations tend to have wide spans of control and work with relatively small sales forces. Inhibiting organizations are relatively small in size, have few formalized policies/procedures, and if they have codes of ethics, they are generally not enforced.

Span of Control

The term "span of control" refers to the relative number of salespeople reporting to a manager. Managers who have many salespeople reporting to them are said to have wide spans of control. We argue that as the managers' spans of control widen, internal forces tend to move the organization away from being a facilitator toward being an inhibitor of ethical behavior. Sales managers who have wide spans of control experience serious time constraints that prevent them from keeping close tabs on individual salespeople. As more salespeople are added to a manager's span, tasks become more complex and interrelated, control becomes difficult and, consequently, salespeople are increasingly left to their own devices (Still, Cundiff, & Govani, 1988; Van Fleet, 1983). Thus, managers with many sales personnel reporting to them seem to operate in inhibiting systems. With wide spans of control, salespeople need to be more experienced and better trained than with narrow spans of control (Dalrymple & Cron, 1992).

Sales Force Size

The larger the sales force, the more likely is the organization to be a facilitator. The fixed cost structure associated with larger sales forces leads them to emphasize fixed compensation plans or salaries (Coughlin & Sen, 1989). Because salary compensation is generally considered to be associated with stronger managerial direction and control (Anderson & Oliver, 1987), salespeople in larger sales forces should experience less job ambiguity, leading to better performance (Sohi,

Smith, & Ford, 1996). Larger sales organizations are also more likely than are smaller ones to support well-developed training programs and to have better trained managers. Under such conditions, salespeople will probably have better information to support their judgments. Thus, larger sales forces will likely facilitate performance. The relationship may not be monotonic, however, because as John and Weitz (1989) point out, as the sales force gets larger, bureaucratic inefficiencies make it difficult to monitor activities. Thus, when the sales force is extremely large, the firm may be inhibiting instead of facilitating. Overall, however, the larger the sales force, the more likely the organization is to be a facilitator organization.

Size of Organization

Similar arguments can be advanced about organizational size. The larger the organization, itself, the more likely it is to be a facilitator. Larger organizations are more likely than are smaller ones to have the resources to support extensive programs for orienting new salespeople to company policies and procedures and for training them in appropriate selling behaviors. Larger organizations are also better able to support elaborate supervisory systems to oversee their sales force in the field. Lacking resources to support training programs, smaller organizations generally recruit experienced salespeople because they can function without minimal training and supervision (Smyth, 1968). Anderson and Oliver (1987) argued that managers in smaller organizations avoid using input measures for evaluating their salespeople because they are unable to underwrite the cost involved. This was supported by the findings of Jobber, Holey, and Shipley (1993), that in comparison with smaller organizations, larger organizations tend to: (a) use a wider range of quantitative criteria for evaluation purposes, (b) use more formalized methods of evaluation, and (c) make greater use of predetermined performance standards. A positive effect of company size on entrepreneurial behavior has also been reported (Caruana, Morris, & Vella, 1998). All of this suggests that sales force organizational frameworks in larger companies function as facilitators. In addition, large companies are more likely than smaller ones to use Management By Objectives (MBO) as a supervisory tool (Dubinsky & Barry, 1982), and MBO seems more consistent with the firm's role as facilitator (Muczyk & Gable, 1987).

Formalization

The more the policies and procedures of a company are formalized, the more likely is the organization to act as a facilitator in ethical decision making. Organizational formalization refers to the use of written rules and procedures to standardize operations (Pugh & Hickson, 1973) and to the degree to which work activities are formally defined by administrative guidelines and rules (Hall, Haas, & Johnson, 1967). Greater organizational formalization was found to (a) influence organizational commitment (an individual desirable outcome) indirectly by its effects on lower levels of role ambiguity and role conflict (Agarwal, 1993; Mellor, Mathieu, & Swim, 1994; Michaels, Cron, Dubinsky, & Joachimsthaler, 1988); (b) lessen the effects of salespeople's role conflict, role ambiguity, and work satisfaction (Sohi, Smith, & Ford, 1996); (c) facilitate problem solving by providing procedures that can be used to deal with task-related problems (Malik & Wilson, 1995); (d) reduce work alienation (Podsakoff, Williams, & Todor, 1986); (e) reduce deviant discretion (Kelley, Longfellow, & Malehorn, 1996); (f) enhance trust in the user-researcher relationship (Moorman, Deshpande, & Zaltman, 1993); and (g) raise performance (Chan, 1996; Dahlstrom & Nygaard, 1995; Guest & Peccei, 1994; Menon, Bharadwaj, & Howell, 1996; Moenaert, Souder, De Meyer, & Deschoolmeester, 1994). Apparently, more explicit management guidance can be beneficial for boundary-spanning professionals such as salespeople.

Salespeople receive important direction from clear-cut policies and procedures (Childers, Dubinsky, & Skinner, 1990); thus, salespeople in highly formalized organizations should have a clear understanding of policies and rules, suggesting that sales force organizational frameworks operate as facilitators. In addition, managers in formalized organizations are able to maintain strong behavioral control over the persuasive communication of their sales personnel by providing them with memorized scripts, or training them in presentations that are "canned" in whole or in part (Jolson, 1989). Such organizations are able to furnish salespeople with detailed policy manuals to help them understand the type of actions that are appropriate for them to take and statements that are appropriate for them to make.

Thus, organizational frameworks within formalized companies are likely to facilitate control over salespersons' activities. Moreover, the formalization of corporate values seems to be the key to influencing employee behavior by facilitating job and role clarity (Nwachukwu & Vitell, 1997). While current organizational thought supports the elimination of bureaucratic formalization (an extreme version of formalization) and its coercive impact (Adler & Borys, 1996; Bozeman & Scott, 1996), we argue that moderate formalization enables employees better to master their tasks. We also argue that without formal policies and procedures, individuals lack direction and, because there is no consensus on underlying value systems, also lack appropriate criteria on which to base ethical decisions. In the long run, confusion will inevitably result because salespeople and their managers lack clear agreement about the appropriate bases on which to make ethical judgments.

Enforcement of Policies

When management is perceived to enforce their established standards for ethical decision making, firms are likely to be facilitating organizations. Such firms have both written and unwritten rules. The mere exist-

Table 1. Indicators of Organizational Framework, Nature of the Relationship, and Rationale for its Use

Indicator of Organizational Framework	Nature of Relationship	Rationale	Direction of Relationship with Facilitating Organizational Framework
Width of Span of Control	The narrower the span of control, the more the organizational framework is a facilitator.	The fewer salespeople under the manager's control, the more an organizational framework can facilitate individual ethical behavior.	Inverse
Sales Force Size	The larger the sales force, the more the organizational framework is a facilitator.	The larger the sales force, the more likely to have fixed compensation, formal training programs, and a well-developed supervisory system. Thus, a facilitating organizational framework is more likely.	Direct
Company Size	The larger the company, the more the organizational framework is a facilitator.	The larger the company, the more likely to have the resources to implement a facilitating organizational framework.	Direct
Degree of Formalization	The more formalized the company, to a point, the more the organizational framework is a facilitator.	The more formalized the company, the more clearly are expectations spelled out to salespeople. Thus, a facilitating organizational framework is more likely.	Direct
Enforcement of Policies	The more the organization enforces its rules, the more the organizational framework is a facilitator.	The more a company enforces its policies, the more likely salespeople will take them seriously and adhere to them. Thus, a facilitating organizational framework is more likely.	Direct

ence of rules (e.g., codes of ethics), however, may be insufficient to either encourage acceptable conduct or discourage unacceptable behavior (Bingham & Raffield, 1989; Laczniak & Inderrieden, 1987). In contrast, a corporation which stands behind its rules of conduct, in that punishment for infractions is clearly expected, will exert stronger control over actions of salespeople than will one in an organization in which infractions are overlooked (Ferrell & Fraedrich, 1988; Murphy & Laczniak, 1981; Weaver & Ferrell, 1977). Thus, the degree to which the organization is perceived to enforce its rules and regulations is a further indication of the extent to which the organization facilitates ethical decision making.

The relationship between the five indicators of organizational framework and the two models—facilitator (F) and inhibitor (I), the nature and direction of the relationships, and a rationale for the use of each, are spelled out in Table 1.

SALES ETHICS MANAGEMENT

Sales managers are genuinely concerned about the ethical behavior of salespeople who, on their side, face many ethical dilemmas in the course of performing their jobs (Dubinsky, Jolson, Michaels, Kotabe, & Lim, 1992; Marden, 1989; Wotruba, 1990). Ethical dilemmas in sales are particularly troublesome when the best course of action seems to be the one that involves unethical behavior (e.g., lying to the buyer regarding the actual available price range in order to sell the most expensive items), or when behaving ethically is likely to result in negative consequences (e.g., losing sales of the more expensive items after providing the buyer with full price information).

Vásquez-Párraga (1990) and Hunt and Vásquez-Párraga (1993) reported that 95 percent of sales and marketing managers viewed telling the truth about price ranges to be ethical when the consequences were positive, but only 82 percent viewed it as ethical when the consequences were negative. Conversely, 85 percent of respondents viewed over-recommending expensive products to be unethical when the consequences were negative, but only 78 percent viewed it as unethical when the consequences were positive. Thus, the presence of negative consequences in ethical situations or positive consequences in unethical situations may create confusion in the formation of ethical judgments. It is not always clear to the salesperson whether it is, for example, ethical to lie to achieve quotas (benefiting both company and achiever), or whether it is more ethical to disclose complete and truthful information about prices when it causes harm to the company and/or to shareholders by doing so.

Sales managers who experience difficulty in arriving at an ethical judgment may also be unsure about the appropriate action (whether reward or punishment), to best influence salespeople's ethical conduct. Should they reward *unethical* behavior that produces *good* results? Is punishment appropriate when *ethical*

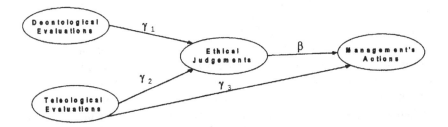

Figure 1. Basic Model of Sales Ethics Management

behavior produces *negative* outcomes? Addressing this dilemma, Vásquez-Párraga (1990) and Hunt and Vásquez-Párraga (1993) found that 92 percent of sales managers punished unethical behavior (over-recommending expensive products) that brought negative consequences to the company (lost sales), but only 77 percent did when the consequences were positive. Vice versa, 98 percent of managers rewarded ethical conduct (providing complete and truthful price information) that produced positive consequences, but only 62 percent did so when ethical conduct produced negative consequences. Again, the contradicting presence of positive or negative consequences when making management decisions creates ethical "confusion."

Thus, two critical research questions in ethical decision making must be addressed: (1) how managers arrive at and evaluate ethical judgments, and (2) how managers decide on the action to take (e.g., rewarding or punishing a salesperson), in order to encourage ethical behavior and discourage unethical behavior.

Sales Managers' Ethical Decision Making

Several theoretical frameworks have been offered to use in exploring these and other ethical issues. From the various frameworks addressing ethical decision making by business people (Ferrell & Gresham, 1985; Ferrell, Gresham, & Fraedrich, 1989; Hunt & Vitell, 1986; Jones, 1991; Velasquez, 1982; Wotruba, 1990), the Hunt-Vitell theory of marketing ethics offers both an operational set of variables and a parsimonious structure of relationships. It includes the basic DU (deontological and utilitarian) model, which is considered to be superior to other basic models (Brady & Dunn, 1995), and attempts to explain ethical judgment and management's actions, key outcomes of the decision-making process followed by business people. It focuses on the joint impact of deontological evaluations and teleological evaluations on ethical judgments and management's actions, as shown in Figure 1.

The deontological moral philosophy focuses on *norms* referred to as duties, responsibilities, and the rights of others. Strict deontologists rely on norms alone to judge ethical conduct (Kant, 1959). Moderate deontologists rely on the norms first, but also on other criteria (Etzioni, 1988). The teleological philosophy focuses on the *consequences* of the various alternatives or preferences for either the acting person (egoism) or others (utilitarianism). Deriving from neoclassical economics, the teleological moral philosophy assesses that all preferences, including the preference of others, encompass one utility, the individual's pleasure or interests (Wallach & Wallach, 1983), and pleasure is judged by its consequences. When using deontology, persons consider only the inherent "ethicalness" of an act. For example, when a salesperson lies to make a sale, the act of lying is bad in and of itself, even when no apparent harm results to either the customer or the salesperson's company. When using teleology, persons consider the consequences of the individual behavior to either the company and related instances or the acting individual. For instance, the act of lying is bad *only* if it results in harm to the customer and/or the company.

Ethical Judgments

When forming ethical judgments, most individuals combine both considerations, deontological evaluations (DEs) and teleological evaluations (TEs). Hunt and Vitell (1986) argued that people use deontology, teleology, or a combination, to solve ethical problems. Vásquez-Párraga (1990) and Hunt and Vásquez-Párraga (1993) empirically tested the Hunt and Vitell (1986) theory by use of an experimental design and found that (1) sales and marketing managers rely on DEs rather than on TEs in arriving at their ethical judgments, and (2) sales and marketing managers rely on both ethical judgments and TEs in rewarding or punishing salespeople. Similarly, Fraedrich, Ferrell, and Jones (1991) found that the logic of managers in general is more deontological than teleological in nature. A focus on TEs may be short-sighted. Moreover, unethical behaviors that have no apparent negative consequences in the short run may have disastrous consequences for the firm in the long term. Unethical statements made during sales presentations, for example, may generate quick sales, but lead to serious ethical and legal consequences for the firm (Boedecker, Morgan, & Stoltman, 1991).

Management's Action

According to Bellizzi and Hite (1989) sales managers deal more severely with unethical behaviors that have negative consequences to the organization (teleological) than those that are merely unethical per se (deontological). Vásquez-Párraga (1990) and Hunt and Vásquez-Párraga (1993) confirmed Bellizzi and Hite's findings and also found that ethical behaviors resulting in negative consequences are rewarded less than those having positive consequences. Sales and marketing managers actually *encouraged* unethical behavior by rewarding unethical acts that had positive consequences for the firm and, conversely, *discouraged* ethical behavior by punishing ethical behavior that has negative consequences for the firm.

ORGANIZATIONAL FRAMEWORK AND SALES ETHICS MANAGEMENT

Previous studies have linked key indicators of organizational framework—span of control of managers, size of company and sales force, formalization, and enforcement of policies—to some ethical outcomes.

Span of Control

Sales managers with wide spans of control tend to spread their attention among a number of salespeople and, hence, are limited in the amount of attention they can pay to any one individual's actions. Consequently, they may be less able to monitor ethical infractions or to evoke disciplinary action. Width of span of control may be linked to ethics indirectly through an accompanying increase in role conflict. Salespersons whose managers have wide spans of control show increased levels of role stress (Chonko, 1982), and as role conflict increases, they may be less able to handle ethical problems (Chonko & Burnett, 1983).

Size of Organization and Sales Force

On the one hand, more ethical conflict seems to exist in large firms (Chonko & Hunt, 1985), and perception of unethical behavior by coworkers seems to be positively related to the size of the firm (Hoffman, Howe, & Hardigree, 1991). On the other hand, large organizations seem to be well suited to handle those conflicts and perceptions as they have the resources to support extensive orientation programs, elaborate supervisory systems, and permanent training programs for their sales forces. Consequently, even though there may be more competitive pressure to advance in larger firms (and hence more motivation and opportunity to behave unethically), there is also a countervailing facilitating environment (Jobber, Holey, & Shipley, 1993) that can help managers better control salespeople's ethical behavior.

Formalization

In the marketing research context, a relationship has been demonstrated between formalization and ethics (Ferrell & Skinner, 1988), although the strength of the explanatory relationship varies considerably by type of firm (from 11.3%

of variance explained in market research firms to only 3.2% in corporate research departments). Highly formalized organizations are likely to have codes of ethics to guide salespeople's decision making/actions. Codes of ethics may help reduce some of the ambiguity about appropriateness of actions and provide some guidance for making decisions in particular situations. However, the existence of such codes alone does not seem to be sufficient to affect ethical outcomes (Akaah & Riordan, 1989; Chonko & Hunt, 1985; Hunt, Chonko, & Wilcox, 1984). Employees need to believe that their managers stand behind the codes. In a laboratory experiment, Hegarty and Sims (1979) demonstrated that unethical behavior was significantly reduced when subjects (graduate-level business students) received a letter from their company president that supported ethical behavior in their company. In a field setting, Akaah and Riordan (1989) confirmed that actions by top management supportive of ethical behavior (or discouraging unethical behavior) influence the behavior of marketing professionals. Seemingly, formalization also affects ethical behavior indirectly through associated decreases in role conflict (Michaels et al., 1988) although the relationship between role conflict and formalization has not been clearly established.

Enforcement of Policies

The existence of a code of ethics alone may merely serve as a "token gesture." Singhapakdi and Vitell (1991) found no relationship between organizational culture, operationalized as the existence of a corporate code of ethics, and deontological norms. The degree of enforcement of the code of ethics may be the important factor in determining how closely salespeople adhere to the ethical prescriptions of their company's code of ethics (Murphy & Laczniak, 1981). It may also be a way to make such prescriptions effective by integrating them into the corporate culture (Akaah & Riordan, 1989; Hunt, Wood, & Chonko, 1989). Supporting this is evidence presented by Weaver and Ferrell (1977), Kaikati and Label (1980), Laczniak and Inderrieden (1987), and Bingham and Raffield (1989), who all noted that ethical behavior increases when corporate policies on ethics are both established and enforced. Congruently, the ethical climate of an organization has the potential to influence sales professionals' perceptions of ethical situations (Singhapakdi & Vitell, 1990, 1991). Thus, on the one hand, employees tend to adopt the ethical beliefs of top management, while on the other hand, managers tend to act unethically if it is to their advantage and if there are no barriers to unethical practices (Caywood & Laczniak, 1986; Ferrell & Fraedrich, 1988; Newstrom & Ruch, 1975; Podsakoff, 1982).

RESEARCH HYPOTHESES

The following research hypotheses are proposed to examine the moderating impact of an organizational framework—indicating either a facilitating

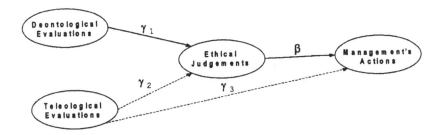

Note: Dotted line indicates a weaker relationship.

Figure 2. Facilitating Organizational Framework

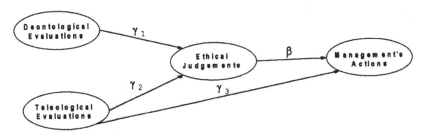

Figure 3. Inhibiting Organizational Framework

or an inhibiting role—on the core relationships of the Hunt-Vitell theory reproducing sales managers' ethical decision making. The hypothesized "facilitator" (hereafter F model) and "inhibitor" (hereafter I model) models of the ethical decision making in sales management are shown in Figures 2 and 3.

Organizational Framework and Ethical Judgment

How do organizational frameworks influence the decision-making process sales managers use to arrive at ethical judgments? In frameworks where monitoring of the sales force is facilitated, control tends to be behavior-based, and sales managers would be expected to rely on DEs to make their ethical judgments. Conversely, when monitoring of the sales force is difficult, managers would tend to focus on outcomes and managers' judgments would be highly influenced by TEs, that is, the positive or negative consequences to the firm irrespective of the ethicalness of the actions, per se.

Table 2. Expected Moderating Effects of Organizational
Framework Indicators on Ethical Judgments/Management Actions

Indicator of Organizational Framework	Ethical Judgments		Management Actions	
	Interaction with Deontological Evaluations	Interaction with Teleological Evaluations	Interactions with Ethical Judgments	Interactions with Teleological Evaluations
Width of Span of Control	Negative [b]	Positive [a]	Negative	Positive
Sales Force Size	Positive	Negative	Positive	Negative
Company Size	Positive	Negative	Positive	Negative
Degree of Formalization	Positive	Negative	Positive	Negative
Enforcement of Policies	Positive	Negative	Positive	Negative

Notes: [a] The higher the value, the more the indicator suggests a facilitating organizational framework.
[b] The lower the value, the more the indicator suggests an inhibiting organizational framework.

Hypothesis 1. Sales managers in facilitating organizational frameworks rely on deontological evaluations, but not on teleological evaluations to form ethical judgments.

Hypothesis 2. Sales managers in inhibiting organizational frameworks rely on both deontological and teleological evaluations for ethical judgments.

Organizational Framework and Management's Actions

How do organizational frameworks influence the decision-making process that determines the type of management's action that should be adopted to either encourage ethical conduct or discourage unethical conduct? In frameworks where managerial direction is facilitated, sales managers will tend to punish (reward) actions that are unethical (ethical) per se, with less emphasis on the consequences of the behavior to the organization. Conversely, where managerial direction is difficult, sales managers will tend to apply more severe punishments when TEs are violated (negative consequences to the organization) than when such considerations are not violated, whether or not the behaviors that produced the outcome were unethical in themselves.

Hypothesis 3. Sales managers in facilitating organizational frameworks rely on ethical judgments, but not on teleological evaluations to take management actions.

Hypothesis 4. Sales managers in inhibiting organizational frameworks rely on both ethical judgments and teleological evaluations to take management actions.

Table 2 summarizes the hypothesized relationships between the organizational framework indicators and the core components of the Hunt-Vitell model.

RESEARCH METHOD

Sample

A national mailing list of 1,000 sales managers representing 1,000 all-industry (including every industrial classification as identified by the SIC) American companies was acquired from a commercial source and used to access an actual sample of 480 sales managers, responding to the self-administered questionnaire and representing an effective response rate of 48 percent (Wiseman & Billington, 1984). Potential nonresponse bias was explored using demographic information supplied by a group of 41 nonrespondent sales managers. No significant differences between the two samples were found using *t*-tests. Moreover, no significant differences among the four experimental groups were detected.

Responding sales managers were primarily male (94.3%), relatively middle aged (median age = 44 years), and relatively well educated (94.6% reported having some college level education while 68.6% were college graduates or better). They were experienced managers, having a median business experience of 20 years and had been with their companies a median of 8.5 years.

Design

The hypotheses were tested in the context of an experimental design. Subjects were first grouped according to the type of organizational framework in which they were operating: facilitating or inhibitory. Following the Vásquez-Párraga (1990) and Hunt and Vásquez-Párraga (1993) approach, subjects were randomly assigned to four treatment groups, each representing a different combination of DE and TE as follows: (a) unethical DE with negative TE, (b) unethical DE with positive TE, (c) ethical DE with positive TE, and (d) ethical DE with negative TE. Two selling situations representing (un)ethical problems were used: overstating plant capacity utilization and over-recommending expensive products. Subjects were exposed to both scenarios, each under the same combination of DE and TE treatments. The precise wording associated with each experimental cell for both scenarios appears in the Appendix.

Situations

Two selling situations were used to stimulate the respondent with two different themes, to facilitate the discovery of method artifacts in the issues, and to replicate the measurement within exactly the same sample. Subjects were instructed to read each situation separately and for each to answer the questions about their ethical judgment and management's action.

The first situation involved a case of overstating plant capacity utilization. It described a salesperson's attempt to convey favorable demand conditions by suggesting product popularity to customers and, as a result, discouraging price negotiations. In the unethical condition, this situation involved lying to the customer and violated the "truth-telling" deontological norm. A dilemma was created when telling the lie benefitted the company by giving the salesperson more leverage in negotiations with a potential result in the form of a more favorable price. In the ethical condition, the salesperson told the truth, but a dilemma was generated when such an approach produced negative consequences to the firm.

The second situation involved over-recommending expensive products of the company. It described a salesperson's attempt to build the dollar size of an order to perhaps earn higher commissions by selling a customer a better quality product than is actually needed. The situation involved deceiving the customer and violated the deontological norm of "trust" and is deontologically unethical because the salesperson shows a blatant disregard for the welfare of the customer and in solving his/her needs. This unethical act has a much stronger potential for negative consequences to the firm than does the preceding one. The seriousness of this situation is underscored by a study of sales managers' perceptions of unethical actions (Dubinsky et al., 1992) in which "making statements to an existing purchaser that exaggerate the seriousness of his/her problem in order to obtain a bigger order or other concession" was rated as the single most serious unethical action (p. 12). The action carries a much greater risk of negative consequences to the firm (teleologically risky). The salesperson was clearly acting in a way that was not in the interests of solving the customer's needs. If found out, both salesperson and company would surely lose credibility, the potential for developing a good long-term relationship with the customer would be lost, and the reputation of both company and salesperson would be tarnished. The true state of the customer's product-related situation, as well as the size/quality of the order are easily verifiable. In the ethical condition, although the norm of trust was not violated, the risk of negative consequences to the firm was introduced. The risk would be large should the salesperson's action be found out.

Measures

Dependent Variables

The dependent variables were "ethical judgment" and "rewards/punishments." Each was a single item measure. After reading each scenario, managers responded to two items concerning the nature of their ethical judgments and the type of reward or punishment they would recommend. Managers evaluated the quality of the ethical response on a 7-point scale ranging from "1" (very unethical) to "7" (very ethical). They described the appropriate reward/punishment from "1" (employment termination) to "9" (pay raise and promotion).

Organizational Framework

Each manager was classified as operating in a facilitating (F) organization, an inhibiting (I) organization, or a *mixed* organization by an index created for this purpose. Five criteria were used to classify salespeople: width of the span of control, size of the sales force, size of the company, degree of formalization, and likelihood of enforcement of stated policies and procedures. Each of these were measured separately and the five were combined to create a single index. The numerical levels that were used to create the index are described below.

Width of managers' span of control was operationalized as the number of persons regularly supervised by the respondent. Size of sales force was operationalized by the approximate number of salespeople employed by the company. Size of firm was measured by the total number of permanent employees in the responding manager's firm. Size of firm was trichotomized: companies with fewer than 50 employees were designated as small, those with 50 to 99 employees were designated as medium sized, while those with 100 or more employees were designated as large.

Degree of formalization was measured by a unidimensional 6-item scale developed by Vásquez-Párraga (1990) with an acceptable internal consistency (α = .83). Perceived likelihood of enforcement was measured by respondent's answers to the questions: (1) "Does your company have a code of ethics?" and (2) "How strictly does your company enforce its code of ethics?" Responses of those managers who reported that their firm did not have a code of ethics were assigned the value of zero. Respondents whose firms had a code of ethics responded on a scale from 1 ("not strictly at all") to 5 ("very strictly"). In this way a continuous 5-point scale was developed indicating the degree of ethical enforcement.

Responding sales managers were classified into an F organization when the company had narrow managerial spans of control, large sales force size, large company size (large number of permanent employees), a moderately high degree of formalization, and a code of ethics that was strongly enforced. Conversely, they were classified into an I organization when the company had wide manage-

Table 3.   Pearson Correlation Coefficients
Facilitating vs. Inhibiting Organizations

Variables	DE	TE	EJ	MA	X	SD
Case 1: Overstating Plant Capacity Utilization						
Facilitating Organizations						
X_1 DE--Deontological Evaluations	1.000				.20	.98
X_2 TE--Teleological Evaluations	.026	1.000			.27	.97
Y_1 EJ--Ethical Judgment	.854*	.107	1.000		4.78	2.00
Y_2 MA--Managerial Actions	.628*	.237*	.764*	1.000	5.69	1.60
Inhibiting Organizations						
X_1 DE--Deontological Evaluations	1.000				.06	1.00
X_2 TE--Teleological Evaluations	.076	1.000			.004	1.002
Y_1 EJ--Ethical Judgment	.824*	.176	1.000		4.52	1.99
Y_2 MA--Managerial Actions	.632*	.319*	.767*	1.000	5.44	1.69
Case 2: Over-recommending Expensive Products						
Facilitating Organizations						
X_1 DE--Deontological Evaluations	1.000				.20	.98
X_2 TE--Teleological Evaluations	.026	1.000			.27	.97
Y_1 EJ--Ethical Judgment	.846*	.122	1.000		4.89	2.02
Y_2 MA--Managerial Actions	.712*	.328*	.797*	1.000	5.59	1.83
Inhibiting Organizations						
X_1 DE--Deontological Evaluations	1.000				.06	1.00
X_2 TE--Teleological Evaluations	.076	1.000			.004	1.002
Y_1 EJ--Ethical Judgment	.855*	.199*	1.000		4.54	2.13
Y_2 MA--Managerial Actions	.704*	.305**	.817*	1.000	5.24	1.86

Note: * $p < .01$.

rial spans of control, small sales force size, small company size (few permanent employees), a low degree of formalization, and no code of ethics or a code of ethics that was weakly enforced. About 3 out of 10 ($n = 165$) were classified as being strongly F type, about 5 out of 10 ($n = 250$) were classified as strongly I type, and slightly more than 1 out of 10 ($n = 65$) were neutral. The latter group was deleted from the analysis and the other two were used to test the hypotheses.

ANALYSIS

Descriptive analyses were first performed using correlations. Structural equation modeling was then performed to address the four hypotheses. The simultaneous direct and indirect effects of the independent or exogenous variables (DEs and TEs) on the dependent or endogenous variables (ethical judgments

Table 4. Estimated Unstandardized Structural Parameters and Goodness of Fit Measures (Facilitating vs. Inhibiting Organizations)

Situation 1: Overstating Plant Capacity Utilization			
Direct and Indirect Effects among Variables and Measures of Overall Fit	Unstandardized ML Parameter Estimates		
	Estimate	S.E.	t-Value
Model 1: Facilitating Organizations			
Direct Effects: DE → EJ (γ_1)	.852	.038	22.684
TE → EJ (γ_2)	.053	.038	1.340
TE → MA (γ_3)	.072	.046	1.978
EJ → MA (β)	.747	.046	16.228
Indirect Effects: DE → MA ($\gamma_1\beta$)	.636	.048	
TE → MA ($\gamma_2\beta$)	.063	.028	
Total Effects: TE → MA ($\gamma_3\beta+\beta$)	.157		
Total coeffient of determination for structural equations = .752			
χ^2 (df = 1, $p < .546$)	.36		
Goodness-of-fit Index	.999		
Adjusted Goodness-of-fit Index	.990		
Root Mean Square Residual	.004		
Model 2: Inhibiting Organizations			
Direct Effects: DE → EJ (γ_1)	.815	.035	22.972
TE → EJ (γ_2)	.114	.035	3.213
TE → MA (γ_3)	.190	.040	4.776
EJ → MA (β)	.734	.040	18.452
Indirect Effects: DE → MA ($\gamma_1\beta$)	.598	.042	
TE → MA ($\gamma_2\beta$)	.084	.026	
Total Effects: TE → MA ($\gamma_3\beta+\beta$)	.274		
Total coeffient of determination for structural equations = .718			
χ^2 (df = 1, $p < .550$)	.36		
Goodness-of-fit Index	.999		
Adjusted Goodness-of-fit Index	.993		
Root Mean Square Residual	.004		

and managerial actions), and between the two dependent variables were estimated using the LISREL subprogram for directly observed or manifest variables (Jöreskog & Sörbom, 1989). Two separate LISREL analyses were conducted: one with the responses of managers who were classified within facilitator organizations ($n = 165$) and the other with responses of managers within inhibitor organizations ($n = 250$).

Table 5. Estimated Unstandardized Structural Parameters and
Goodness of Fit Measures (Facilitating vs. Inhibiting Organizations)

Situation 2: Over-recommending Expensive Products

Direct and Indirect Effects among Variables and Measures of Overall Fit	Unstandardized ML Parameter Estimates		
	Estimate	S.E.	t-Value
Model 1: Facilitating Organizations			
Direct Effects: DE → EJ (γ_1)	.843	.038	22.015
TE → EJ (γ_2)	.061	.038	1.822
TE → MA (γ_3)	.065	.041	1.853
EJ → MA (β)	.768	.041	18.710
Indirect Effects: DE → MA ($\gamma_1\beta$)	.648	.045	
TE → MA ($\gamma_2\beta$)	.077	.030	
Total Effects: TE → MA ($\gamma_3\beta+\beta$)	.132		

Total coeffient of determination for
  structural equations = .766

X^2 (df = 1, p < .008)	6.94		
Goodness-of-fit Index	.982		
Adjusted Goodness-of-fit Index	.823		
Root Mean Square Residual	.018		

Model 2: Inhibiting Organizations

	Estimate	S.E.	t-Value
Direct Effects: DE → EJ (γ_1)	.845	.032	26.374
TE → EJ (γ_2)	.135	.032	4.209
TE → MA (γ_3)	.148	.036	4.085
EJ → MA (β)	.787	.036	21.691
Indirect Effects: DE → MA ($\gamma_1\beta$)	.665	.040	
TE → MA ($\gamma_2\beta$)	.106	.026	
Total Effects: TE → MA ($\gamma_3\beta+\beta$)	.254		

Total coeffient of determination for
  structural equations = .765

X^2 (df = 1, p < .282)	1.16		
Goodness-of-fit Index	.998		
Adjusted Goodness-of-fit Index	.977		
Root Mean Square Residual	.006		

Preliminary Analysis

Table 3 contains the correlation coefficients resulting from the two models, F and I, for each ethical situation. A preliminary examination of these
shows: (a) significant and strong correlations between DEs and ethical

judgment for both situations, suggesting that DEs are more important for both organizational frameworks than TEs; (b) significant (but not as strong) correlations between TEs and ethical judgment, implying that TEs acquire some importance in the formation of ethical judgments in the I model only; and (c) significant correlations between both ethical judgments and TEs and the managerial decision to punish (reward) a salesperson's unethical (ethical) behavior.

Overall Fit of the Models

Both models, the "facilitator" (F) and the "inhibitor" (I), fit the data very well as assessed by the four criteria recommended by Jöreskog and Sörbom (1989): χ^2, goodness-of-fit index (GFI), adjusted goodness-of-fit index (AGFI), and root mean square residual (RMSR). The exact indices for each model are given in Tables 4 and 5.

Despite a relatively large sample size, in relation to which the χ^2 measure is sensitive, both models in both situations result in a χ^2 that is acceptably small (ranging from .36 to 6.94). Both GFI and AGFI are regarded as better measures because they are independent of the sample size and relatively robust against departures from normality. Both indices are high (close to one) for both models (ranging from .982 to .999), indicating that the models fit the data very well. In addition, the RMSR is very small for both models, ranging from .004 to .018. Small RMSRs minimize both the values expected from sampling error (Anderson & Gerbing, 1984) and the discrepancies between the observed covariances and the model-implied covariances (Hayduk, 1987). Finally, the total coefficient of determination for structural equations is high for both models (ranging from .718 to .766). This shows the overall strength of the modeled relationships jointly, so that the larger the value of the coefficients (from zero to one), the better the model.

Both models (F and I) provide a similar test of the basic theory (Hunt-Vitell model) in which: (a) both DEs and TEs determine the formation of ethical judgments, (b) TEs have a direct impact on the decision to reward and punish, and (c) DEs do not affect the decision to reward or punish directly, but indirectly through the formation of ethical judgments.

Results of Hypotheses Tests

The hypotheses were tested by the application of LISREL techniques on models representing sales managers in companies characterized by F and I organizational frameworks (Bagozzi & Li, 1989). They were tested in each situation separately. Table 4 shows the LISREL estimates for situation 1 (overstating plant capacity utilization), while Table 5 shows the results for situation 2 (over-recommending expensive products). Statistical significance requires that the *t*-values

Table 6. Summary of Hypotheses and Results

	Organizational Framework	Effects on the Dependent Variable	Nature of Hypothesis Test	Result of the Hypothesis Test in Situation 1	Result of the Hypothesis Test in Situation 2
Hypothesis 1	Facilitator	Ethical judgments are influenced by deontological, but not by teleological evaluations.	γ_1 significant γ_2 not significant	Corroborated	Corroborated
Hypothesis 2	Inhibitor	Ethical judgments are influenced by both deontological and teleological evaluations.	γ_1 significant γ_2 significant	Corroborated	Corroborated
Hypothesis 3	Facilitator	Managerial actions are directly influenced by ethical judgments, but not by teleological evaluations, and thus indirectly influenced only by deontological evaluations through their effects on ethical judgments.	γ_1 significant γ_2 not significant γ_3 significant β significant $(\gamma_1 \times \beta) > \gamma_3 + (\gamma_2 \times \beta)$	Corroborated	Corroborated
Hypothesis 4	Inhibitor	Managerial actions are directly influenced by ethical judgments and teleological evaluations, and thus indirectly influenced by both deontological and teleological evaluations through their effects on ethical judgments.	γ_1 significant γ_2 significant γ_3 significant β significant	Corroborated	Corroborated

corresponding to a path be greater than 2.0 (Jöreskog & Sörbom, 1989). The outcomes of the hypotheses tests are summarized in Table 6.

Organizational Framework and Ethical Judgment

Hypothesis 1 concerns relationships between ethical judgments of sales managers and both DEs and TEs in the F model. Support for Hypothesis 1 requires the presence of a significant path between DEs and ethical judgments and no path or a weaker path between TEs and ethical judgments. For situation 1 (Table 4), the path between DEs and ethical judgments is highly significant ($\gamma_1 = .852$, $t = 22.684$), whereas the path between TEs and ethical judgments is not significant ($\gamma_2 = .053$, $t = 1.340$). Similarly, for situation 2 (Table 5), the path between DEs and ethical judgments is highly significant ($\gamma_1 = .843$, $t = 22.015$) and the path between TEs and ethical judgments is not significant ($\gamma_2 = .061$, $t = 1.820$). Thus, Hypothesis 1 is supported in both situations.

Hypothesis 2 concerns the same paths in the I model. Support for Hypothesis 2 requires significant paths from both TEs and DEs to ethical judgments in the I model. For the first situation (Table 4), significant paths appear between both DEs and ethical judgments ($\gamma_1 = .815$, $t = 22.972$) and TEs and ethical judgments ($\gamma_2 = .114$, $t = 3.213$). Similarly, in the second situation (Table 5), both paths are significant ($\gamma_1 = .845$, $t = 26.374$; $\gamma_2 = .135$, $t = 4.209$). Thus, Hypothesis 2 is supported for both situations.

These suggest that in both the F and I models managers rely primarily on DEs when forming their ethical judgments. However, the managers in the I model rely on TEs in addition to DEs to a greater extent than the managers in the F model do.

Organizational Framework and Management's Actions

Hypotheses 3 and 4 concern the relationship between both DEs and TEs and management's actions in both frameworks. A common base for both hypotheses is a significant and large indirect path from DEs ($\gamma_1\beta$), through ethical judgments to management's actions in both models. Corroboration of both hypotheses requires a greater total effect of TEs on management's actions in the I model (Hypothesis 3) than in the F model (Hypothesis 4) ($[\gamma_3 + \gamma_2\beta]_I > [\gamma_3 + \gamma_2\beta]_F$).

The LISREL estimates for the I model in situation 1 (Table 4) show highly significant paths between both DEs and ethical judgments ($\gamma = .852$, $t = 22.684$) and ethical judgments and management's actions ($\beta = .747$, $t = 16.228$), producing a large and significant positive indirect effect between DEs and management's actions ($\gamma_1\beta = .636$). Similarly, in the I model, there are positive highly significant paths between DEs and ethical judgments ($\gamma_1 = .815$, $t = 22.972$) and between ethical judgments and management's actions ($\beta = .734$, $t = 18.452$), indicating the presence of a significant and large indirect effect from DEs to management's actions through ethical judgments ($\gamma_1\beta = .598$).

The direct effects of TEs on ethical judgments ($\gamma_2 = .053$, $t = 1.340$) are not significant in the F model and their direct effects on the manager's decision to reward or punish ($\gamma_3 = .072$, $t = 1.978$) are also not significant. In contrast, the direct path from TEs to management's actions is positive and significant ($\gamma_3 = .190$, $t = 4.776$) in the I model, and there is an indirect path through ethical judgments ($\gamma_2\beta = .084$) to management's actions, adding to a total effect of .274. A total effect of .274 in the I model compares favorably to a total effect of .157 in the F model, and thus Hypotheses 3 and 4 are fulfilled in situation 1.

The results in situation 2 (Table 5) are similar. Once again, the paths are positive and significant between DEs and ethical judgments ($\gamma_1 = .843$, $t = 22.015$ in the F model and $\gamma_1 = .845$, $t = 26.374$ in the I model), and between ethical judgments and management's actions ($\beta = .768$, $t = 18.710$ in the F model and $\beta = .787$, $t = 21.691$ in the I model), indicating a significant indirect effect from DEs to management's actions through ethical judgments ($\gamma_1\beta = .648$ in the F model and $\gamma_1\beta = .665$ in the I model). Subsequently, the direct effects of TEs on the manager's decision to reward or punish in the F model are smaller and not statistically significant ($\gamma_3 = .065$, $t = 1.853$). In contrast, in the I model, both the direct and indirect paths from TEs to management's actions are positive and significant (direct: $\gamma_3 = .148$, $t = 4.085$; indirect: $\gamma_2\beta = .106$), with a combined total effect of .254. A total effect of .254 in the I model compares favorably to a total effect of .132 in the F model, and thus Hypotheses 3 and 4 are also supported in situation 2.

DISCUSSION

The purpose of the study was to empirically test some hypotheses regarding the moderating impact of two organizational frameworks on the sales manager's ethical decision making. Empirical results from this research provide support for previously untested relationships between organizational frameworks and the process of ethical decision making. Although DEs and TEs determine the process of ethical decision making (Hunt & Vásquez-Párraga, 1993; Vásquez-Párraga, 1990), the organizational framework influences the way such considerations impact on both the formation of ethical judgments and the type of action that should be taken to either encourage ethical behavior or discourage unethical behavior.

The results reveal that relatively narrow spans of control, large sales forces, large companies, moderate formalization of policies and procedures, and high likelihood of stated policies and procedures enforcement facilitate the formation of ethical judgments and management's actions on the basis of deontological evaluations alone, thus favoring ethical "clarity." Conversely, wide spans of control, small sales forces, small companies, low degree of formalization, and low likelihood of enforcement inhibit the formation of ethical judgments and management's actions by requiring that both deontological and teleological evaluations be performed, thus favoring ethical "confusion."

Important differences exist between the ethical thinking of sales managers operating in an F model and that in an I model. Managers in an F model rely primarily on DEs when forming their ethical judgments. Because they are involved personally in directing and monitoring the manner in which salespeople perform their jobs, they seem to be better able to judge the behavior as right or wrong based on the moral content of the act with less attention to the consequences produced. Understandably, the clarity of managerial direction to salespeople operating in systems in which appropriate behavior of sales personnel is spelled out in some detail, translates into the managers' ability in ethical decision making.

In contrast, managers in an I model use DEs but also tend to be influenced by TEs. Because they evaluate salespeople's performance by monitoring their results, they tend to pay more attention to the consequences of the behavior, regardless of the moral content of the act, to judge them right or wrong.

The findings also support the notion that in an F model, as opposed to an I model, sales managers are more likely to focus on the deontological nature of ethical situations rather than on TEs when deciding on the managerial action to follow. Such managers seem to have a moral understanding of what constitutes an unethical behavior, as distinguished from a behavior that is merely bad for the firm, and thus punish it based on the gravity of the violation of the moral standard. Conversely, managers in an I model are somewhat deceived by the consequences because they combine moral evaluations with utilitarian or egoist concerns to both judge the behavior and determine the degree of punishment or reward.

MANAGERIAL IMPLICATIONS

A sales manager's ability to accurately distinguish between unethical selling actions and negative consequences to the firm is important, because the manager is the one who supervises sales personnel. If sales managers cannot distinguish between ethical and unethical outcomes, how are they going to train, instruct, and coach salespeople to behave ethically in the field? There is frequently a good deal of ambiguity in ethical situations that arise on the sales job, that is, when a moral condition is combined with negative consequences or an immoral condition is combined with positive consequences to the firm. Salespeople need some basis on which to make decisions when ambiguous situations arise. At times, ambiguity can be lessened by the manager's leadership. Indeed, there is a good deal of evidence that employees adopt the ethical perspective of their managers (Caywood & Laczniak, 1986; Ferrell & Fraedrich, 1988; Newstrom & Ruch, 1975; Podsakoff, 1982). Hence, sales managers need to be very clear in their own minds about what constitutes ethical actions and how they should be enforced if they expect their subordinate salespeople to act ethically in their sales interactions.

In line with behavioral learning theory that suggests that salespeople will increase behavior that is rewarded and decrease behavior that is punished (Scott, Swan, Wilson, & Roberts, 1986), this study shows that the severity with which a manager punishes ethical infractions or the benevolence with which he/she rewards ethical behavior reflects the type of behavior that is discouraged or encouraged, respectively, in a given firm. Implementation of a reward/punishment system, however, is facilitated or restricted depending on the type of framework that prevails in the organization.

The findings of this study strongly suggest that the F organization facilitates the ability on the part of managers to make correct ethical judgments and to take appropriate actions that either encourage ethical behavior or discourage unethical behavior. Firms that are sincerely interested in making certain that their sales forces are performing ethically, should adopt an F model of sales management, as opposed to an I model. As an example, in an F model an appropriate managerial strategy would be to discuss the outcomes with the salesperson from the point of view of selling strategy/actions, and to use the information feedback received from the negative consequence as the basis for improving later sales efforts.

Yet, not many companies seem to support an F model and, thus, managers in I companies have to, on the one hand, adapt to the conditions of their work and, on the other hand, look for change. Managers in an I model can help identify and start changing particular elements of the organization that can be improved in the short term (e.g., width of span of control and enforcement of policies). Company size, sales force size, and formalization can only change slowly, over time. Span of control and enforcement of rules can change faster. Thus, smaller, less formalized organizations may improve their ethical climate by narrowing their spans of control, implementing policies (e.g., formalization of procedures), and enforcing policies, so that managers can monitor and direct more closely salespeople's behavior. Guidance can be obtained from the results of this research, that is, the relationships between ethical outcomes and some indicators of organizational framework.

In this study, the severity of the punishments and the benevolence of the rewards were affected by span of control and by the degree of enforcement of ethical codes, as well as by the managers' ethical judgments. Managers with wide spans of control were more likely to punish salespeople for teleological infractions and less likely to punish them for perceived deontological infractions. This strongly suggests that those firms who wish to encourage ethical actions on the part of salespeople should not overburden their managers with so much supervisory responsibility that they are not able to give sufficient attention to individual salespeople. By not being aware of the details of each salesperson's situation, a manager can lose sight of the ethical issues underlying a sales outcome and reward/punish the salesperson inappropriately, thus encouraging unethical behavior.

This also suggests that the approach of decreasing the numbers of sales supervisors and increasing their spans of control (Taylor, 1992), is a dangerous one, likely to result in increased ethical problems in the field. The decreased contact between supervisors and salespeople is likely to result in a decreased understanding of the moral dilemmas a salesperson is facing and the giving of inappropriate rewards/punishments for ethical infractions. Companies that are eliminating middle managers must be certain that they are not also removing management's ability to stay on top of factors impacting upon the ethical behavior of sales personnel. Such firms might attempt to counteract the problems by enacting strong codes of ethics and making certain that they are enforced strongly. Managers operating in firms in which codes of ethics are enforced are more likely than others to reward/punish ethical/unethical behavior appropriately.

Formalization can be achieved with more time and more effort. Moderate formalization seems to support the manager's ability to make appropriate ethical judgments. In a moderately formalized organization (avoiding extreme bureaucratic formalization), rules and regulations are spelled out in order to fulfill stated objectives. Managers and salespeople are likely to be more confident of the appropriateness of their actions. Salespeople are likely to feel more confident that they are carrying out the wishes of their companies. Ambiguities are resolved, and the ethical nature of the situation is made clear. In a formalized company, ethical policies are likely to be spelled out, once again removing ambiguity (Nwachukwu & Vitell, 1997).

The parameters of appropriate actions need to be spelled out. Salespeople in the field frequently must take action without having the opportunity to consult with their managers, and need to have the bases for making ethical decisions ingrained in their minds. Salespeople also need the ability to recognize situations and actions that are inherently unethical when they arise. Thus, the ethical implications of different situations need to be clarified.

Dubinsky et al. (1992) underscored the extent of the ethical confusion by salespeople in the marketplace. They found that salespeople do not always know whether their firms have company directives that focus on particular situations. Thus, rules should be "formalized" both for recognizing ethical problems and choosing appropriate selling actions when they arise. Companies must make certain that they are communicated to their managers and to sales personnel.

Limitations of the Study and Suggestions for Future Research

This study is limited by the number of situations used. New situations will allow for replication, for testing the role of each indicator of organizational framework in the process of ethical decision making. Replications using different situations will also reveal the level of generality of the basic relationships examined in this research and the level of specificity of the relationships between indicators and ethical outcomes.

Respondents to this study were largely male (94.3%), thus it was not possible to examine gender differences in ethical judgments and managerial actions. Prior research has suggested gender differences in the bases of moral reasoning (e.g., Gilligan, 1987; Thoma, 1986), and these differences have been observed in the sales force context (Dawson, 1992, 1997; Stevenson & Bodkin, 1994). Similarly, gender differences have been observed in responses to organizational indicators (Tharenou, Latimer, & Conroy, 1994). Future research should consider the moderating impact of gender differences in the manner in which organizational factors facilitate or inhibit ethical decision making.

Although we were able to analyze the key elements of organizational frameworks and their impact on salespeople's ethical decision making, future studies should include others, particularly those that are new in ever-changing organizations particularly in the area of information and communication. In addition, further research can address other important relationships. In particular, the relationship between ethical outcomes and the nature and extent of management coordination and the type and complexity of performance evaluation procedures should be investigated.

APPENDIX

Table A1. Experimental Treatment

	Deontologically Unethical Condition	Deontologically Ethical Condition

Scenario 1: Overstating Plant Capacity

Positive Consequences

Deontologically Unethical Condition:

Larry Wilson, a salaried salesperson you supervise, has been one of your top performers over the last several years. Recently, in an attempt to negotiate the best price, Larry has been telling purchasing agents that the utilization of plant capacity is at a very high level because of the popularity of his company's product. Larry does this even when utilization of plant capacity is low. Purchasing agents are generally unaware of Larry's overstatements. Indeed, Larry's tactic has resulted in his average prices being higher than most other salespeople's and a rise in his total dollar sales.

Deontologically Ethical Condition:

Larry Wilson, a salaried salesperson you supervise, has been one of your top performers over the last several years. Salespeople at Ajax Manufacturing sometimes overstate their present plant capacity utilization, believing this will help them negotiate the best price with customers. Larry thinks that overstating plant utilization is an improper sales tactic and expressed this opinion in a recent sales meeting. Larry discussed the case of a colleague in another company who had been overstating capacity utilization until he lost credibility with many of his customers as they discovered he was misleading them. Larry obtained some support in the meeting but also received some criticism. Several months later, salespeople who joined Larry's side had increased sales, whereas those who did not follow Larry's advice had lost credibility and experienced declines in their sales.

(continued)

167

Table A1. (Continued)

	Deontologically Unethical Condition	Deontologically Ethical Condition
Scenario 1: Overstating Plant Capacity		
Negative Consequences	Larry Wilson, a salaried salesperson you supervise, has been one of your top performers over the last several years. Recently, in an attempt to negotiate the best price, Larry has been telling purchasing agents that the utilization of plant capacity is at a very high level because of the popularity of his company's product. Larry does this even when utilization of plant capacity is low. However, during a recent sales call, Larry lost all credibility with a prospect because the prospect knew through a personal friend that Larry's plant was operating significantly below capacity. The prospect figured that if Larry was willing to mislead a customer with inflated accounts of plant usage, he might also be less than honest with regard to other, more important issues. From that point on, Larry had trouble just getting in to see this prospect.	Larry Wilson, a salaried salesperson you supervise, has been one of your top performers over the last several years. Salespeople at Ajax Manufacturing sometimes overstate their present plant capacity utilization, believing this will help them negotiate the best price with customers. Larry thinks that overstating plant utilization is an improper sales tactic and expressed this opinion in a recent sales meeting. Larry discussed the case of a colleague in another company who had been overstating capacity utilization until he lost credibility with many of his customers as they discovered he was misleading them. Larry obtained some support in the meeting but also received some criticism. Several months later, salespeople who followed Larry's recommendation had experienced declines in their sales, whereas those who did not follow Larry's advice had increased sales.

(continued)

Table A1. (Continued)

	Deontologically Unethical Condition	Deontologically Ethical Condition
Scenario 2: Over-recommending Expensive Products		
Positive Consequences	Tom Hansen, a salaried salesperson you supervise, has been one of your top performers over the last several years. Occasionally, Tom's customers ask him which of his products he recommends for their company. Regardless of real customer needs, Tom recommends one of the more expensive items in his product line. His practice has been relatively effective, resulting in increased sales of the more expensive products and higher profits for the company.	Tom Hansen, a salaried salesperson you supervise, has been one of your top performers over the last several years. Some salespeople at Century Fashion tend to "over-recommend" the company's products by encouraging customers to buy the more expensive items in the product line regardless of actual customer needs. Tom does not engage in this practice, believing it to be an improper sales tactic. When asked for advice about products, Tom first asks the customer what his/her needs are and then recommends the product that will best satisfy the customer at the minimum price. One customer learned of Tom's good recommendation and called him to examine the possibility of buying other products. Similarly, other customers learned about Tom's approach and soon Tom's sales increased substantially.
Negative Consequences	Tom Hansen, a salaried salesperson you supervise, has been one of your top performers over the last several years. Occasionally, Tom's customers ask him which of his products he recommends for their company. Regardless of customer needs, Tom recommends one of the more expensive items in his product line. One customer learned of Tom's over-recommending of more expensive products from a competing rep and all future business with this customer was lost.	Tom Hansen, a salaried salesperson you supervise, has been one of your top performers over the last several years. Some salespeople at Century Fashion tend to "over-recommend" the company's products by encouraging customers to buy the more expensive items in the product line regardless of actual customer needs. Tom does not engage in this practice, believing it to be an improper sales tactic. When asked for advice about products, Tom first asks the customer what his/her needs are and then recommends the product that will best satisfy the customer at the minimum price. However, Tom's recent sales have lagged far behind those of salespeople who have adopted the "over-recommending" sales tactic. Some managers at Century Fashion believe that recent declines in sales and profits are the result of salespeople like Tom not emphasizing enough expensive products in their sales presentations.

REFERENCES

Adler, P.S., & Borys, B. (1996). Two types of bureaucracy: Enabling and coercive. *Administrative Science Quarterly, 41*(March), 61-89.

Agarwal, S. (1993). Influence of formalization on role stress, organizational commitment, and work alienation of salespersons: A cross-national comparative study. *Journal of International Business Studies, 24*(4), 715-739.

Akaah, I.P., & Riordan, E.A. (1989). Judgments of marketing professionals about ethical issues in marketing research: A replication and extension. *Journal of Marketing Research, 26*(February), 112-120.

Anderson, J.C., & Gerbing, D.W. (1984). The effect of sampling error on convergence, improper solutions, and goodness-of-fit indices for maximum likelihood confirmatory factor analysis. *Psychometrica, 49*(June), 155-173.

Anderson, E., & Oliver, R.L. (1987). Perspectives on behavior-based versus outcome-based sales force control systems. *Journal of Marketing, 51*(October), 77-88.

Bagozzi, R.P., & Yi, Y. (1989). On the use of structural equation models in experimental designs. *Journal of Marketing Research, 26*(August), 271-284.

Bellizzi, J.A., & Hite, R.E. (1989). Supervising unethical sales force behavior. *Journal of Marketing, 53*(April), 36-47.

Bingham, F.G., & Raffield, B.T., III. (1989). An overview of ethical considerations in industrial marketing. In J.M. Hawes & J. Thanopoulos (Eds.), *Developments of marketing science* (Vol. XII, pp. 17-20). Orlando, FL: Academy of Marketing Science.

Boedecker, K.A., Morgan, F.W., & Stoltman, J.J. (1991). Legal dimensions of salespersons' statements: A review and managerial suggestions. *Journal of Marketing, 56*(January), 70-80.

Bozeman, B., & Scott, P. (1996). Bureaucratic red tape and formalization: Untangling conceptual knots. *American Review of Public Administration, 26*(March), 1-17.

Brady, F.N., & Dunn, C. (1995). Business meta-ethics: An analysis of two theories. *Business Ethics Quarterly, 5*(3), 385-398.

Brigley, S. (1995). Business ethics research: A cultural perspective. *Business Ethics: A European Perspective, 4*(1), 17-23.

Caruana, A., Morris, M.H., & Vella, A.J. (1998). The effect of centralization and formalization on entrepreneurship in export firms. *Journal of Small Business Management, 36*(January), 16-29.

Caywood, C.L., & Laczniak, G.R. (1986). Ethics and personal selling: Death of a salesman as an ethical primer. *Journal of Personal Selling and Sales Management, 6*(August), 81-88.

Chan, R.Y. (1996). Organizational practices and management style of major multinational banks in Hong-Kong: An exploratory study. *International Journal of Management, 13*(September), 314-322.

Childers, T.L., Dubinsky, A.J., & Skinner, S.J. (1990). Leadership substitutes as moderators of sales supervisory behavior. *Journal of Business Research, 21*, 363-382.

Chonko, L.B. (1982). The relationship of span of control to sales representatives' experienced role conflict and role ambiguity. *Academy of Management Journal, 25*(2), 452-456.

Chonko, L.B., & Burnett, J.J. (1983). Measuring the importance of ethical situations as a source of role conflict: A survey of salespeople, sales managers, and sales support personnel. *Journal of Personal Selling and Sales Management, 3*(May), 41-47.

Chonko, L.B., & Hunt, S.D. (1985). Ethics and marketing management: An empirical examination. *Journal of Business Research, 13*(August), 339-359.

Collier, J. (1995). The virtuous organization. *Business Ethics: A European Perspective, 4*(3), 143-149.

Coughlin, A.T., & Sen, S. (1989). Sales force compensation theory and managerial implications. *Marketing Science, 8*(Fall), 324-342.

Dahlstrom, R., & Nygaard, A. (1995). An exploratory investigation of interpersonal trust in new and mature market economies. *Journal of Retailing, 71*(Winter), 339-361.

Dalrymple, D.J., & Cron, W.L. (1992). *Sales management* (4th ed.). New York: Wiley.

Dawson, L.M. (1992). Will feminization change the ethics of the sales profession? *Journal of Personal Selling and Sales Management, 12*(Winter), 21-32.

Dawson, L.M. (1997). Ethical differences between men and women in the sales profession. *Journal of Business Ethics, 16*, 1143-1152.

Di Toro, P. (1995). Building an ethical organization. *Business Ethics: A European Perspective, 4*(1), 43-51.

Dubinsky, A.J., & Barry, T.E. (1982). A survey of sales management practices. *Industrial Marketing Management, 11*(April), 133-141.

Dubinsky, A.J., Jolson, M.A., Michaels, R.E., Kotabe, M., & Lim, C.U. (1992). Ethical perceptions of field sales personnel: An empirical assessment. *Journal of Personal Selling and Sales Management, 12*(Fall), 9-22.

Etzioni, A. (1988). *The moral dimension: Toward a new economics.* New York: The Free Press.

Ferrell, O.C., & Fraedrich, J.P. (1988). A descriptive approach to understand ethical behavior. In S. Shapiro & A.H. Walle (Eds.), *Marketing: A return to the broader dimensions*, Winter Educator's Conference. Chicago: American Marketing Association.

Ferrell, O.C., & Gresham, L.G. (1985). A contingency framework for understanding ethical decision making in marketing. *Journal of Marketing, 49*(Summer), 87-96.

Ferrell, O.C., Gresham, L.G., & Fraedrich, J. (1989). A synthesis of ethical decision models for marketing *Journal of Macro-marketing, 9*(Fall), 55-64.

Ferrell, O.C., & Skinner, S.J. (1988). Ethical behavior and bureaucratic structure in marketing research organizations. *Journal of Marketing Research, 25*(February), 103-109.

Fraedrich, J.P., Ferrell, O.C., & Jones, K. (1991). An empirical investigation into the ethical philosophies of managers. In Terry Childers et al. (Eds.), *AMA Winter Educator's Conference* (p. 463). Chicago: American Marketing Association.

Gilligan, C. (1987). Moral orientation and moral development. In E.F. Kittay & D.T. Meyers (Eds.), *Women and moral theory* (pp. 19-33). Totowa, NJ: Rowman and Littlefield.

Guest, D.E., & Peccei, R. (1994). The nature and causes of effective human resource management. *British Journal of Industrial Relations, 32*(June), 219-242.

Guzzo, R., & Gannett, B. (1988). The nature of facilitators and inhibitors of effective task performance. In D. Schoorman & B. Schneider (Eds.), *Facilitating work effectiveness* (pp. 148-155). Lexington, MA: Lexington Books.

Hall, R.H., Haas, J.E., & Johnson, N.J. (1967). Organizational size, complexity, and formalization. *American Sociological Review, 73*, 903-912.

Hayduk, L.A. (1987). *Structural equation modeling with LISREL: Essentials and advances.* Baltimore: The Johns Hopkins University Press.

Hegarty, W.H., & Sims, H.P. (1979). Organizational philosophy, policies, and objectives related to unethical decision behavior: A laboratory experiment. *Journal of Applied Psychology, 64*(3), 331-338.

Hoffman, K.D., Howe, V., & Hardigree, D.W. (1991). Ethical dilemmas faced in the selling of complex services: Significant others and competitive pressures. *Journal of Personal Selling and Sales Management, 11*(Fall), 13-25.

Hunt, S.D., Chonko, L.B., & Wilcox, J.B. (1984). Ethical problems of marketing researchers. *Journal of Marketing Research, 22*(August), 309-324.

Hunt, S.D., & Vásquez-Párraga, A.Z. (1993). Organizational consequences, marketing ethics, and salesforce supervision. *Journal of Marketing Research, 30*(February), 78-90.

Hunt, S.D., & Vitell, S. (1986). A general theory of marketing ethics. *Journal of Macromarketing, 6*(Spring), 5-16.

Hunt, S.D., Wood, V.R., & Chonko, L.B. (1989). Corporate ethical values and organizational commitment in marketing. *Journal of Marketing, 53*(July), 79-90.

Jobber, D., Holey, G.J., & Shipley, D. (1993). Organizational size and sales force evaluation practices. *Journal of Personal Selling and Sales Management, 13*(Spring), 37-48.

John, G., & Weitz, B. (1989). Sales force compensation: An empirical investigation of factors related to use of salary versus incentive compensation. *Journal of Marketing Research, 26*(February), 1-14.

Jolson, M.A. (1989). Canned adaptiveness: A new direction for modern salesmanship. *Business Horizons* (January-February), 8-13.

Jones, T. (1991). Ethical decision making by individuals in organizations: An issue-contingent model. *Academy of Management Review, 16*(2), 366-395.

Jöreskog, K.G., & Sörbom, D. (1989). *LISREL 7: A Guide to the program and applications.* Chicago: SPSS.

Kaikati, J., & Label, W.A. (1980). American bribery legislation: An obstacle to international management. *Journal of Marketing, 44*(Fall), 38-43.

Kant, I. (1959). *Foundations of the metaphysics of morals* (L.W. Beck, trans.). New York: Bobbs-Merrill. (Originally published in 1785)

Katz, D., & Kahn, R. (1978). *The social psychology of organizations.* New York: Wiley.

Kelly, S.W., & Dorsch, M.J. (1991). Ethical climate, organizational commitment, and indebtedness among purchasing executives. *Journal of Personal Selling and Sales Management, 9*(4), 55-66.

Kelly, S.W., Longfellow, T., & Malehorn, J. (1996). Organizational determinants of service employees' exercise of routine, and deviant discretion. *Journal of Retailing, 72*(Summer), 135-157.

Laczniak, G.R., & Inderrieden, E.J. (1987). The influence of stated organizational concern upon ethical decision making. *Journal of Business Ethics, 6*(May), 297-307.

Malik, S.D., & Wilson, D.O. (1995). Factors influencing engineers' perceptions of organizational support for innovation. *Journal of Engineering and Technology Management, 12*(December), 201-218.

Marden, M.J. (1989). The salesperson: Clerk, con man, or professional. *Business and Professional Ethics Journal, 8*(1), 3-23.

McMahon, C. (1995). The ontological and moral status of organizations. *Business Ethics Quarterly, 5*(3), 541-554.

Mellor, S., Mathieu, J.E., & Swim, J.K. (1994). Cross-level analysis of the influence of local union structure on women's and men's union commitment. *Journal of Applied Psychology, 79*(April), 203-210.

Menon, A., Bharadwaj, S.G., & Howell, R. (1996). The quality and effectiveness of marketing strategy: Effects of functional and dysfunctional conflict in intraorganizational relationships. *Journal of the Academy of Marketing Science, 24*(Fall), 299-313.

Michaels, R.E., Cron, W.L., Dubinsky, A.J., & Joachimsthaler, E.A. (1988). Influence of formalization on the organizational commitment and work alienation of salespeople and industrial buyers. *Journal of Marketing Research, 25*(November), 376-383.

Moenaert, R.K., Souder, W.E., De Meyer, A., & Deschoolmeester, D. (1994). R&D—Marketing integration mechanism, communication flows, and innovation success. *Journal of Product Innovation Management, 11*(January), 31-45.

Moorman, C., Deshpande, R., & Zaltman, G. (1993). Factors affecting trust in market research relationships. *Journal of Marketing, 57*(January), 81-101.

Muczyk, J.P., & Gable, M. (1987). Managing sales performance through a comprehensive performance appraisal system. *Journal of Personal Selling and Sales Management, 7*(May), 41-51.

Murphy, P., & Laczniak, G.R. (1981). Marketing ethics: A review with implications for managers, educators and researchers. In B.M. Enis & K.J. Roering (Eds.), *Review of marketing* (pp. 251-266). Chicago: American Marketing Association.

Newstrom, J.W., & Ruch, W.A. (1975). The ethics of management and the management of ethics. *MSU Business Topics, 23*(Winter), 29-37.

Nwachukwu, S., & Vitell, S.J. (1997). The influence of corporate culture on managerial ethical judgments. *Journal of Business Ethics, 16*(June), 757-776.

Phillips, M.J. (1995). Corporate moral responsibility: When it may matter. *Business Ethics Quarterly, 5*(3), 555-576.

Podsakoff, P.M. (1982). Determinants of a supervisor's use of rewards and punishments: A literature review and suggestions for further research. *Organizational Behavior and Human Performance, 29*(February), 58-83.

Podsakoff, P.M., Williams, L.J., & Todor, W.T. (1986). Effects of organizational formalization on alienation among professionals and nonprofessionals. *Academy of Management Journal, 29*(December), 820-831.

Pugh, D.S., & Hickson, D.J. (1973). The comparative study of organizations. In G. Salaman & K. Thompson (Eds.), *People and organizations* (pp. 50-66). London: Longman.

Scott, R.A., Swan, J.E., Wilson, M.E., & Roberts, J.J. (1986). Organizational behavior modification: A general motivational tool for sales management. *Journal of Personal Selling and Sales Management, 6*(August), 61-70.

Singhapakdi, A., Kraft, K.L., Vitell, S.J., & Rallapalli, K.C. (1995). The perceived importance of ethics and social responsibility on organizational effectiveness: A survey of marketers. *Journal of the Academy of Marketing Science, 23*(1), 49-56.

Singhapakdi, A., & Vitell, S.J. (1990). Marketing ethics: Factors influencing perceptions of ethical problems and alternatives. *Journal of Macromarketing* (Spring), 4-18.

Singhapakdi, A., & Vitell, S.J. (1991). Analyzing the ethical decision making of sales professionals. *Journal of Personal Selling and Sales Management, 11*(Fall), 1-12.

Smyth, R.C. (1968). Financial incentives for salesmen. *Harvard Business Review, 46*(January-February), 109-117.

Sohi, R., Smith, D.C., & Ford, N.M. (1996). How does sharing a sales force between multiple divisions affect salespeople? *Journal of the Academy of Marketing Science, 24*(Summer), 195-207.

Steel, R.P., & Mento, A.J. (1986). Opportunity knocks: The impact of situational constraints on relationships between job performance criteria. *Organizational Behavior and Human Decision Processes, 37*, 254-265.

Stevenson, T.H., & Bodkin, D.C. (1994). Sales ethics: Are there gender-related differences in the ranks of potential salespeople? In E.J. Wilson & W.C. Black (Eds.), *Developments in marketing science* (Vol. 17, pp. 20-23). Coral Gables, FL: Academy of Marketing Science.

Still, R.R., Cundiff, E.W., & Govoni, N.A.P. (1988). *Sales management* (5th ed.). Englewood Cliffs, NJ: Prentice-Hall.

Taylor, T.C. (1992). Back from the future. *Sales and Marketing Management, 144*(June), 46-56, 60.

Tharenou, P., Latimer, S., & Conroy, D. (1994). How do you make it to the top?: An examination of influences on women's and men's managerial advancement. *Academy of Management Journal, 37*, 899-931.

Thoma, S.J. (1986). Estimating gender differences in the comprehension and preference of moral issues. *Developmental Review, 6*, 165-180.

Van Fleet, D.D. (1983). Span of management research and issues. *Academy of Management Journal, 4*, 546-552.

Vásquez-Párraga, A.Z. (1990). *Organizational consequences and marketing ethics: A study of marketing managers' propensity to reward or discipline salespeople's ethical and unethical behavior*. Doctoral dissertation, College of Business Administration, Texas Tech University.

Velasquez, M. (1982). *Business ethics: Concepts and cases*. Englewood Cliffs, NJ: Prentice-Hall.

Victor, B., & Cullen, J.B. (1988). The organizational bases of ethical work climate. *Administrative Science Quarterly, 33*(March), 101-125.

Wallach, M.H., & Wallach, L. (1983). *Psychology's sanction for selfishness*. San Francisco, CA: W.H. Freeman.

Weaver, K.M., & Ferrell, O.C. (1977). The impact of corporate policy on reported ethical beliefs and behavior of marketing practitioners. In B.A. Greenberg & D.N. Bellenger (Eds.), *Contemporary marketing thought* (pp. 477-481). Chicago: American Marketing Association.

Wiseman, F., & Billington, M. (1984). Comment on a standard definition of response rates. *Journal of Marketing Research, 21*(August), 336-338.

Wotruba, T.R. (1990). Comprehensive framework for the analysis of ethical behavior, with a focus on sales organizations. *Journal of Personal Selling and Sales Management, 10*(Spring), 29-42.

"SOME DAYS ARE BETTER THAN OTHERS":
BEER COMMERCIALS AND A QUESTION OF ETHICS

Joyce M. Wolburg, Roxanne Hovland, and Ronald E. Hopson

ABSTRACT

This research addresses the ethical question of whether beer ads contain elements that directly tap into the psychological profile of recovering alcoholics—a special market whose needs have not been addressed by advertisers. The study explores two alternative ethical stances on the issue of alcohol advertising, and it examines the content of beer advertising for elements associated with problematic modes of experience previously identified for people in treatment for alcohol addiction: difficulties with relationships, a disrupted sense of time, an inability to express intense emotions, and a lack of self-efficacy.

Beer ads contained appeals to all of these elements—a finding that suggests the persuasive strategy may be particularly compelling to alcoholics. Consequently,

Research in Marketing, Volume 15, pages 175-202.
Copyright © 1999 by JAI Press Inc.
All rights of reproduction in any form reserved.
ISBN: 0-7623-566-5

further research is needed to investigate the impact of these commercials on alcoholics in order to provide guidelines for advertisers.

INTRODUCTION

The relationship between the advertising of alcoholic beverages and the consumption of alcohol has been the subject of considerable research and debate. Most researchers have attempted to discover a linear, cause and effect relationship between advertising and consumption; however, research has failed to provide definitive answers. While some studies have reported that brand-level advertising only resulted in brand switching and did not increase the overall size of the market (Duffy, 1989; Guis, 1996; Lee & Tremblay, 1992), others claimed that measurement difficulties in econometric analyses may have limited the ability to detect effects (Smart, 1988). Given that the research comes from a limited effects paradigm and the emphasis on communication has been the transmission of information rather than ritual aspects (Carey, 1989), it is not surprising that the results have been insignificant. For many, the lack of a clear relationship has minimized the role of advertising to that of a factor that merely enables manufacturers to gain market share at the expense of rival brands. By taking this position, other effects of alcohol advertising may have gone undetected.

Other research has shown that advertising bears a different type of influence than the linear, cause and effect relationship. In a study that examined the effects of advertising on recovering alcoholics, advertising was identified as a factor that triggers the impulse to drink (Treise, Taylor, & Wells, 1994). Certain images with music and party scenes were particularly troubling, and many recovering alcoholics reported a variety of coping strategies including reinterpreting the ads by recalling negative aspects of alcohol and attempting to avoid beer advertising altogether, lest they jeopardize their recovery. Additional studies support these findings and show that alcoholics in treatment often try to counterargue the advertising appeal (Fisher & Cook, 1995; Sobell, Sobell, Toneatto, & Leo, 1993). Treise, Taylor, and Wells (1994) further note that their examination of recovering alcoholics in a natural setting revealed an advertising effect not found in studies using the more traditional methods of surveys, laboratory experiments, field studies, and content analyses.

When these findings are examined in light of psychological research on the addictive experience, a new question arises. Do beer ads contain elements that directly tap into the psychological profile of those recovering from alcohol addiction? This study seeks to answer the question by examining the elements in televised ads for both beer and a control product; however, it begins by recognizing the scope of the problems associated with alcohol, examining the ethical and legal issues surrounding alcohol advertising, addressing theoretical perspectives, reviewing the advertising and psychological literature, and describing four problematic modes of experience in alcohol addiction. Within this context we discuss the meaning of the elements and return to the issue of ethics.

Scope of the Problem

Alcohol abuse and dependence directly affect about 10 percent of the U.S. adult population, with the total economic cost in 1990 including treatment, support of persons with alcohol problems, value of lost output from reduced productivity, lost work days, and losses because of premature death estimated at $98.6 billion (Rice, 1993). These figures show a 40 percent increase during the five-year period from 1985 to 1990. Statistics further define the magnitude of the problem, for the National Highway Traffic Safety Administration (NHTSA, 1994) reports that 50 percent to 60 percent of the fatal highway accidents involve alcohol, while 35 percent of all accidental fall fatalities, 28 percent of all suicides, 45 percent of all accidental fire fatalities, and 38 percent of all accidental drownings are alcohol related (Archer, Grant, & Dawson, 1995). Alcohol consumption has also been associated with unplanned and unsafe sexual activity, physical and sexual assault, unintentional injuries, other criminal violations, interpersonal problems, physical or cognitive impairment, and poor academic performance (Hanson & Engs, 1992; Presley, Meilman & Lyerla, 1993; Wechsler & Issac, 1992).

Ethical and Legal Issues

For a legal but potentially harmful product, the advertising of alcoholic beverages raises ethical considerations beyond those for more benign products. In an evaluation of business ethics, Rotzoll and Haefner (1996) find that advertising is criticized either for being "unprincipled or for utilizing principles seen as inadequate for the task" (p. 198). Essentially, they note two fundamental ethical systems that operate in the business world: deontological principles, which are standards to be held regardless of effects, and utilitarianism, which weighs the effects. Deontological principles carry rules that apply to all situations, for example, ads must not be deceptive, while utilitarianism tolerates some degree of negativity as long as it brings the greatest good for the greatest number. Rotzoll and Haefner find utilitarianism (advertising's predominant ethical system) problematic in the case of alcohol advertising, due to the ambiguity of effects reported.

At issue is the protection of special markets, including underage drinkers and alcoholics. Proponents of the deontological ethical system consider effects upon these markets regardless of their size in the marketplace, while proponents of utilitarianism prioritize the rights of the majority. In the case of alcohol advertising, those who take the deontological view are likely to favor restrictions that protect members of special groups even though they may be more restrictive than necessary for the majority, while utilitarians are likely to oppose restrictions because they serve a minority at the expense of the majority.

Considering the legal environment, the three primary sources of regulation of alcohol advertising are government organizations, the media companies' clearance departments, and self-regulatory organizations. At the federal government level, the Federal Trade Commission takes the most active role and is charged with examining advertising content for deceptive claims and blocking alcohol advertising that targets underage drinkers. As long as beer ads contain no deceptive claims and are targeted to adults, they pass FTC standards.

The Federal Communications Commission (FCC) has no direct power over advertisers but also bears influence on advertising content by granting operating licenses to broadcast stations and reviewing stations' service to the public interest. A third government organization, the Bureau of Alcohol, Tobacco, and Firearms (BATF), oversees guidelines for the advertising and promotion of alcoholic beverages, restricts active sports figures from appearing in ads, and also prohibits health claims in alcoholic beverage advertising (U.S. Department of the Treasury, 1996).

Ads must also pass media clearance departments, which weigh the benefits of accepting ads as a source of revenue against possible negative consequences. As long as beer ads are not judged offensive by the media companies, they pass the clearance process.

Self-regulation comes from a number of organizations including the National Advertising Review Board (NARB) and the National Advertising Division (NAD) of the Council of Better Business Bureaus. In the alcohol industry, trade associations such as the Beer Institute, the Wine Institute, and the Distilled Spirits Association also engage in self-regulation by agreeing to abide by certain standards of advertising practice. Self-regulation has resulted in a number of voluntary guidelines, which clearly state that beer ads should not (1) encourage or condone drunk driving, (2) depict an illegal use of the product, (3) show people intoxicated, (4) use cartoon characters, (5) show actual consumption of the product, (6) use underage models, (7) "portray sexual passion, promiscuity or any other amorous activity as a result of consuming beer," (8) claim that individuals cannot "obtain social, professional, educational, athletic or financial success or status without beer consumption," nor (9) claim that "individuals cannot solve social, personal or physical problems without beer consumption" (Beer Institute, 1997).

Theoretical Framework

Several theoretical perspectives offer insight into the meaning of advertising messages. The first is phenomenology, an interpretive inquiry that directs attention to "lived experience" (Polkinghorne, 1986), and is often used to frame qualitative research. While phenomenological studies typically use in-depth interviews to provide insight into the experiences of participants, this study extends the perspective to gain insight into the experiences portrayed or depicted in ads.

Because this study is an investigation of text that alcoholics and general members of the population are exposed to rather than an examination of the way these groups interpret ads, we cannot test theories that address the decoding process. However, we make note of several to provide a basis for speculating that the content of beer ads may be an issue for alcoholics. Goldberg and Kozlowski (1997) summarize a number of theories that meaningfully addressed possible effects of imagery in advertising and particularly note the explanatory value of classical conditioning. Stuart, Shimp, and Engle (1987) showed significant effects by pairing attractive nature scenes and objects such as toothpaste. Based on the results of Stuart et al. (1987), Goldberg and Kozlowski (1997, p. 346) propose that the "repeated juxtaposition of Joe Camel's coolness or the Marlboro Man's rugged individualism and the advertised cigarette leads the target audience to conjure up images of coolness or individualism when seeing the cigarette by itself." In like manner, the repeated juxtaposition of images associated with beer advertising may lead consumers to conjure up images when seeing the product by itself.

While classical conditioning explains human behavior from the point of view of environmental forces, social learning theory (Bandura, 1977) combines both environmental and internal determinants to explain the learning of behavior through observation and modeling. Tan (1986) has reviewed media effects associated with television violence from a social learning perspective, and when the perspective is applied to beer advertising, the ads can focus attention on drinking, depict people in situations that are rewarding or reinforcing, and offer vicarious satisfaction.

A different perspective comes from the persuasion literature. Goldberg and Kozlowski (1997) note that the Elaboration Likelihood Model provides additional insight into the information processing of advertising images. Petty, Caccioppo, and Schumann (1983) demonstrated that peripheral cues in advertising can be not only persuasive but also more influential than reasoned claims about a product's central benefits. Peripheral cues can include the imagery associated with the product, which is particularly relevant for alcohol advertising because it is almost exclusively image based.

These theories apply to all consumers—not just alcoholics—and the differences between alcoholics and others in the general population regarding the processing of information are not fully known. The use of denial (Wurmser, 1978) suggests that alcoholics may not question the logic or accuracy of the imagery used in ads and may more readily engage in wishful thinking and/or peripheral processing than others. While this needs further investigation, the results reported by Treise, Taylor, and Wells (1994) add credence to this proposition because some alcoholics in treatment found it necessary to counterargue the ads.

Individual differences in the interpretation process are well documented. Scott (1994) introduced reader-response theory (from literary criticism) to advertising research and repositioned the reader as the dominant partner in the triad of author, text, and reader. Following this perspective, ads are open texts for consumers (readers), and their interpretation is independent of the intent of the creators (authors) of the ads. Accordingly, ads are open to interpretation among all members of society, but because of their experiences with alcohol, one might expect alcoholics to systematically interpret the ads differently than others.

Perspectives on Addiction

The phenomena of addiction has been of concern to scholars since the first century BC when Seneca observed that some persons who became intoxicated were not able to control their alcohol consumption. Drug and alcohol abuse was included in the second edition of Kraeplin's 1887 textbook on mental disease, and since the beginning of this century, addiction has been the subject of theoretical discussion in the psychological literature (Adams, 1978; Fenichel, 1945; James, 1961).

Several perspectives have been offered for the understanding of addiction. Marlatt and Gordon (1985) have contrasted four models with differing views toward responsibility including (1) the medical model, which purports that addiction is a physical disease for which the addict bears no responsibility; (2) the moral model, which holds the addict responsible for change; (3) the enlightenment model, which places recovery in the hands of a higher power, for example, God, others, or self-help programs; and (4) the compensatory model, which defers understanding of etiology and focuses on developing self-mastery strategies.

Psychodynamic theoreticians have offered an alternative conceptualization (Mack, 1981; Wurmser, 1978) that places substance abuse as a symptom of underlying psychological problems (Berger, 1991). Issues such as the management of affect, aggression, primitive forms of guilt and shame, as well as inadequate ego development have been cited as relevant in the etiology of addiction (Adams, 1978). Khantzian (1981) and Mack (1981) maintain that the alcoholic is impaired in two areas: self-care (Khantzian) or self-governance (Mack), and regulation of feelings.

Wurmser (1978) suggests that psychological factors constitute the necessary preconditions for the development of addictive problems including intense emotionality and use of more primitive defenses (e.g., denial, dissociation, and splitting). Here the addictive experience is seen as fundamentally a problem in self/affect regulation. An emotional event ensues, resulting in dysphoric affect and the attendant plummeting of self-esteem. This leads to intense potentially overwhelming feelings and the inability to articulate those feelings (affect regression and generalization/totalization of archaic preverbal affects). In an attempt to defend against these affects, the addicted person is driven to action (acquiring drugs/alcohol) to aid in the denial and subsequent elimination of the overwhelming affect.

Valliant's Study

Valliant's (1983) findings from a longitudinal study of hundreds of alcoholics suggest that there are no easily ascertained personality or biological markers for the problem of addiction. Some persons in Valliant's study (approximately 5% to 15%) were able to return to controlled drinking while others could not. Most showed no correlation between problematic histories or personality problems, although there was a greater incidence of pre-morbid "acting out" among those who had become alcoholics. The only similarities found were that those persons who were to become alcoholics evidenced "hyperactivity," "pushing limits," and "rapid tempo" during childhood and adolescence, and were reared by either alcoholic parents or "tea totallers." Although Valliant denies that psychological factors underlie addiction, these characteristics suggest psychological involvement.

One significance of this study is that it recommends concentrating on the psychological involvement and experience of addiction among alcoholics rather than attempting to identify underlying factors for addiction. Furthermore, the evidence of hyperactivity, pushing limits, and rapid tempo offer insight into alcoholics' pre-morbid experiences.

Hopson's Study

Noting the reported findings from past research regarding affect regulation (Khantzian, 1981; Mack, 1981; Wurmser, 1978), self-governance (Khantzian, 1981; Mack, 1981; Valliant, 1983), disruption of tempo (Valliant, 1983) and other psychological factors, Hopson (1993) conducted phenomenological research to identify feelings associated with the experience of addiction as reported by the alcoholic. His findings provide first-person accounts of what previous researchers reported from a third-person perspective. These findings indicate that the addictive experience is characterized by four problematic modes: (1) intense feelings for which language is inadequate, (2) a disruption in the experience of time, (3) alienation from oneself and others, and (4) lack of sense of agency, self-efficacy, or capacity for self-regulation. These four experience modes serve as a foundation for the present study.

Hopson's study utilized in-depth interviews of recovering alcoholics. Transcript analysis was completed by a team of researchers utilizing the phenomenological method to obtain a thorough description of the essential characteristics of the addictive experience (Husserl, 1970; Merleau-Ponty, 1962; Valle & Halling, 1989). The team worked to determine the thematic structure of the reported experiences of the participants, and the synthesis of the multiple perspectives represented by each team member was utilized to enhance the reliability of the themes (Giorgi, 1975; Polkinghorne, 1986; Thompson, Locander, & Pollio, 1986).

While phenomenology and other forms of qualitative research are often criticized for (1) lack of generalizability based on small numbers of participants and (2) subjectivity on the part of the researchers, some marketing researchers encourage its use and have cautioned against too heavy a reliance on quantitative research (Seymour, 1985) because "the metaphors used in marketing [rationality, measurement, and problem solving] limit the insights generated" (Arndt, 1985, p. 3). The four experiential modes found by Hopson (1993) are described below.

Intense Feelings.   The life-world of the alcohol addicted person is set within intense feelings which form the context within which the person lives. The world is ordered by feelings, and actions are organized around an attempt to manage them. The feelings are often, though not always, negative, and are experienced as potentially overwhelming and always intense. One participant noted:

> All of my life I held my feelings inside. I was unable to identify my feelings and whenever I'd come in from work, I might not realize what I was feeling...I learned that if I started first of all identifying my feelings and then talking about it...I had always gone on the assumption that actions speak louder than words...I wasn't able, first of all to figure out what I was feeling and second of all to communicate it.

Disruption in the Experience of Time

Within the context of these wordless, intense, affective experiences, the sense of temporal flow is disrupted. The usual sense of temporality and flux is interrupted, and time moves exceedingly slowly, or ceases to move at all. Giving time almost an adversarial role, one participant said:

> I felt frozen, yeah, very trapped, very trapped...like time had ceased to exist...so to get beyond this I've got to realize I'm not here forever...the illusion is I'm stuck, it's like we don't recognize that it's going to go away...I found out that things do pass.

Alienation from Oneself and Others

The third area of difficultly is that of intra/interpersonal relationships. The world of the addicted person is a world of disconnection from oneself and others and a sense of alienation. One participant said:

> I was alone and it was loneliness, it was intense...I just felt so alone...I was sad, so lonely, so isolated, I wasn't me, but as far as having some friends, really being close to somebody, there wasn't anybody...I was unable to keep those connections.

Lack of Sense of Agency, Self-efficacy, and Capacity for Self-regulation

The final area of difficulty relates to efficacy. The failure of words or time to adequately represent, symbolize, and modulate affective states appear to be related to a relative lack of sense of agency, self-efficacy, and capacity for self-regulation (Khan, 1983). In the words of another participant:

> [in nightmares]...things are so unreal, so frighteningly unreal, and so unescapable, sort of like the common dream I think of trying to run away from something that's after you and you can't move your feet. Or they feel like they've got lead boots on or something like that. And it never catches you. But you're always struggling to get away from it.

These findings characterize the alcohol addictive phenomena as a manifestation of particular perceptual and experiential anomalies.

METHODOLOGY

The Interpretive Approach

A qualitative design was utilized to investigate the complex nature of the content of beer advertising. Document analysis was the method chosen in order to allow researchers to examine the content of ads without losing rich, descriptive material (Denzin, 1978; Taylor, 1994). This method differs from traditional content analysis in which elements in the content are numerically counted by independent coders using predetermined coding categories in a manner that is objective, systematic, and quantitative (Kassarjian, 1977). Document analysis, a more subjective method, allows the coding categories to emerge from the data. Thus, instead of applying preexisting categories used in previous research (none existed for the four experiential modes) or creating them prior to examining the data, the method allows the researcher to create categories *while* examining the data (Altheide, 1996). This results in a trial and error method using a continuous interplay between the ads and analysis. By utilizing analytic induction and comparative analysis (Glaser and Strauss, 1967; Strauss and Corbin, 1994), tentative categories are tested and refined until final categories can fit the data without being either too inclusive or too restrictive. The identification of patterns that emerge is part of the findings for document analysis, not a preliminary step as in the case of content analysis.

Because the three researchers brought different interests and expertise to the study including legal and social issues in advertising, existential-phenomenological psychology, and advertising as a form of cultural communication, the researchers worked as a team in viewing and coding a sample of commercials. Known as "investigator triangulation" (Denzin, 1978, p. 245), the team approach in qualitative research benefits from expanding the interpretive base of the research by revealing elements of the phenomenon that are not necessarily seen by just one researcher. The researchers worked until reaching a consensus on all issues; thus, no unresolved differences occurred. Unlike quantitative research, which relies on hypothesis testing and requires the use of independent coders to avoid bias, qualitative research states no up-front hypotheses; thus, the use of independent coders and subsequent tests of intercoder reliability are not part of the research method.

Because no previous research operationalized how the four experiential modes might be depicted in ads, the researchers examined sources for creative strategy to generate initial ideas. Advertising strategies have been classified as either transformational or informational, with the former based on emotion and the latter based on logic (Laskey, Day, & Crask, 1989). Also, a standard list of advertising appeals includes a number of emotions such as excitement, fear, love, and pleasure, which are commonly used in ads as part of the creative strategy (Moriarty, 1991). These emotional appeals indicate a way in which ads may resonate with those who have intense feelings for which language is inadequate.

An advertising study that identified five ways in which time is depicted in ads (Wolburg & Taylor, 1997) generated ideas concerning the second mode—a disruption in the experience of time. According to the study time was expressed as (1) a commodity that can be saved or spent, (2) an orientation to past, present, and future, (3) something that "marks" events including birthdays and anniversaries, (4) a way of noting pace through editing, and (5) a way of noting passage (old versus new). These provided a basis for examining time messages in the beer and car product ads.

The advertising appeals also included the need for affiliation or belonging, which seems to resonate with the third mode—alienation from oneself and others. Finally, appeals to challenge, achievement, and accomplishment resonate with the fourth mode—the lack of sense of agency or self-efficacy. These sources generated initial ideas prior to viewing the ads, and during the process of viewing the ads themselves the researchers continued to refine the list of elements that pertain to each mode.

The team approach used in phenomenological research was used for this study, although the analysis of text (transcripts of the ads) was the focus instead of interview transcripts. The researchers sought to explicate any and all ways that the execution of the ads related to the four problematic modes by identifying related elements. While the study applies a nontraditional approach, a host of advertising studies have employed various interpretive methodologies (McCracken, 1989; Mick & Buhl, 1992; Scott, 1990; Stern, 1996; Stern & Holbrook, 1994; Taylor, Hoy, & Haley, 1996).

Obtaining the Sample

The sample was drawn from weekend television sports programming including professional football games, basketball games, and car racing on cable and broadcast channels over a four-month period. Sports programming was chosen due to the large volume of beer advertising and for its appeal to men, who represent about 60 percent of beer consumers and are the primary target market (Simmons Market Research Bureau, 1996). Figures also support the choice of television as a medium because 83 percent of beer ads are placed on TV (Leading National Advertisers, 1996). Beer ads were dubbed to another tape until 50 unduplicated national beer ads had been compiled (41 hours of programming were required). Fifty unduplicated, national ads for automotive products and services (motor oil, batteries, fuel additives, etc.) were also dubbed to serve as a comparison product. After compiling the tapes, the ads were transcribed.

Although quite dissimilar to beer as a product category, automotive products had the advantages of being targeted to the same demographic group and at the same frequency (41 hours of programming also generated 50 automotive product and service ads). Products more similar to beer such as soft drinks are not addictive and are targeted to different demographic groups, for example, both males and females, teenagers and older people. Cigarettes are another legal, addictive product, but they are not advertised on television. Illegal drugs (e.g., cocaine) are addictive but not advertised; thus, no ideal comparison product exists. Given these differences, the use of a comparison product was included primarily for illustrative purposes.

The Research Questions

The study posed three research questions, each of which directed a stage of the analytical process. The three questions are presented together, and the stages are presented afterward.

RQ1: Does beer advertising contain any elements that directly relate to Hopson's four problematic modes of experience for people recovering from alcohol addiction?

RQ2: If so, when beer advertising depicts various situations and experiences, what key elements in the ads relate to these problematic modes?

RQ3: How does beer advertising differ from the advertising for other products in its use of the elements associated with the problematic modes?

The Research Process

Stage 1

RQ1 asks if beer advertising contains elements related to the four modes. A preliminary viewing of the sample provided overwhelming support that beer ads do depict situations and experiences that can directly appeal to people who have difficulties with (1) intense feelings, (2) disruption in the experience of time, (3) alienation from oneself and others, and (4) lack of agency, self-effi-cacy, or self-regulation.

The relationship between the ads and the modes of experience is complex. The ads never visually depict consumption as part of the four problematic modes, and the ads make very few rational, testable statements—certainly no ads claim that consumption will overcome problematic modes, for problems were never acknowledged. However, by consistently showing beer as a product for popular fun-seekers who spend their time enjoying life, expressing emotions, celebrating occasions, and performing at high levels of skill, the ads focus on the very quali-ties and experiences most elusive to those recovering from alcohol addiction. The ads contain both verbal and visual elements that can make promises through imagery and encourage the belief that people who drink experience none of these problems. These initial findings directed the next stage.

Stage 2

RQ2 asked what specific elements relate to the modes. A more thorough view-ing of the ads was required to address this question, and a coding sheet was cre-ated to capture the variety of advertising elements related to these modes (see the Appendix). Rather than presenting the coding sheet as a finite or exhaustive list of elements related to the problematic modes, it is offered as a list of the elements most apparent to the researchers.

Given that people with alcohol addiction experience intense feelings for which language is inadequate, both verbal and visual expressions of emotion were noted using Moriarty's list of appeals in addition to actions that take the place of verbal communication. This is exemplified by "act, don't think" behavior. Because alcohol addiction carries the experience of disruption of time, the study identified all verbal and visual references to time including use of time for celebrations, prominent use of fast or slow paced music, and ideali-zation of past, present, or future. Given the feelings of alienation, the study also noted all interaction, particularly the nature of the relationship (friendship, romance, etc.). Finally, because recovering alcoholics experience a lack of agency and self-efficacy, the study coded the overcoming of physical laws including defiance of gravity, use of anthropomorphism, "scoring" in sports or in sex, and use of special effects.

Each ad for both product categories was viewed using the coding sheet in order to gain a count of how frequently each element occurred and to gain insight into their use. Examples of the elements are provided among the findings.

Stage 3

RQ3 asked how beer advertising differs from the advertising of other products. To address this question, differences in usage and frequency of the elements were noted and compared. Although the interpretation of qualitative research primarily relies on insight, the collection of numerical data allowed for chi-square analysis as well. In cases where cell values were less than ten, Yates' correction was applied.

FINDINGS

The following provides a description and analysis of how the elements were used in the ads. Results of the chi-square analysis are also included.

Intensity of Feelings

A number of elements in the ads addressed emotion, and the beer commercials outnumbered the car category commercials in both verbal and nonverbal expressions of emotion. Chi-square analysis showed that the combined use of verbal and nonverbal emotion was significantly greater for beer ads (Table 1), as was the use of emotion in advertising appeals (Table 2). Emotional appeals as a whole and specific emotions of love (romance) and pleasure (humor) were also significantly greater for beer ads. However, the number does not do justice to the intensity of emotion. The following Bud Light ad expresses that emotional intensity using quick cuts of various beach, boat, and pool scenes with a large cast of fun-loving sunbathers on a hot day.

Man: Live from the beach, it's Bud Light!!!

Woman: Where the weather's always hot and the Bud Light's cold!

Man: Bud Light for all my friends!

Woman: What if we get stranded???

Man: Ha... (He implies that being stranded would be an opportunity to "score.")

Woman: It's perfect on a cold winter day—like today! (In reality, it's hot).

Man: Unbelievable! The official beer of winter. Sure beats rush hour. Bud Light!!!

The quick editing style, special effects, enthusiasm in their voices, and pulsating background music all gave the dizzying impression of emotion in the midst of intense activity.

Fast action for its own sake was even more prominent in a series of Coors Light ads that depicted swimming, rollerblading, and volleyball in one spot and skiing, ice skating, and hang gliding in another, all fused with dancing scenes and images of the Coors can breaking through a mountain of snow. The words "keep on movin'" were repeated while a voiceover sang:

Table 1. Frequency of Appeals

Appeals	Clarification of Some Appeals	Incidence in Beer Ads	Incidence in Car Ads	Chi-square
Aesthetics***	Appreciation of the beautiful	22 (44%)	0 (0%)	25.60
Affiliation**	Belonging to a group	16 (32%)	2 (4%)	11.40
Appetite**	Hunger, taste, cravings	7 (14%)	0 (0%)	5.52
Aspiration**	Achievement, accomplishment	14 (28%)	2 (4%)	9.00
Attractiveness		0 (0%)	0 (0%)	NA
Avoidance1		(2%)	5 (10%)	2.83
Cleanliness		0 (0%)	3 (6%)	3.09
Comfort		0 (0%)	1 (2%)	1.01
Convenience	Saving time and effort	0 (0%)	5 (10%)	3.36
Economy***	Saving money	0 (0%)	18 (36%)	19.50
Efficiency***		2 (4%)	32 (64%)	37.40
Egoism	Recognition, prestige	24 (48%)	23(46%)	0.04
Total emotions**		47 (94%)	36 (72%)	8.57
Excitement		10 (20%)	5 (10%)	1.96
Fear	Danger, embarrassment	0 (0%)	4 (8%	2.34
Family	Love, protection	0 (0%)	4 (8%)	2.34
Love***	Affection, romance	12 (24%)	0 (0%)	13.60
Nostalgia		2 (4%)	0 (0%)	2.04
Pleasure*	Humor, happiness, laughter	23 (46%)	11 (22%)	6.41
Poignancy		1 (2%)	0 (0%)	1.01
Pride		9 (18%)	12 (24%)	0.54
Relief		1 (2%)	0 (0%)	1.01
Identification	Respect, hero worship	29 (58%)	21 (42%)	2.56
Mental stimulation	Curiosity, challenge	3 (6%)	0 (0%)	3.09
Responsibility		2 (4%)	4 (8%)	0.70
Safety/security***		1 (2%)	16 (32%)	13.80
Sensory pleasure***	Touch, taste, sound, sight	28 (56%)	0 (0%)	38.80
Sex***		22 (44%)	1 (2%)	20.20
Thriftiness		0 (0%)	9 (18%)	9.89

Notes: * $p = < .05$ for chi-square analysis with Yates' correction for small cells.
    ** $p = < .01$,
    *** $p = < .001$.

And the Silver Bullet has the taste to keep it movin.' Coors Light. Naturally brewed for a taste that goes down easy. Coors Light. Keep on movin.'

The words "keep on movin'" kept the pace rapid and depicted an action-packed life that left little time to reflect. The words contrast markedly with one alcoholic's description of wearing lead boots that make you feel "you can't move your feet" (Hopson, 1993).

The "act, don't think" theme occurred only in beer ads, and it implied that the generation of emotion through activity could substitute for genuine emotion. While car product ads also used emotions, the nature of the emotions differed. For

Table 2.   Elements in Ads by Product Category

Elements in Ads	Incidence in Beer Ads	Incidence in Car Part Ads	Chi-square
Elements Associated with Intense Emotion			
Verbal expression of emotion	15 (30%)	8 (16%)	2.76
Nonverbal expression of emotion	23 (46%)	16 (32%)	2.05
Total verbal and nonverbal expression**	38 (76%)	24 (48%)	8.31
Emphasis on "act don't think"***	18 (36%)	2 (4%)	14.00
Elements Associated with Time			
Verbal references	16 (32%)	17 (34%)	0.04
Visual references	14 (28%)	7 (14%)	2.95
Celebrations*	14 (28%)	2 (4%)	6.49
Special editing**	15 (30%)	4 (8%)	9.00
Compressed or non-real time*	40 (80%)	31 (62%)	3.93
Prominent use of music for pace**	27 (54%)	13 (26%)	8.16
Idealization of past, future, present	5 (10%)	0 (0%)	3.36
Time as a limited commodity***	0 (0%)	15 (30%)	15.30
Time passage, longevity	2 (4%)	5 (10%)	1.38
Elements Associated with Relationships			
No beings depicted	4 (8%)	9 (18%)	2.21
Single being depicted*	4 (8%)	14 (28%)	5.48
Nonhuman interaction	3 (6%)	1 (2%)	1.04
Total human interaction**	39 (78%)	25 (50%)	8.50
Family members	0 (0%)	3 (6%)	3.09
Friends*	24 (48%)	3 (6%)	20.20
Acquaintances	6 (12%)	6 (12%)	0
Strangers	8 (16%)	6 (12%)	0.33
Coworkers, team members	1 (2%)	7 (14%)	3.39
Romantic interest present***	22 (44%)	1 (2%)	13.80
Predator/victim	4 (8%)	0 (0%)	2.34
Physical contact	15 (30%)	8 (16%)	2.76
Identity disclosed	4 (8%)	12 (24%)	3.64
Recognizable, familiar music	7 (14%)	2 (4%)	3.05
Elements Associated with Efficacy			
Total limit violations***	36 (72%)	9 (18%)	27.30
Anthropomorphism	7 (14%)	1 (2%)	3.39
Defiance of gravity	5 (10%)	1 (2%)	2.83
Defiance of nature***	24 (48%)	3 (6%)	20.20
Other special effects	12 (24%)	4 (8%)	3.64
Scoring***	30 (60%)	6 (12%)	22.90
Product as reward***	14 (28%)	0 (0%)	14.00
Product empowers	9 (18%)	5 (10%)	1.32
Objectifying other people*	6 (12%)	0 (0%)	4.43
Others shown for validation*	6 (12%)	0 (0%)	4.43

Notes: * $p = < .05$ for chi-square analysis with Yates' correction for small cells.
      ** $p = < .01$.
    *** $p = < .001$.

example, some car product ads played off the fear of injury to a family member by using the wrong brand. The following ad for Interstate Batteries also uses a fear appeal with visuals indicating "the day is coming" and sounds of an unseen man praying plaintively with soft religious music in the background.

> Man: Oh please, oh please, oh please. (pause) Just help me this once, and I'll never ask for anything again ever. On the count of three. One…two…three.
>
> (sound of a dead battery)
>
> VO: Next time get a dependable Interstate Battery. We check 'em before you buy 'em for fresh power. Guaranteed.

The use of occasional negative emotions for the car product category contrasted with the beer commercials' consistently positive tone. As a result, consumers know that there are risks in purchasing car products and services, such as the dissatisfaction that comes from buying a product that doesn't live up to expectations. Consumers may even overestimate the risk of physical injury from suing a product of lower quality, for example, having an accident for lack of Michelin tires. Ironically, the statistics leave no doubt that alcohol is a risky product, but the lack of negative emotions in beer ads effectively conceals any evidence of risk.

Time

A number of elements are associated with the passage of time, most of which were used significantly more often in beer ads including references to celebrations and prominent use of music for pace (Table 1 and 2). Beer ads were also more likely to use special editing devices that either compressed time or presented the sequence of events as a montage of images rather than in "real" time. The use of time as a limited commodity was used significantly fewer times in beer ads than for car product commercials, which relied heavily on claims such as "while supplies last," "lifetime guarantee or your money back," and "quickest service around." These messages focus on "clock time," while one could say beer ads suspend clock time.

Miller beer has incorporated time in a long-standing campaign of ads using "Miller Time," which appears significant given the alcoholic's distorted sense of temporal flow. One ad in the sample opened with the words to the song, "Time is on my side," while the visuals showed men quitting work at the auto shop and going to a bar to drink beer.

> Song: Time is on my side. Yes it is. Time is on my side. Yes it is.
>
> VO: The time is 5:01. The beer is Miller High Life. And the reason is clear.
>
> When the time is your own, it must be Miller Time.
>
> Song: Time, time, time…
>
> VO: Miller Time. Miller Beer.

Not only is the association with time meaningful, but the use of lyrics conveying that time is "on my side" encourages thinking that by drinking Miller, time is "my friend" instead of the adversary that Hopson's participants described.

Michelob has also used a long-standing time-oriented campaign using the slogan, "Some days are better than others." In an ad that commemorated PGA golfers, a number of spectacularly executed golf shots were shown including one in which the ball bounced off the water and landed in the hole.

VO: Did you ever have one of those days that starts off with a bang?

When things take a turn for the best?

When you practically walk on water?

VO: Michelob salutes the PGA golfers and golfers everywhere, and those special moments that make some days better than others.

The ad sends two messages: first, by associating Michelob with success the ad encourages viewers to believe that "if I drink Michelob, things will take a turn for the best. Maybe I can practically walk on water, too." Second, by "saluting...special moments that make some days better than others," the ad goes beyond the context of golf and encourages the belief that "Michelob can turn the ordinary moments of my life into special moments that make the days better." This could be a compelling message for the person who feels that time is never-ending.

Pace featured prominently in the ads through slow, sexy music; fast, rhythmic music; editing devices that changed the feel of the passage of time; and use of special content in visuals. For example, the Busch "be a mountain man" ads used music with a prominent beat, quick editing, and visuals that rushed the viewer to the mountains. The heavy reliance on pace and images of movement for Busch beer and the previously described Coors ads convey the notion that beer offers an escape from feeling "stuck" in time.

Hopson's participant who described feeling "trapped" implies a spatial component in addition to a temporal one. The mountain man ads not only transported people through time but literally to another place. The place metaphor was also vivid in Miller Genuine Draft's use of the line, "The world is a very cool place; get out of the old and into the cold," and in the Busch ads that worship the cowboy and idealize the land:

There's no place on earth that I'd rather be, out in the open where it's all plain to see. The land is pure, unchained and free, and there's no place that I'd rather be. Come on, come on, head for the mountains of Busch Beer. Head for the mountains, it's cold and it's smooth, it's waiting for you. Come on, head for the mountains of Busch Beer.

Interpersonal Alienation

Because the participants in Hopson's study spoke of extreme loneliness and isolation from others, both sets of ads were examined for appeals to affiliation and the nature of interpersonal relationships. Overall, beer ads were significantly stronger in the appeal to affiliation, the portrayal of interaction, which was most commonly between friends, and sexual or romantic interest. Absence of any people or the use of a single spokesperson occurred significantly more often in car category ads, and when interaction occurred it was more often between coworkers or with customers (Tables 1 and 2).

Celebrity spokespersons rarely appeared in beer ads because retired sports celebrities can appear but current sports figures cannot. Because these restrictions do not apply to car part and service commercials, more celebrities appeared. As a result, car category ads encouraged viewers to identify psychologically with an individual (e.g., Richard Petty or Mario Andretti), while the beer ads encouraged viewers to identify with a character type, e.g., "the mountain man" or "the modern day hero."

The vast majority of beer commercials presented the drinker in social settings. In contrast with the feelings of alienation experienced by people addicted to alcohol, many beer ads used casts in social settings where belonging was easy and befriending strangers was natural. Even when nonhumans were shown, they were socializing (the Budweiser frogs, the Molson bears, people on billboards who came to life, etc.).

Many beer ads emphasized friendship, and a Molson ad featured two anthropomorphic bears conversing as buddies in a humorous play on words.

Bear 1: Hey, whatcha doin' down there?

Bear 2: Trying to cool off.

Bear 1: Yeah, the heat's unbearable.

Bear 2: I was gonna hit the beach but it's a zoo on weekends.

Bear 1: Yeah, parking can get really hairy.

Bear 2: You know, I could go for a nice cold beer.

Bear 1: Hey, how'd you like to wrap your paws around a nice cold Molson?

Bear 2: Molson? Hey. Now you're talking.

    VO: Molson—of Canada. Because good friends deserve a great beer.

Bear 1: Whatcha wanna do tomorrow?

Bear 2: Hey, it's the weekend. Let's go scare some tourists.

While this exchange included bears, a Heineken ad between two men had the same degree of humor and male bonding.

Several ads used strong sexual innuendo such as a Miller Genuine Draft ad played to the tune of "The Good, The Bad, and The Ugly." The ad featured a sweaty, sexy woman in a hot apartment who called a repairman to fix her air conditioner. She opened the door to a stranger wearing cowboy boots, who unplugged the AC and opened a bottle of MGD. Instantly the room became filled with snow and strong sexual undercurrents. The real repairman drove up, saw the snow coming from the apartment, and examined the bottle cap with an amused but knowing expression. Viewers heard the familiar words:

> for those who've discovered its smooth draft taste, the world is a very cool place. So get out of the old and into the cold.

The ad is one of a series, all of which center on strong sexual attraction between a man and woman who are strangers, while a second male bystander, who is older, less attractive, not drinking, and presumably not "cool," watches with an expression of envy and surprise. In each ad, beer and sex are associated only with the attractive young man and woman, not the "outsider."

Other ads had a large cast of characters such as the Bud Light series of beach party ads and the Busch mountain man ads. Each type of relationship depicted in the ad, whether it involved strong male bonding, intense male/female sexual attraction, or casual party scene encounters, showed an ease and naturalness as though beer was the essential element that brought people together. This could be a powerful association for those who experience extreme loneliness and feelings of isolation.

In contrast, one of the closest relationships in the car ads depicted a bond between a race car driver and his pit crew. An Autolite Spark Plug ad showed driver John Force in playful comradery with his crew as he joked about switching to a different plug.

> Force (to viewers): I love my new hot rod. Those flames scare the other guys. 5,000 horsepower helps too—and a fat bank roll. You know, we've been running Autolite Spark Plugs forever, but I can wring more money outta someone else. (pause) Money's good. My crew burns it, so I tell the guys we're going to run a different plug. They say no. I say I'm the boss. They say Autolite keeps this monster lit. So I tell them (pause) I was just kidding.

The relationship between Force and his crew is strong but by delivering lines to viewers, Force's main relationship is shifted from the crew to viewers. In contrast, beer ads most often communicated with viewers through the use of voiceovers instead of dialogue directed at them. This allows the focus of the beer ads to remain on the relationship between cast members, and it facilitates viewers' involvement with that relationship.

Agency and Self-efficacy

The commercials were examined for evidence of efficacy through activities involving such things as skill, power, and accomplishments. Appeals to aspiration (accomplishment) and references to agency and self-efficacy were significantly more frequent in the beer commercials, especially through "scoring" in sports and in sex (Tables 1 and 2). People in the beer ads operated at a high level of skill when athletic ability was required and easily succeeded in attracting members of the opposite sex.

In fact, people in beer ads had superhuman abilities, particularly through the use of "limit violations"—a term that denoted the stretching of reality beyond its limits. Examples included people in billboards who came to life and people who performed daredevil acts of skill that defied gravity. This took place in a world where beer cans forged through mountains, snowstorms came out of beer bottles, frogs and bears talked, monsters walked through cities while women watched in amusement, and buildings became bottle openers. Many beer ads combined the use of limit violations with a positioning of the product that either empowered or rewarded the user.

An example is a series of commercials that implied that Miller beer can do anything including resolving disagreements over which TV programs to watch. When one ad depicted a group of men arguing over whether to watch a cooking show or a wrestling match, the cook suddenly became part of the match and defeated the wrestler. A different ad in the series combined golf and football into a single sport. Both closed with the line, "Can your beer do this?"

Similarly, a series of Busch ads challenged viewers by asking if they have what it takes. The answer is "yes" for those who drink Busch. Each ad showed a young man picking up two kinds of Busch beer while young, attractive, admiring women were on hand.

> Have you got what it takes to be a mountain man? All it really takes are the two cool beers of the mountain man. Smooth Busch Beer and easy drinking Busch Light. So, be a mountain man. All you gotta do is head for the mountains.

An unspoken implication is that the Busch-drinking mountain man has "what it takes" to sexually satisfy the many women he attracts.

Foster's beer used a series of humorous ads that contained subtle limit violations. These ads identified objects in a very exaggerated way, either through understatement or overstatement. For example, one showed a shark and redefined it as a "guppy." Other ads redefined a sprig of parsley as "salad" and a crocodile's mouth as a "can opener." The next image in all ads showed a can of Foster's, which was defined as beer. When the same redefining process is used for beer, the ad encourages viewers to use their imagination to exaggerate the meaning of beer and redefine it in a new way.

Limit violations were significantly less frequent in car parts commercials. One featured an interview at a BP station with a man and a series of cars that "talk" about how clean their fuel injectors feel. Another showed a bottle of 4 X 4 Quaker State Oil breaking out of a box and turning into a 4 X 4 vehicle. While the ad recommends the "intelligent oil for hard working engines," the vehicle climbs over the merchandise in an auto parts store, hauls items, and breaks through ice.

Efficacy was observed to be a recurring theme in both beer and car product ads; however, in beer commercials the efficacy almost always enhanced the user, and limit violations were achieved as a result of using the product. The efficacy involved in the car product commercials predominantly referred to the product's efficacy in fulfilling its intended purpose. In other words, the car product empowered the car, not the driver. In a few instances the car product empowered the user by making him/her more competitive, but the product claims and imagery were within realistic limits, unlike the magical world of beer imagery.

SUMMARY AND CONCLUSIONS

Revisiting the Research Questions

These results offer some convincing insights into the original research questions. RQ1 and RQ2 asked whether beer advertising contains any elements that directly relate to the four problematic modes of experience for people recovering from alcohol addiction, and if so, what key elements relate to these problematic modes? A list of elements emerged from the study that formed a coding sheet, which was used in a succession of viewings to gather descriptive data and frequency counts. Not only did specific elements differ significantly between the two product categories, but as a whole the elements presented an exaggerated, unrealistic view of the drinking experience. A heavy reliance on emotional appeals, sensory pleasure, music, and hyperactivity evoked a magnified intensity of emotion, while the use of occasions and pace depicted a world where time never slows down and all the days are special.

Beer commercials depicted people who enjoy a variety of intensely satisfying and successful relationships including friendship and sex, and they have a general feeling of belonging instead of loneliness and isolation. Success extends beyond sex and other relationships to sports and leisure activities, and the limit violations allow people to experience the impossible.

RQ3 asked how beer advertising differs from the advertising for other products. In response, no elements appeared to be exclusive to either product category, and nothing in the intrinsic nature of the product dictated the use of any particular creative strategy. However, more elements of the problematic modes occurred in beer ads, perhaps with different results due to differences in context.

The beer ads generally used more expressions of emotion, more emphasis on the experience of time for celebrations than the finite limits of time, more interaction between people, and more emphasis on efficacy through limit violations. Not only did they outnumber the car product and service ads for these elements, but they used them in a qualitatively different manner that took on a potentially harmful meaning when associated with alcohol.

For example, most of the car commercials presented the product or service as the hero; yet many of the beer commercials not only made the product the hero, but also the user. Giving hero status to the user enables the drinker to maintain control and deny that problematic modes of experience have any power over him or her, and elevating beer to hero status gives power to the product. For beer drinkers the message is that social interactions are many and always satisfying; time is for celebrating, and one should live for the moment; emotions are intense but most often expressed effectively through action; and there are no limits, personal or otherwise.

The "no consequences" messages contrasts sharply with what we know can be the long-term (and sometimes even short-term) negative effects of alcohol abuse and addiction: isolation or social stigma, accidents and physical injury and death, physiological deterioration, poor performance on the job, and many others. Perhaps the most significant difference between the advertising for the two products is the degree of realism. Car product and service advertising occasionally used puffery to exaggerate the perception of safety, endurance, or quality, but distortions of reality through limit violations were rare. Beer advertising, in contrast, frequently presented images of fantasy that exaggerate the reality of the experience.

Returning to a consideration of theory, beer ads present the experience of drinking in a way that for many contrasts with reality. Ads were deconstructed beyond the surface level to see what elements exist that might have a special meaning for alcoholics. While reader response theory emphasizes the need to understand what alcoholics experience, an equally important step is an analysis of the text itself.

The Elaboration Likelihood Model, classical conditioning, and social learning theory provide three means for understanding the potential meaning of beer ads to alcoholics. By associating certain positive imagery with beer, alcoholics may continue to deny the negative reality of beer. The heavy use of elements associated with experience modes may be persuasive peripheral cues, and alcoholics may try to model the behavior seen in ads. Further research may reveal more about the processing of information among alcoholics.

Limitations and Future Research

This study is an examination of the text of the ads given what we know about alcoholics, rather than an investigation of alcoholics' perceptions of the ads. While previous research has broadly recorded this group's difficulties with alcohol advertising, more research is needed to gain insight from the alcoholic's perspective into the meaning of the elements identified in this study. However, research will have to be done in such a way that no interference with the treatment process occurs. This study was an important transition project between what's already known about alcoholics and what's known about the advertising of alcoholic beverages.

One concern regarding the findings is the frequent turnover of messages due to changing ad campaigns. While no evidence suggests that these elements are unique to this set of ads or limited to selected brands, longitudinal research could evaluate the endurance of these underlying messages and their ability to differentiate brands.

Future research might also continue exploring the psychological context surrounding advertising for various kinds of products. The comparison of car category ads provided an opportunity to stay within the same target market, but as noted previously, no ideal product exists for comparison without introducing a host of other factors. Even though nonalcoholic beverages such as soft drinks are not considered harmful products and are usually marketed to a distinctly different target audience, their use in social occasions may make them a logical product for comparison to beer. Advertising for other harmful but legal products such as cigarettes, gambling, and liquor may also prove useful.

Ultimately, the importance of the study is the discovery that elements associated with problematic modes are present in beer advertising. Regardless of their presence or absence in other products, their presence in beer advertising should be taken seriously.

Implications

With $786 million at stake in mass media advertising (Leading National Advertisers, 1996), many would claim that there is nothing inherently unethical or illegal about the tactics used by beer advertisers. Supporters might argue that beer advertisers are merely employing tactics available to all advertisers. Unfortunately, while beer advertising is aimed at a general audience, it reaches especially vulnerable audiences—those who are in the throes of alcohol addiction, heavy drinkers who have the potential to become alcoholics, and those in recovery programs who are actively committed to overcoming alcohol addiction. The traditional marketing notion of maximizing advertising efficiency by targeting those who are likely to consume relatively more of the product has unique implications when the product is addictive, and when the heaviest users include alcoholics.

Beer advertisers often defend their position by arguing that restrictions go against the utilitarian notion of the greatest good for the greatest number by putting the needs of a small group above those of the majority who otherwise have a right to see these ads. This study takes the position that while advertisers are meeting minimum expectations by law, they should be held to a higher standard due to the addictive nature of the product.

The inevitable question is whether this form of beer advertising should go unrestricted. While the results of any one study may not produce sufficient evidence to make this decision, it shows the need to investigate the issue further using a wide range of research methods that go beyond econometric studies in order to come to terms with the potential harm to society. If further investigation provides evidence that these ads are compelling to the heaviest drinkers, the argument can be made that this type of commercial should be prohibited because it is impossible to target nonalcoholics exclusively, and the consequences of alcohol addiction are so costly to the individual and to society. Unlike children and other vulnerable groups that can be targeted separately on the basis of age or other demographics, alcoholics blend into society and cannot be differentiated in their use of media, and so on.

Essentially, we propose a shift from utilitarianism to the deontological view. Less restrictive measures than the outright banning of beer advertising can be utilized including the limitation of creative strategy to "tombstones," which provide only the brand name without the use of imagery, and counter-advertising, which can provide an alternative view of the reality of drinking.

A second question addresses whether advertisers knowingly exploit the weaknesses of a potentially lucrative but highly vulnerable audience. Due to the proprietary nature of advertising research, we have no basis for leveling the charge of intent against advertisers; however, it is presumed that advertisers know this audience well. Regardless of whether or not they have knowingly tried to tweak the needs and feelings of their "best" customers, public policy decisions regarding beer advertising should be made based on the effects upon alcoholics regardless of intent. The defense that beer advertisers have done nothing that most other advertisers wouldn't also do is unacceptable given the consequences of the product.

Aside from the focus on legal and ethical issues, a different approach requires experts in addiction recovery to carefully explore the impact of advertising on the recovery process. Helping the recovering alcoholic understand the potential impact of these commercials, as well as the reasons underlying it, could be a significant part of the recovery process. Complicated legal issues and questions about the advertiser's intent notwithstanding, the potential impact of these ads on a significant segment of the population deserves special attention.

This research constitutes a step toward understanding the unique interaction between advertising messages and the experience mode of the alcohol addicted consumer. Given the importance to individuals and society, it is essential to investigate the power of advertising for this group.

APPENDIX:
CODING SHEET

Intense Feelings

_____ overt expression of emotion: _____ verbal; _____ nonverbal
_____ product serves as substitute expression
_____ emphasis on "act, don't think"

The Experience of Time

_____ verbal references to time
_____ visual references to time
_____ references to celebrations
_____ editing effects
_____ use of "real" time in editing
_____ use of "compressed" time or other non-real time
_____ use of music: _____ fast tempo; _____ slow tempo; _____ nostalgia
_____ idealization of: _____ past; _____ future; _____ present
_____ time as a limited commodity
_____ time passage (longevity)

Interaction, Relationships, Alienation

_____ no beings depicted
_____ single being shown
_____ nonhuman interaction
_____ human interaction
    Nature of relationship: _____ family members
                            _____ friends
                            _____ acquaintances
                            _____ coworkers, team members
                            _____ strangers
_____ romantic interest
_____ predator/victim
_____ physical contact
_____ identity disclosed
_____ recognizable music

Lack of Agency, Self-efficacy, or Self-regulation

_____ limit violations: _____ anthropomorphism
                             _____ defiance of gravity
                             _____ defiance of nature
                             _____ other special effects

_____ "scoring:" _____ sports, _____ sex
_____ product as reward
_____ product empowers
_____ objectifying other people
_____ others shown for validation of efficacy

REFERENCES

Adams, J. (1978). *Psychoanalysis of drug dependence: The understanding of a particular form of pathological narcissism.* New York: Grune and Stratton.

Altheide, D.L. (1996). *Qualitative media analysis.* Thousand Oaks, CA: Sage.

Archer, L., Grant, B.F., & Dawson, D.A. (1995). What if Americans drank less? The potential effect on the prevalence of alcohol abuse and dependence. *American Journal of Public Health, 85,* 61-66.

Arndt, J. (1985). The tyranny of paradigms: The case for paradigmatic pluralism in marketing. In N. Dholakia & J. Arndt (Eds.), *Research in marketing,* Supplement 2: *Changing the course of marketing: Alternate paradigms for widening market theory* (pp. 3-26). Greenwich, CT: JAI Press.

Bandura, A. (1977). *Social learning theory.* Englewood Cliffs, NJ: Prentice-Hall.

Beer Institute. (1997). *Advertising and marketing code.* Washington, DC: Author.

Berger, L. (1991). *Substance abuse as symptom.* Hillsdale, NJ: Analytic.

Carey, J.W. (1989). *Communication as culture.* New York: Routledge, Chapman and Hall.

Denzin, N.K. (1978). *The research act: A theoretical introduction to sociological methods.* Englewood Cliffs, NJ: Prentice-Hall.

Duffy, M.H. (1989). Measuring the contribution of advertising to growth in demand: An econometric-accounting framework. *International Journal of Advertising, 8,* 95-110.

Fenichel, O. (1945). *The psychoanalytic theory of neurosis.* New York: W.W. Norton.

Fisher, J.C., & Cook, P.A. (1995). *Advertising, alcohol consumption, and mortality: An empirical investigation.* Westport, CT: Greenwood Press.

Giorgi, A. (1975). An application of phenomenological method in psychology. In A. Giorgi, C.T. Fischer, & E.L. Murray (Eds.), *Duquesne studies in phenomenological psychology* (Vol. 2, pp. 82-103). Pittsburg: Duquesne University Press.

Gius, M.P. (1996). Using panel data to determine the effect of advertising on brand-level distilled spirits sales. *Journal of Studies on Alcohol, 57,* 73-76.

Glaser, B.G., & Strauss, A.L. (1967). *The discovery of grounded theory: Strategies for qualitative research.* Chicago: Aldine.

Goldberg, M.E., & Kozlowski, L.T. (1997). Loopholes and lapses in the "1997 tobacco agreement": Some devils in the marketing details. *Journal of Public Policy & Marketing, 16*(2), 345-351.

Hanson, D.J., & Engs, R.C. (1992). College students' drinking problems: A national study. *Psychological Report, 71,* 39-42.

Hopson, R.E. (1993). A thematic analysis of the addictive experience: Implications for psychotherapy. *Psychotherapy, 30*(Fall), 481-494.

Husserl, E. (1970). The *crisis of the European sciences and transcendental phenomenology: An intro-duction to phenomenological philosophy* (trans. by D. Carr). Evanston, IL: Northwestern University Press.

James, W. (1961). *The varieties of religious experience: A study in human nature.* New York: Collier MacMillian.

Kassarjian, H.H. (1977). Content analysis in consumer research. *Journal of Consumer Research, 4,* 8-18.

Khan, M. (1983). *Hidden selves.* New York: International Universities Press.

Khantzian, E.J. (1981). Some treatment implications of the ego and self disturbances in alcoholism. In M. Bean & N.E. Zinberg (Eds.), *Dynamic approaches to the understanding and treatment of alcoholism* (pp. 147-169). New York: Free Press.

Krugman, D., Reid, L.N., Dunn, S.W., & Barban, A.M. (1994). *Advertising: Its role in modern marketing.* Fort Worth, TX: Harcourt Brace.

Kvale, S. (1983). The qualitative research interview: A phenomenological and a hermeneutical mode of understanding. *Journal of Phenomenological Psychology, 14*(Fall),171-196.

Laskey, H.A., Day, E., & Crask, M. (1989). Typology of main message strategies for television commercials. *Journal of Advertising, 18*(1), 36-41.

Leading National Advertisers/Mediawatch Multi-Media Service. (1996). Competitive Media Reporting and Magazine Publishers of America.

Lee, B., & Tremblay, V.J. (1992). Advertising and the U.S. market demand for beer. *Applied Economics, 24,* 69-76.

Mack, J. (1981). Alcoholism, AA and the governance of the self. In M. Bean & N.E. Zinberg (Eds.), *Dynamic approaches to the understanding and treatment of alcoholism* (pp. 98-113). New York: Free Press.

Marlatt, G.A., & Gordon, J.R. (1985). Relapse prevention in theoretical rationale and overview of the model. In G.A. Marlatt & J.R. Gordon (Eds.), *Relapse prevention.* New York: Guilford.

McCracken, G. (1989). Who is the celebrity endorser? Cultural foundations of the endorsement process. *Journal of Consumer Research, 16*(December), 310-321.

Merleau-Ponty, M. (1962). *The phenomenology of perception.* London: Routledge & Kegan Paul.

Mick, D.G., & Buhl, C. (1992). A meaning-based model of advertising experiences. *Journal of Consumer Research, 19*(December), 317-338.

Moriarty, S.E. (1991). *Creative advertising: Theory and practice.* Englewood Cliffs, NJ: Prentice-Hall.

National Highway Traffic Safety Administration. (1994). *Fatal accident reporting system.* Washington, DC: U.S. Department of Transportation.

Petty, R.E., Caccioppo, J.T., & Schumann, D. (1983). Central and peripheral routes to advertising effectiveness: The moderating role of involvement. *Journal of Consumer Research, 10,* 135-146.

Polkinghorne, D.E. (1986). Conceptual validity in a non-theoretical human science. *Journal of Phenomenological Research, 17*(2), 129-149.

Presley, C.A., Meilman, P.W., & Lyerla, R. (1993). *Alcohol and drugs on American college campuses: Use, consequence, and perceptions of the campus environment,* Vol. 1: *1989-1991.* Carbondale, IL: The Core Institute.

Rice, D.P. (1993). The economic cost of alcohol abuse and dependence: 1990. *Alcohol Health Research World, 17,* 16-18.

Rotzoll, K.B., & Haefner, J.E. (1996). *Advertising in contemporary society: Perspectives toward understanding* (3rd ed.). Urbana: University of Illinois Press.

Scott, L.M. (1990). Understanding jingles and needledrop: A rhetorical approach to music in advertising. *Journal of Consumer Research, 17*(September), 223-236.

Scott, L.M. (1994). The bridge from text to mind: Adapting reader-response theory to consumer research. *Journal of Consumer Research, 21*(December), 461-480.

Seymour, D.T. (1985). Marketing—A retrenchment exercise. In N. Dholakia & J. Arndt (Eds.), *Research in marketing*, Supplement 2: *Changing the course of marketing: Alternate paradigms for widening market theory* (pp. 219-234). Greenwich, CT: JAI Press.

Simmons Market Research Bureau. (1996). Vol. P-14. *The Study of Media and Markets*, 147.

Smart, R.D. (1988). Does alcohol advertising affect overall consumption? A review of empirical studies. *Journal of Studies on Alcohol, 49*(4), 314-323.

Sobell, L., Sobell, M., Toneatto, T., & Leo, G. (1993). Severely dependent alcohol abusers may be vulnerable to alcohol cues on television programs. *Journal of Studies on Alcohol, 54*, 85-91.

Stern, B. (1996). Textual analysis in advertising research: Construction and deconstruction of meanings. *Journal of Advertising, 25*(3), 61-73.

Stern, B., & Holbrook, M.B. (1994). Gender and genre in the interpretation of advertising text. In J.A. Costa (Ed.), *Gender issues and consumer behavior* (pp. 11-41). Thousand Oaks, CA: Sage.

Strauss, A., & Corbin, J. (1994). Grounded theory methodology: An overview. In N.K. Denzin & Y.S. Lincoln (Eds.), *Handbook of qualitative research* (pp. 273-285). Thousand Oaks, CA: Sage.

Stuart, E.W., Shimp, T.A., & Engle, R.W. (1987). Classical conditioning of consumer attitudes: Four experiments in an advertising context. *Journal of Consumer Research, 14*, 334-349.

Tan, A. (1986). Social learning of aggression from television. In J. Bryant & D. Zillmann (Eds.), *Perspectives on media effects* (pp. 41-55). Hillsdale, NJ: Lawrence Erlbaum.

Taylor, R.E. (1994). Qualitative research. In M.W. Singletary (Ed.), *Mass communication research* (pp. 265-279). New York: Longman.

Taylor, R.E., Hoy, M.G., & Haley, E. (1996). How French advertising professionals develop creative strategy. *Journal of Advertising, 25*(1), 1-14.

Thompson, C.J., Locander, W.B., & Pollio, H.R. (1989). Putting consumer experience back into consumer research: The philosophy and method of existential-phenomenology. *Journal of Consumer Research, 16*(September), 133-146.

Treise, D., Taylor, R.E., & Wells, L.G. (1994). How recovering alcoholics interpret alcoholic-beverage advertising. *Health Marketing Quarterly, 12*(2), 125-139.

U.S. Department of the Treasury, Bureau of Alcohol, Tobacco and Firearms. (1996, September). Laws and regulations under the Federal Alcohol Administration Act. *Code of Federal Regulations* (Title 27). Washington, DC: GPO.

Valle, R.S., & Halling, S. (1989). *Existential-phenomenological perspectives in psychology*. New York: Plenum.

Valliant, G. (1983). *The natural history of alcoholism*. Cambridge, MA: Harvard University Press.

Wechsler, H., & Isaac, N. (1992). "Binge" drinkers at Massachusetts colleges. *Journal of the American Medical Association, 267*(21), 2929-2931.

Wolburg, J.M., & Taylor, R.E. (1997). *An investigation of three cultural values in American advertising: The role of the individual, the depiction of time, and the configuration of space*. Paper presented at the national conference of the Association for Education in Journalism and Mass Communication, Chicago.

Wurmser, L. (1978). *The hidden dimension psychodynamics of compulsive drug use*. New York: Jason Aronson.

CPSIA information can be obtained
at www.ICGtesting.com
Printed in the USA
LVHW081251310122
709859LV00002B/4